JOHNSONIAN GLEANINGS

BY ALEYN LYELL READE
Hon. M.A. Oxon. & Liverpool

PART X

JOHNSON'S EARLY LIFE: THE FINAL NARRATIVE

1968
OCTAGON BOOKS, INC.
New York

Originally published in 1946

Reprinted 1968

by

OCTAGON BOOKS, INC.
175 FIFTH AVENUE
NEW YORK, N. Y. 10010

LIBRARY OF CONGRESS CATALOG CARD NUMBER: 68-15885

Printed in U.S.A. by

NOBLE OFFSET PRINTERS, INC.
NEW YORK 3, N. Y.

PREFACE

IN August 1903, while working out the history of my own family, I applied to Mr. Gainsborough Harward, a solicitor at Stourbridge, in Worcestershire, for some information I required in connexion with certain very humbly placed kinsfolk in the Staffordshire Potteries, who, through some queer trick of *mésalliance*, had intermarried with the Hickman family of Stourbridge, for one of whom Mr. Harward had acted professionally. He very kindly told me what he could, and enclosed a sketch pedigree showing all he knew of the Hickmans, including the Dorothy Hickman who married Dr. John Turton, and to whom Johnson wrote an early sonnet. A little further enquiry brought me into much fuller touch with the Johnsonian associations of the family, to which Mr. Harward had briefly alluded. The results to me were momentous. My family history duly appeared, in June 1906, as a large quarto, and the title tells its own tale as to what had happened. *The Reades of Blackwood Hill, in the Parish of Horton, Staffordshire, A Record of Their Descendants, with a Full Account of Dr. Johnson's Ancestry, his Kinsfolk and Family Connexions*, contained a detailed record of all the ramifications of my own family, yet the Johnsonian matter had accumulated to such an extent, largely while the earlier portion was passing through the press, that it easily exceeded in bulk what was originally intended to be the main part of the volume. In fact, the tail had come to wag the dog.

Once I had put my hand to the plough (to disengage myself from the preceding metaphor) it was never willingly withdrawn. In October 1907 I began to contribute to *Notes and Queries* a series of articles embodying fresh information and entitled "Notes on Dr. Johnson's Ancestors and Connexions," which concluded in June 1909. In August of the same year I privately reprinted these articles, with various additions, and with a number of portrait plates, as a slim volume, which constituted the now very rare Part I. of my *Johnsonian Gleanings* and had the sub-title of "Notes on Dr. Johnson's Ancestors and Connexions and Illustrative of his Early Life." Part II. of the series, "Francis Barber, the Doctor's Negro Servant," a very full biography of that worthy, which had not been printed elsewhere, appeared in June 1912. Then came a long interval, for which the first Great War was principally responsible, as it not only made printing economically out of the question, but also led to my serving some three years, in

England and France, in the disguise of a private soldier. It was not till March 1922 that Part III. appeared, "The Doctor's Boyhood." My work had been growing increasingly biographical in character, and thenceforward it took the form of a continuous enquiry into the facts and circumstances of Johnson's early life, in which genealogy was subordinated to be merely the useful handmaid of such research. Part IV., issued in March 1924, consisted of the "Appendices" to Part III. Part V., "The Doctor's Life 1728–35," issued in May 1928, continued the story, as did also Part VI., "The Doctor's Life 1735–40," issued in April 1933. Part VII., issued in December 1935, had as its subject, "The Jervis, Porter and Other Allied Families." Part VIII., issued in October 1937, gathered together fresh matter I had accumulated as the work proceeded, under the title of "A Miscellany," and Part IX., issued in May 1939, was of a similar character and entitled "A Further Miscellany."

The great object of this present Part is to place in the hands of those who are not specialists, and who cannot be expected to wade through the great bulk of my previously printed material, the main results of my researches, in the form of a succinct and readable narrative of the first cycle of Johnson's life, ending in 1740. In this narrative, which is as complete as I can now make it, the whole of the evidence, whether derived from the authors of the various 'lives,' from the mass of printed memoirs and letters of contemporaries, or from the deliberate enquiries of myself and others, is generally so thoroughly digested that it cannot be discerned at any point whether the authority is Johnson himself, or Boswell, or an exponent of modern systems of research, or any other of the countless sources that have been drawn upon. In a few instances, here and there, it has seemed necessary to depart from this principle. One would not, for example, quote Miss Seward's statements without the qualification of her name, for they carry hardly any authority unless corroborated from some other source. But most of the principal witnesses to Johnson's early life, Boswell, Hawkins, William Shaw, and Mrs. Piozzi, are good witnesses, in varying degree, and what they tell us I accept as fact unless it is inherently improbable or conflicts with other evidence. This is a rule by which all biographers must work in that big field where actual proof is lacking. Quite frequently, of course, the same incident is related by several witnesses in different versions, and it has then been my business to consider all the probabilities, and to sift the truth (as far as possible) out of these different versions before presenting it to my readers. A pretty thorough account of his origins is given, both in relation to the direct and inescapable suasions of actual heredity and to those more general influences of domestic and social environment that are seen to play so large a part in shaping his early career.

The writing of this Part has involved far more than merely condensing the narrative as given in previous volumes of the *Gleanings*. A change of scale and method always necessitates a large amount of recasting and re-arrangement. In some cases even the conclusions drawn have had to be changed or modified. And it has been necessary to scour the whole field of evidence again to make sure that nothing has been omitted which throws light upon this first and potentially most important cycle of Johnson's life.

It is not a brilliant narrative, partly because of the limitations so unkindly imposed upon the author by nature (who got in the first blow), and partly because of the limitations he has deliberately imposed upon himself. But it is one that should wear well, and enable future biographers to deal with this period of Johnson's life in a way they could hardly have attempted without its aid. Coming from one who has devoted himself so closely to the subject, and whose methods and judgment have been well tried in a long struggle to achieve accuracy of deduction as well as accuracy of fact, it can hardly fail to be definitive within its narrow bounds. Everything is founded upon substantial evidence, and even the lightest statements are not lightly made. It would scarcely have been possible for any one else to have extracted all the implications of so varied a mass of records as thoroughly as their collector and editor.

In the whole narrative there is not a single reference, or a single footnote. Pedantry (not that I would ever really plead guilty to that humourless fault) has been ruthlessly excluded. Quotations have been almost entirely avoided, as conflicting with the aim at complete assimilation of the material: the few given are only short, for all passages of any length have been resolved. The story is purged of all the elaborate presentations of evidence, the ponderous marshalling of authorities, the intricate arguments, the laborious explanations, the careful qualifications, the nice splitting of hairs, and the solemn weighing of probabilities, that go to make up "the hideous apparatus of research." For those, the reader with sufficient stamina may go to the previous volumes of the *Gleanings*, where the whole story can be seen with the "scaffolding" unremoved, and to the references there given, by which my conclusions can be tested. The sweat and tears that went to the erection of the scaffolding have here all been wiped away.

The *Gleanings*, of course, contain an immense amount of illustrative material about this period of Johnson's life, as well as about later periods, that will not be found in my essay, for all has been excluded which does not seem to me to bear closely upon the narrative. In some cases solid pages of evidence may be reflected by a single adjective. I can take some pride in the thought that the intimidating number of closely reasoned pages in which the century-old problem of Johnson's Oxford residence is finally settled, founded upon long months of arduous labour over and tabulation of the Pembroke College records, finds no echo here, except in the bare statement of when that residence ceased, and that all the intricate puzzles connected with "buttery books" and "battels" have been sternly kept from my readers' sight.

There are a number of minor points throughout the narrative for which chapter and verse cannot actually be found in the *Gleanings*. Some of the references in previous Parts have been more fully exploited than seemed necessary when I used them before, and it is therefore necessary in a few cases to go back to the original source.

If some complain that genealogy fills too big a place in my scheme, let them remember that the work was conceived in genealogy, and largely intended to show to how great an extent that exacting science may be made to serve the purposes of biography. Everyone acquainted with the research work of modern literary students, particularly those in this country and America who follow the elusive trails of the Elizabethan actors and dramatists, can see how increasingly, and how successfully, they use many of the tools of the working genealogist. There certainly could not be a better training in accuracy and factual discrimination than that supplied by a study which demands such scrupulous attention to the correctness of names and dates, and necessitates weighing the validity of so many different classes of evidence.

There is another factor to be considered in this connexion, that from the first I have had a considerable number of subscribers whose interest in my work is almost entirely genealogical, and without whose loyal support (and active help) it could not have been produced. The genealogies, too, serve a double purpose, reflecting my aim not only to identify all the people with whom the young Johnson came into contact in any way but also to enable the descendants of those people to associate themselves hereditarily with him, and so spread the number of his vicarious progeny. It is, moreover, the ideal practice now for those engaged in serious biographical research to get into touch wherever possible with present representatives of the persons associated with their subject, in order to find out whether any relevant records have come down in the family, and from my own experience much is to be gained by this excess of zeal.

I have made practically no attempt to supply a "background" to the story I tell, for to do so would have confused my purpose of simply presenting the ascertained facts of Johnson's early life, leaving it almost entirely to the future biographers for whose benefit I write to put their own interpretation on those facts and to paint in their own background.

It has been remarked with some truth that the series labours under a certain disadvantage by reason of its title, for "Johnsonian Gleanings" does not suggest the scope or the serious intention of the work. At this distance of time I do not recollect exactly how I came to fix that title, but as at the inception there was no intention of following any set scheme in the succeeding volumes it must have seemed an obvious enough selection. Indeed, in the preface to Part I., I described it as "the first of a series of small volumes dealing with various obscure phases of Johnsonian biography." The second Part was intended originally to deal with "Dr. Johnson's Household," but the accumulation of material in regard to Francis Barber alone led to him being the sole hero of the volume, to the exclusion of Anna Williams, Robert Levett, and other minor figures of that queer London *ménage*. It was not till after the first Great War, as already stressed, that work upon Part III. definitely committed me to the scheme of concentrating my researches upon the successive stages of Johnson's early life. It was then too late to alter the title, and I can only hope that its inadequacy may be lived down. If it comes to be considered almost as inappropriate as "*Literary Anecdotes*" seems to us now for Nichols's huge dump of undigested biographical information about the minor figures of eighteenth century letters, I shall be amply satisfied.

Out of all those who have assisted me in my work, and to whom, in their hundreds, my gratitude cannot be too warmly expressed, it is permissible here to mention a few to whom I am under very special obligations. Mr. A. W. Read, of Leicester, since an early stage in my studies, has made searches for me in his own Midland area of such an extent as to leave the imprint of his genealogical enthusiasm, as well as of his extreme kindness, on almost the whole series. I have never sought his help in vain, and rarely failed to profit by it. Like all who study any aspect of Johnson's life or work, I have constantly had recourse to the knowledge, particularly the local knowledge, of the late Dr. Ernest A. Sadler, who at Ashburne in Derbyshire extended a never failing welcome to all Johnsonians who cared to visit him in the beautiful house where Johnson spent so many holidays with his friend Dr. Taylor, and who never sought an excuse in his busy professional life for neglecting to answer with the most scrupulous care all queries addressed to him by his numerous literary correspondents, even when they involved, as they often did, considerable fresh research. Mr. P. Laithwaite, of Lichfield, has explored his local records for Johnsonian material with such success as to place all of us under a great debt of obligation to him for the energy and acumen that have led to so many fresh discoveries, and I am proud to think that his work was largely inspired by my own researches, and by our frequent and friendly correspondence. Until ten or a dozen years ago I never attacked any problem of Midland genealogy without seeking the skilled help of the Rev. F. A. Homer, of West Bromwich, with his remarkable knowledge and his great collection of material, and his death left a gap that could not be filled in the ranks of my helpers. His assistance was nominally of a professional nature, but it far transcended all the bounds of self-advantage.

On the literary side I need scarcely say how much I have profited by the help of my friend Dr. L. F. Powell, of Oxford, whose long and exacting labours in re-editing Birkbeck Hill's *Boswell* have made him the most widely informed Johnsonian scholar of his day—or any preceding day. Students not only in this country but from over many seas gratefully acknowledge his unfailing accessibility, and the generous way in which he is ever ready to place his great store of information at the service of all serious enquirers. His study, indeed, may almost be described as the world's clearing house in the matter of Johnsonian investigation. His encouragement, together with that of other accomplished literary scholars, such as Dr. R. W. Chapman, of Oxford, Mr. H. Gordon Ward, of the University of Liverpool, and the late Mr. Leonard Whibley, who have all given me specific and valuable help on innumerable issues where my own knowledge was particularly defective, has been a great stimulus to work, as has also been the fact that the Universities of Oxford and my own native Liverpool have both seen fit to confer upon me an Honorary Mastership of Arts. A warm supporter whose death robbed me of a friend with a singularly gracious personality, compound of rare qualities of modesty, simplicity and unselfishness, was the late Mr. Algernon Gissing, who, though his own work lay mostly in very different literary fields, maintained an enthusiastic interest in all the minutiæ of biographical research, and himself, when occasion offered, displayed the patient accuracy of the professed scholar.

To four of those to whom I have expressed my indebtedness I am under a further great obligation for having carefully read through the typescript of this Part, correcting me and advising me on many points. They are Dr. Powell, Mr. Laithwaite, Mr. H. Gordon Ward, and the late Dr. Sadler, who must not, however, be held responsible for any part of it, as their advice has not always been followed. If blemishes are too apparent such must be attributed to an obstinate adherence to my own methods rather than to their failure as critics.

This Part concludes with a number of appendices. The first two are pedigrees respectively of the Johnsons and the Fords, presented in the final form in which my researches have left them. The Ford pedigree has never been re-drafted since the issue of the parent work in 1906, and in the forty intervening years I have constantly been adding fresh details, as the successive Parts of the *Gleanings* bear witness. The Johnson pedigree, which in 1906 had hardly taken form, has also similarly received many accretions, and now for the first time appears in full shape. These pedigrees, though not included with that object, may help the readers of my story to understand the relationships mentioned therein. It is true that their narrative form does not illustrate such relationships as graphically as would the tabular form, but on the other hand it allows the inclusion of all that essential detail which could not have been presented on a chart. The remaining appendices tell their own story, and most of them have a direct bearing upon some part of Johnson's early life.

The next Part will consist of the consolidated index of names to the whole series, as well as to the Johnsonian portion of the parent work, *The Reades of Blackwood Hill and Dr. Johnson's Ancestry*. On the construction of this index I spent a hard year's work at the beginning of the late War, leaving it then in card form ready to receive its final entries when this Part X. was set up in type. It should add very greatly to the value of the series, for it will not only obviate the heart-breaking necessity of looking through eleven separate indexes for any desired name and so make the mass of information far more easily accessible, but in addition will define all the persons much more thoroughly. It will also help to establish the *Gleanings* as an indispensable source book for students, particularly to all those dealing with eighteenth century biography, literary history and genealogy.

It has been seen that one Great War caused a break of nearly ten years between the issue of Parts II. and III. And now a second (and even greater) Great War has caused an interval of over seven years between the issue of Parts IX. and X. As Hitler would have said, "My patience is almost exhausted," and I must demand at least a few years of moderately settled world conditions in which to carry my scheme to a conclusion. And though at three-score-and-ten one must not count too gaily on a continuance of health and strength, my outlook is still sufficiently optimistic to breed the hope that I shall be able later on to continue my work by endeavouring to elucidate Johnson's life for the period after he settled in London in 1740, by methods similar to those which I have applied to his earlier life. It is painfully evident to all students of Johnson's career how little we really know of those long years of struggle preceding his introduction to Boswell in 1763. I can scarcely hope to add much to our actual knowledge, but the methodical examination of all the information we do possess and the construction therefrom of an ordered narrative, on a strict basis of chronology, and expanded as much as possible by research, will mark a considerable step forward, and perhaps lead to the filling up of some of the numerous gaps in the story, as well as to the solution of various problems that still puzzle the biographers.

I must add in conclusion that the scholarly edition of *The Poems of Samuel Johnson*, by David Nichol Smith and Edward L. McAdam, 1941, has enabled me to make a number of minor corrections and additions to my narrative, originally written in 1934.

All the dates in this Part are given in *new style*, as regards the year, unless otherwise stated. The dates in connexion with Johnson's own life, of course, are printed in full, but in the case of incidental dates, or those relating to subsidiary characters, the year alone has usually been considered sufficient.

ALEYN LYELL READE.

Treleaven House, Blundellsands,
near Liverpool.
7 August, 1946.

LIST OF CONTENTS

CHAPTER I.

HIS FATHER AND MOTHER

THE townsman, of a stock usually transplanted from its native soil, is often quite ignorant of his family origins, even when not naturally blind to their significance. But with the countryman, bred up among the traditions of a past which still speaks to him every day through many visible records, and living in a narrow circle where intellectual preoccupations have not killed his simpler curiosities, such things are an ordinary topic of conversation and pass into the fund of common knowledge. His memory is tenacious of all he hears about his kith and kin, and links him indissolubly with forefathers who are substantial figures in his imagination if not actually pictureable in the flesh.

There are few countrymen, even in these days of change, who could honestly confess to ignorance of their grandfathers. It may perhaps be doubted whether Samuel Johnson, who in the solemn pages of the great *Dictionary* proudly turned aside to salute the ancient city of Lichfield, in the Virgilian phrase, as his *magna parens*, considered himself a countryman. But he came on both sides of a country stock, and Lichfield itself, though in his young days the second largest town in the county, with a population of about 3,000, was really not much more than a semi-rural community when stripped of its official and ecclesiastical dignity. When, therefore, we find him telling Boswell that he could scarcely say who his grandfather was, we realise a significance in the confession that might not attach to it had he been the product of real urban conditions.

Markedly patriarchal in his attitude towards family descent, Johnson was here undoubtedly thinking of his father's father, and taking no credit for his mother belonging to a family with more 'gentle' associations: it was always his father's social status he accepted as the index of his own origin. His father's father is indeed a shadowy figure, even to us who are better informed about him. William Johnson first emerges out of the mists of obscurity in 1657, when his son Michael, to become the far from negligible genealogical link between one man utterly unknown and another whose fame has assumed the character of a legend, was baptized on 2 April at the little Derbyshire village of Cubley, where in due course followed further children, Benjamin in 1659, Andrew in 1660, and Margaret in 1663. Local tradition, for a long time back, has connected William Johnson's actual home with a small thatched cottage (now rebuilt) some little distance from the village and standing high on Cubley Common, along the road to Ashburne. The 'Common' now rather belies its name, for it consists of cultivated farm land, and the fields are pleasantly fringed with trees.

Johnson, however lacking in precise information of his grandfather, was well aware that his father's native place was Cubley, and recorded it on his gravestone. The village, such as it is, lies about half-a-dozen miles south of Ashburne, where Johnson in later life stayed so often and long with his old school friend, John Taylor, the opulent and somewhat gross-minded clerical dictator of the place. He probably often saw the modest home of his grandfather from the windows of his host's "large, roomy post-chaise," with its "four stout, plump horses," and "two steady, jolly postillions." Standing in a rather remote part of Derbyshire, that has never figured prominently in historical records, or been invaded by industry, the quiet little parish, with its few hundreds of inhabitants, has always been dependent almost entirely on agriculture. William Johnson provided no exception to the general rule. According to Shaw, the historian of Staffordshire, who wrote at the end of the eighteenth century, the family were but day-labourers at Cubley. William Johnson's sons, in their apprenticeship papers, agreed in describing him as a yeoman, or gentleman, and though it is probable that they were putting the best possible interpretation on his social status we can hardly believe that all three would conspire to misrepresent it so completely, and over a period of ten years. But it is at least certain that his share of the world's goods was extremely small, when, soon after the birth of his children, he moved to Lichfield.

There were Johnsons in plenty scattered through the hills and dales of that corner of Derbyshire, and William Johnson was no doubt a product of the local soil. The story that he was "an Annandale Johnstone," who anglicised the spelling of his name, was a pretty piece of humour which tickled Sir Walter Scott, well able to imagine the grandson's reaction to such a suggestion. The family connexion with Cubley itself, where, it is rather curious to find, the lords of the manor were the titled predecessors of Johnson's own particular Earl of Chesterfield, was but a fleeting one, and between the years 1663 and 1666 William Johnson, for some cogent reason of which we are totally ignorant, moved with his wife and children from his primitive little village to the dignified cathedral city of Lichfield, in Staffordshire, more than twenty miles to the south, and, one might think, as different in its interests, in its social atmosphere, and in its general conditions of life, as well could be outside an industrial area. Apart from recent development on its outskirts, Lichfield cannot then have been very unlike the town the visitor sees today.

Whatever the reason for the move, and however it was dictated by some declension in the family fortunes, it was to have a profound influence on the future of the children. Three young boys, instead of being dependent for their learning on some tiny village school, now came within reach of an education, and general educative influences, that might enable them to escape from the bondage of mere physical toil. William Johnson first appears in Lichfield in 1666, when he was living in Tamworth Street, in a small house, which he vacated in 1668 for another as small, some distance away, in Bird Street or Sandford Street. In 1670 he came back on his tracks as far as Bore Street, and it was probably here that he died, early in 1672, being buried at St. Michael's church. What occupation he followed while living in Lichfield there is no evidence to show, but it can hardly have been agriculture, and he had almost the lowest assessment in the parish.

The widow, Catherine Johnson, left with a family of young children, was now poorer than ever, and hard put to it to make both ends meet. She went back to the little house in Bird Street or Sandford Street, and was in such want that in the first year of her widowhood she got one of the "women's waistcoats" provided under Smith's Charity, the funds of which were administered by the St. Mary's parish officers, on behalf of "the poor inhabitants of the city." She was similarly helped in 1673 and 1679, during which period she had ceased even to be a householder. Fortunately, there were other charities which extended help to her children, and just at a time when such help was vital to their future. Not many weeks before William Johnson's death, his "boy"—assuredly Michael—had received a grant towards his "placing and preferment" from the Feoffees of the Conduit Lands Trust, an excellent body which, after it had done its duty as regards the city water supply, was empowered to expend the surplus income for the common weal of the inhabitants, to support the Grammar School, and to make grants to poor children to assist their advancement in life. Whether Michael and his younger brothers went to the Grammar School cannot be definitely said, but his respectable Latin, and the good education they must all have received, makes it extremely probable. The grant to Michael may have been for school fees, as it is known to have been in other cases, for he did not begin his vocational training until over a year later.

At a meeting of the Feoffees at the end of 1672 it was agreed that Michael, son of the late William Johnson, be paid £4 towards his "preferment and binding apprentice," another half-dozen children of the town being allotted £3 apiece. This was only prospective, but on 12 April 1673 the widowed Mrs. Johnson was actually paid the sum mentioned, towards placing her son Michael, then aged sixteen, as apprentice to Richard Simpson, of London, stationer, for eight years, from 11 April, ten shillings of it being allocated for his journey and the various charges on the way.

Richard Simpson, son of an Oxfordshire shoemaker, was himself apprenticed as far back as 1653. He took up the Company livery on the very day when Michael was bound his apprentice, and his bookselling business was established in St. Paul's Churchyard, at the sign of The Harp. Here he was in partnership with Ralph Simpson, whom he left in 1692 to carry on his business at The Three Trouts, also in the Churchyard. A man of some position in the trade, he in due course became Master of the Stationers' Company. Whatever it was that caused the Lichfield widow to entrust her son to his care, he must have proved a satisfactory master, for less than three years later Benjamin Johnson, the second son, went up to join his brother at The Harp. His apprenticeship was from 6 December 1675, and was for seven years only. The Feoffees of the Conduit Lands had been active here again, and had granted Mrs. Johnson £3 for his apprenticeship to Richard Simpson.

Michael Johnson was a keen observer of his times, and one memory of his apprentice days related to the occasion in December 1680 when Gilbert Burnet, afterwards Bishop of Salisbury, and Thomas Sprat, afterwards Bishop of Rochester, both preached before the House of Commons on the same day. He also recollected the almost unexampled run on Dryden's satire, *Absalom and Achitophel*, at the end of 1681. It was in the April of this same year that his apprenticeship expired. A young man of twenty-four, evidently ambitious at the outset of his career, he returned immediately to his native city, and by July was already established in business on his own account, as a bookbinder and bookseller, in Sadler Street, or Market Street as it was alternatively called, the best business part of the town, where he remained all his life, in premises assessed at a pretty high figure. Perhaps he was the first bookseller in Lichfield, but William Bailye, who came from Wolverhampton, where he had been a favourite apprentice of Edward Gough, traded close-by, in the same street, as bookseller and stationer, from at least 1683. William Bailye married in 1677 one of the well known Pershouses, and founded a family of some repute in Lichfield.

The most surprising thing about Michael Johnson's career, considering that it started in poverty, and dragged out its later stages in chronic impecuniosity, was the rapid headway he made at the outset. The establishment of a new business, where there is no capital and no influence, is usually a very uphill task. The circumstances almost suggest that he must have got financial backing from some unknown source, and as we know that in his early life he contracted a burden of debt which oppressed him ever afterwards, this may mean that he borrowed the capital on which he set up business. It is true that he was in his own town, but he came of poor and obscure people, and those who know us best are not always the most easily convinced of our capacity. At any rate, by 1684, when he was but twenty-seven, he was elected a Warden of the Conduit Lands Trust, a position which carried considerable responsibility, and it was during his year of office that a scheme was put in hand for building the house for the headmaster of the Grammar School—a house, by the way, which still delights the visitor to Lichfield. In 1687 he became an Overseer of the Poor; while in 1688 "Mr. Johnson, stationer," achieved great respectability as churchwarden of St. Mary's church.

The poor boy of the previous decade had thus suddenly become the privileged dispenser of the very charities that had so recently helped him and his family to emerge from straightened obscurity. This is indirect but striking proof of an initial success in business, and makes us wonder all the more what really caused its later decline. In 1687 he published Sir John Floyer's *Touchstone of Medicines*, the earliest work of the famous Lichfield physician ; and in the same year a *Syncritical Grammar*, for Samuel Shaw, Master of the Grammar School at Ashby-de-la-Zouch. By this time he boasted branches at Ashby, which is in Leicestershire, as well as at Uttoxeter, in Staffordshire, both full fifteen miles away, though probably they were only weekly stalls in the market-place. In 1687, too, he subscribed the decent sum of ten shillings towards re-casting the Cathedral bells. In 1690 he appears as one of the booksellers to take subscriptions for Anthony à Wood's *Athenæ Oxonienses* and *Fasti Oxonienses*. That he did not, even then, confine himself purely to literary wares is evidenced by a pamphlet of 1691, entitled *The Happy Sinner : or the Penitent Malefactor*, in which a very respectable Lichfield murderer bequeathed to his country a number of choice remedies, one of which, the " Queen of Hungary's Water," was to be retailed by Michael Johnson himself, whose name also appears as publisher on the title-page. In October 1685 he had been made free of the Stationers' Company, but he never took up the livery. Possibly he jibbed at the fee, and thought that in the provinces the formality would not impress his customers.

During this period of expansion he did not escape the private troubles that beset us all. In 1686 he became engaged to Mary Neild, the twenty-three-year-old daughter of one Luke Neild, a leading tradesman at Derby—barber, innkeeper and churchwarden—and matters got so far as the issue of a licence for their marriage at the end of the year. But they got no farther, and Mary was soon after married to another man. Without postulating any Freudian complexes we can imagine that this frustration of his hopes, whatever its cause, must have affected him deeply. It may have helped to develop that intense melancholy which troubled him in after life, and it probably explains why he came to wait until late middle-age before contracting a marriage not very romantic in its circumstances, however fruitful for the world in its results. Perhaps his wife and children never heard the story of Mary Neild.

Michael's sudden rise to prosperity meant better times for his mother, who about 1683 gave up the small house to which she had returned in 1679, and probably went to live with him. Her "waistcoats" had no longer to be supplied by the parish. She survived until January 1692, as the register of St. Mary's church (where there was no burial ground) tells us. Michael paid for her grave, which no doubt was by her husband's at St. Michael's. He had not acquired a sitting at St. Mary's until 1690. Earning the reputation of being a "zealous high-church man," he yet delighted, in later years, to send his horses out on a Sunday, in order to annoy the great Mrs. Harriotts, his wife's rich cousin.

Miss Seward told a most romantic story about Michael Johnson, that during his apprenticeship at Leek (!) a young woman became so violently enamoured of him that she followed him to Lichfield, took lodgings opposite his house, and "indulged her hopeless flame." The good Michael took pity on her, and promised marriage, but she died before she could take advantage of his self-sacrificing offer. All he could do was to bury her, and put a stone in the Cathedral to mark where lay "the body of Mrs. Elizabeth Blaney, a stranger," who died on 2 September 1694. But in cold, prosaic fact the young woman was a superior servant, greatly valued, and "gentle" as often was the case in those days, in the well ordered establishment of Charles Hinton, and afterwards of his widow, in the Cathedral Close, where she had been for at least five years and upwards, and a "stranger" only in the sense of not being a native of Lichfield, where, however, her mother was living. And Michael was over thirteen years out of his apprenticeship. So that the whole story is vitiated at the source, and must be rejected. Michael Johnson and his brother Andrew appraised her goods and chattels, so there must have been some tie between them, but she left nothing to either, while bequeathing money to her master's young son for the purchase of a "handsome gold watch."

Andrew Johnson, of whom we have just heard again, has set us a pretty puzzle in regard to his early training for a career. In 1676, at the age of fifteen, he was apprenticed for seven years to John Marriott, a baker at Ashburne, in Derbyshire, only some five miles from his own birthplace at Cubley. His mother had received the sum of three pounds the same year, from the Feoffees of the Conduit Lands Trust, for his 'putting forth.' Yet in 1683, six months after the term of his apprenticeship to John Marriott had expired, and at the mature age of twenty-three, he was again bound apprentice, this time to his brother Benjamin Johnson, bookseller. It seems extraordinary for a man to spend fourteen years of his life in a state of apprenticeship. Whether he served his full term with John Marriott or not, he probably did so with his brother Benjamin, or he would hardly have practised the trade which made the Johnson family into a triumvirate of booksellers. Andrew evidently had some of the physical strength of his brother Michael, for he excelled at the manly sports of wrestling and boxing. In the latter art he gave some instruction to his nephew, who proudly told Mrs. Thrale that his uncle's prowess was such as enabled him to "keep the ring in Smithfield" for a full year and never to suffer defeat in either sport. This glorious spell of athletic supremacy must have been during his apprenticeship to his brother, when he would be at the height of his physical powers. So far as we know he received no assistance for his second apprenticeship from the public authorities at Lichfield, which is scarcely to be wondered at, and probably his brothers were now able to help him.

The benefits conferred upon the Johnson family by the excellent system of local charities at Lichfield can hardly be overestimated: without them it is extremely doubtful whether Boswell's services as a biographer would ever have been required. If the family had remained on in sleepy little Cubley they certainly would not have enjoyed all the advantages which came to them through a move that was, nevertheless, probably made under the pressure of some necessity rather than as a means of advancement.

Immediately his time was up, at the end of 1690, Andrew joined his brother Michael at Lichfield, helped with the business, married, and in due course begat a family. He did not take up the Company's freedom. In 1695, already a widower, he was actually living with Michael, in the Market Street shop, which also housed Simon Marten, the young apprentice, and Anne Deakin, the servant, who a few months later married Jonathan Mallett, Sheriff of Lichfield in 1717. Simon Marten was the son of a notary public in Lichfield, a man of education who must have thought highly of Michael Johnson to place the boy with him: he did well in the trade, and became Mayor of Leicester in

1728. He went to Leicester from Ashby-de-la-Zouch in 1701, so perhaps had been sent from Lichfield to look after Michael Johnson's connexion in the little town where he had so long had a stall.

There was living in Tamworth Street at this time a maltster named Thomas Bromhall, who had in 1692 married Martha, daughter of Thomas Fisher, a substantial yeoman at Elmdon, in Warwickshire. She had a sister Sarah, who would likely enough visit the Bromhalls in Lichfield : at any rate, Andrew Johnson, tired of three years without a home of his own, met her and decided to take her as his second wife, in 1696. Thus equipped, he went to Birmingham and set up his own business there, where in 1702 he issued a volume containing two sermons by a local clergyman, the Rev. Abraham Jeacocke, Minister of Deritend and afterwards Vicar of Ashburne, a small book which used, mistakenly, to be looked upon as the first published in the town. That is the only success we can attribute to the pugilistic bookseller, who in 1708 was sued by his brother Michael for a debt.

In 1696, too, Michael Johnson published another work for Sir John Floyer, *The Preternatural State of Animal Humours Described ;* and in 1699 he published for the Rev. John Bradley, Vicar of Alrewas, close to Lichfield, *An Impartial View of the Truth of Christianity, with the History of the Life and Miracles of Apollonius Tyanœus.* It cannot be said that his publications were on the gay side, and the profits were probably not sufficient to encourage much cheerfulness. Perhaps that is why he launched out into another kind of business, and one which later on contributed a good deal to his financial embarassment. In 1695 he supplied a skin of parchment to his own church, which occasionally bought books from him, but it may not have been his own manufacture. However, by about 1697, when it is rather astonishing to find him able to advance £80 to the Corporation, he had definitely begun the manufacture of vellum and parchment himself. He scoured England, Scotland and Ireland for skins, whether in person or not we do not know. Handicapped by an admitted complete ignorance of the technical side of the trade, he had to employ others to do the actual tanning of the skins he rejected as unfit for parchment (himself selling the leather), relying first upon a Mr. Chaplain and afterwards upon Thomas Rutter. Even had he possessed the requisite knowledge the law would not have allowed him to practise a trade to which he had not been duly apprenticed. Rutter, who had married the eldest daughter of John Perkins, a prominent citizen of Lichfield, died in 1702, and on his death bed requested that Michael Johnson should continue to give the business to his wife and their son John, a request that was generously observed. His parchment factory was placed some third-of-a-mile away from the shop, on the low-lying ground reclaimed from Stowe Pool, and in 1705 the Corporation took action to compel him and others who had similarly encroached to take up formal leases of the land.

Towards the end of 1700 there lay dying in his house at the little hamlet of Woodseaves, in the parish of High Offley, and full twenty-five miles north-west of Lichfield, one Gerard Skrymsher, a Cambridge graduate and Doctor of Medicine. An old man of eighty-two, with but four days to live, he was too weak to make a will, except by the common method of declaring his testamentary wishes before those gathered round the bedside. Among these witnesses was Michael Johnson, and it was on him, as the scholar and amateur lawyer of the party, that the responsibility was placed of putting the declaration on paper and seeing that it was properly witnessed by himself and the other persons. A few months later, when administration of the estate was granted to Catherine Skrymsher, the widow, it was Michael again who stood surety for due performance, and for the "education" (or upbringing) of the children. Years afterwards, when death was knocking at his own door, Samuel Johnson, who always attributed great importance to the bond of kinship, enquired for one of these children, Charles Skrymsher, long dead, who had followed his father to Trinity College, Cambridge, and claimed him as a very near relative.

There appears only one explanation of the relationship, and this is that Catherine Skrymsher, the widow, who was born about 1651, must have been an elder sister of Michael Johnson, which would account for his hurrying all the way from Lichfield to be at the death bed of a man born into a very different class of society from that to which he himself belonged. Gerard Skrymsher came of an old Staffordshire county family: his elder brother had married a sister of the Earl of Chichester and fathered a son who was Adjutant-General to Prince Rupert and Standard Bearer of the Pensioners to Charles II. His sister, Mrs. Elliot—and this might well have thrilled the old lion of

Bolt Court as he thundered forth his contempt for the Hanoverian interlopers—had been nurse to James II., who, when he was Duke of York and she his Duchess's Woman-of-the-Bedchamber, did what he could, though without success, to further her granddaughter's marriage to Lord Abergavenny. Dr. Gerard Skrymsher was an old man when he married, and, as commonly happens in such cases, he may have chosen his wife for her youth, without regard to her pedigree. That the branch of the family to which he himself belonged was said, in 1671, to be "all whoremongers," need not interfere with our appreciation of the virtues attributed to him on a fine marble tablet in High Offley church. At his death he was pretty largely engaged in farming, with twenty-six cows to account for the five thousand pounds of cheese in his cheese chambers.

Early in 1700 Michael Johnson successfully summoned an Atherstone tanner for a debt in respect of some hides, and there were many other actions by him for debt recovery and goods supplied. A year later he sued Edward Howcott, tenant of part of his premises, for £22 10 0, in 1702 for £4 19 0, in 1703 for £30, and in 1704 for £22, sums which may represent rent that had not been paid. By 1705 his neighbour and rival in business, William Bailye, a man who started life with much greater advantages than himself, had been reduced to such poverty as required his dismissal from the Corporation, though we do not know that Michael's success was the cause of his undoing.

We have seen how Andrew Johnson, in 1696, had met and married the sister of a neighbour's wife. Ten years later Michael was to parallel his brother's exploit. Living in Lichfield was a saddler named John Harrison, son of a chandler who had been Sheriff of the city in 1693. This John Harrison, in 1698, had taken to wife Phoebe, eldest daughter of Cornelius Ford, then of Curdworth, in Warwickshire. No doubt it was through the Harrisons that an acquaintance originated between her youngest sister, Sarah Ford, and Michael Johnson—an acquaintance that was to have such tremendous consequences for the literary history of the eighteenth century, and to result in a whole period of mind and manners being remembered under the family name of one impressive and dominating personality.

Johnson himself recognized a clear distinction between his father and mother, as regards origins, and when he composed their epitaph he described her as "of the ancient family of Ford." Her nephew, "Parson" Ford, half-a-century and more earlier, had similarly distinguished his father as "sprung from an ancient stock." Boswell's information was that the Fords were "an ancient race of substantial yeomanry in Warwickshire." It is clear that the Ford family considered itself somewhat above the ordinary, and such consciousness of superiority is an influence to be reckoned with, as potent in itself, even if we dispute the reality of the boast. And there was in the family history evidence of qualities and achievements which the Johnsons could not claim. Michael Johnson, in his rugged strength and great stature, in his strong intelligence, as well as in his brooding melancholy, was truly his son's father. But that son had another heritage on his mother's side. Even if we do not attach particular significance in this connexion to the brilliant natural gifts of his cousin, "Parson" Ford, we must recognize the hereditary influences implied by descent from a family that for several generations at least had enjoyed enough prosperity to gather more education than was common among the yeoman class, to acquire a measure of refinement, and to establish some of its members in the medical, clerical and legal professions. His mother may herself not have displayed any special qualities of mind or character, but there is no doubt that she must have transmitted a good many.

The Ford family history, so far as it is definitely known, and probably for much further back, had its focal centre in Birmingham. Henry Ford, the great-grandfather of Samuel Johnson, bearing a name now so familiar all over the world through the industrial activities of a modern namesake, is first met with at Ward End, in the parish of Aston, on the western side of Birmingham, in 1607. He was a substantial yeoman and miller, who about 1635, after all his children were born, moved some half-a-dozen miles to West Bromwich, east from Birmingham, where he bought property and carried on his milling business, incidentally, in 1641, taking the "Oath of Protestation" against Popery. But by 1643 he was established in Birmingham itself, where he died in 1648.

His widow, Mary Ford, joined the following year with her younger son, Cornelius, in purchasing, for the substantial sum of £750, a property at Kings Norton, called Haunch Hall, for his special use. Kings Norton, a country village with which the family were to be associated for many years, was in Worcestershire, some five miles south of Birmingham. Mrs. Ford came with her seventeen-year-old son to live at Kings Norton, though some of the rooms at Haunch Hall were rented to a stranger. She survived her husband ten years, dying in 1658, and was buried at Kings Norton. In her will, made on her death bed, she remembered the poor of Kings Norton, Birmingham, West Bromwich and Trysull, the last named place, sixteen miles away in Staffordshire, as the home of one of her married daughters, of whom we shall hear later on.

Henry Ford left an elder son Henry, as well as Cornelius. This younger Henry, though he does not come directly into the story, calls for some notice. Born in 1628, and educated for the law, he lived first at Winson Green, Birmingham, on a property probably inherited from his father, in 1661 marrying the daughter of a prosperous yeoman at Hampton-in-Arden. In 1665 he was admitted a Fellow of Clifford's Inn, London, his qualifications gaining him exemption from the usual lectures and "exercises of learning." He secured a room high up in a portion of the Inn that had been rebuilt after the Great Fire, and retained it till 1691, when he was still practising, as an attorney, in the Common Law Courts, and, as a solicitor, in the Equity Courts. He led a very active professional life, and was engaged in much litigation. Selling his Winson Green estate in 1683, he built himself a good three-storeyed house in red brick, called The Manwoods, with about fifty acres of land, at Handsworth, where he was close to Sandwell Park, West Bromwich, the seat of Brome Whorwood, for whose Staffordshire estates he had acted as agent since about 1672, and whose wife will always be remembered for her strenuous endeavours to effect the escape of Charles I. from Carisbrooke Castle. His professional duties often took him to London, and, latterly at least, to Oxford, where Brome Whorwood, who represented the city in Parliament from 1661 to 1681, had another seat at Holton Park. He was so much from home that his brother Cornelius, and other residents of Kings Norton charged with enclosing part of the common there, were constrained to engage another lawyer, with whom they could converse. Henry Ford died in 1691, aged sixty-three, seven months after relinquishing his room at Clifford's Inn—a great-uncle of Johnson's who cannot be overlooked when we discuss the question of hereditary influences.

But we must get back into the main current of the story. Cornelius Ford, the grandfather of Johnson, born in 1632, did not, like his elder brother, adventure into a profession, but remained on the land. When his mother died, in 1658, he was a young man of twenty-six, and out of the care of his guardian, John Smalbroke, whose cousin, Richard Smalbroke, Johnson afterwards knew as Bishop of Lichfield. She left him her farming stock and implements, as well as her household goods, and with Haunch Hall as his inheritance he was well provided for. About 1661 he married, remaining at Kings Norton, where all his children were born. There were four sons who survived, Joseph, born in 1662; Samuel, born in 1672; Cornelius; and Nathaniel, born in 1676; as well as three daughters, Phoebe, born in 1665 and married in 1698 to John Harrison; Mary, born in 1667 and married in 1703 to John Hardwicke; and Sarah, born in 1669 and married to Michael Johnson in 1706. Of all of them we shall hear more later on. As late as 1775 Johnson wrote to his friend, Edmund Hector, at Birmingham, asking him to get the baptisms of the eight children of his grandfather, Cornelius Ford, who lived at "the Haunch," in Kings Norton.

Kings Norton was hardly an intellectual centre, and even the ability to read was considered something of an accomplishment there, at least for members of the older generation. But Thomas Hall, the ejected vicar of 1662, had presented his own collection of books as the nucleus of a small parish library. Cornelius Ford, clearly a man of superior education to most of his neighbours, possessed some of Hall's own works, and as he treasured also volumes by Baxter and others of the evangelical school it is easy to see where his particular sympathies lay—far from the highchurchmanship of Michael Johnson and his more famous son. Cornelius's little library also included a Latin Bible, and a "dictionary" which may have helped him to read it.

Cornelius Ford was still at Kings Norton in 1685, but by 1688 he was living at Curdworth, in Warwickshire, a dozen miles away to the north-east. Here he occupied Dunton House, the principal residence of the place, and here, in 1701, he lost his wife, the companion of forty years. A year or two after her death he made yet another move, back south again over a dozen miles, to Packwood, also in Warwickshire, which was to be his last home.

Sarah Ford, his youngest daughter, who had been born at Haunch Hall, Kings Norton, in the March of 1669, was the last to remain at home, and after her sister Mary's marriage to John Hardwicke in 1703 she was left in sole charge of her father. Though able to write—her letters Johnson destroyed, with tears in his eyes, only in the last week of his life—she had little or no acquaintance with books, and her interests, even with all the opportunities of her later years, never rose above the ordinary domestic round that was her constant lot.

It is quite possible that Cornelius Ford, as an intelligent man appreciating the value of books, had made the acquaintance of Michael Johnson, who travelled the country so much, before he appeared in the guise of a prospective son-in-law. But, as already mentioned, Sarah's sister, Mrs. Harrison, was Michael's neighbour at Lichfield, and this circumstance is more likely to explain the development of the love affair between an elderly couple whose homes lay so far apart, or far apart for those days of difficult travel. When Michael Johnson married Sarah Ford, at Packwood, on 19 June 1706, she was thirty-seven and he within a year of fifty. Physically they could hardly have been more dissimilar, he even bigger and stronger than his son afterwards grew to be, and she rather below middle height and of slight build.

Whatever the speed or character of the courtship, the actual marriage was not lightly embarked upon. Legal formalities had to be observed, and settlements arranged, especially as the bride was to have a very decent portion of her own. Eight days before the wedding the various parties concerned got together, and the document so carefully prepared by the lawyers was duly completed. Cornelius Ford, of Packwood, in the county of Warwickshire, gentleman, undertook that his daughter Sarah should be worth £230 in goods and money at the time of her marriage, and to pay the trustees another £200 within nine months after. Michael Johnson, of the city of Lichfield, bookseller, for his part, undertook to pay in £100 to the trustees within the same limit of time. The combined sum was to be put out at interest till a convenient time came for its investment in land or property, which was to be held in trust for Michael, his widow, and their children. An only child, if a daughter, was to receive a further £300 from Michael's estate at his death ; and if there were two children or more then £500 was to go to them in such proportions as the parents might order. If

Sarah survived him she was to have the use of all his ready money, household goods, and stock-in-trade, or five per cent on their value. Michael undertook that his estate, when he came to die, should be worth at least a clear £500. As we should have to multiply these sums at least by six to get an idea of what they would represent today, the whole arrangement suggests that the happy couple embarked on their great adventure in an atmosphere of considerable prospective prosperity.

The marriage was evidently not unagreeable to Sarah's family, for Michael's signature to the settlement was witnessed by her brother, Samuel Ford, and her brother-in-law, John Harrison, who, as before suggested, may have been indirectly at least responsible for the whole affair. And while one of the trustees was Richard Pyott, esquire, of Streethay, two miles from Lichfield, a county gentleman of some importance, the other was Sarah's eldest brother, Joseph Ford, already a successful medical practitioner at Stourbridge in Worcestershire. Altogether it was quite an impressive document that was to regulate the joint financial affairs of Samuel Johnson's parents, though those affairs turned out to be no more capable of being salved by such paper and pen formalities than many others which "gang aft agley." How a man in Richard Pyott's position came to act as a trustee for the marriage settlement of the local bookseller remains unexplained, for the office is normally undertaken by close relatives or friends, whereas he was not akin and belonged to quite a different stratum of society.

It was only three months after his marriage that Michael Johnson engaged in what, so far as we know, was the most ambitious transaction of his bookselling career. The ninth Earl of Derby, who died in 1702, was possessed of a considerable library in his mansion house at Knowsley, near Liverpool, and his brother, after succeeding, decided to realize, though he had not the modern excuse of death duties to justify him. Running to some 2900 volumes, it consisted preponderatingly of folios, comprising "most of the Fathers," and works on French history, the collection winning from an independent inspector before its sale the description of "great and noble." This library, one might have thought, would have been acquired by one of the big London booksellers, but if they made bids those bids must have been exceeded by Michael Johnson, to whom it was sold early in September 1706.

Nothing is known as to the price paid, or how Michael was able to finance such a venture—a venture suggesting that he must have had clients of much more standing than we should expect in the case of a provincial bookseller. His wife's marriage portion may have encouraged him to undertake the deal, at a time when, as a newly married man, he would naturally be anxious to extend his business. By May of 1707 a catalogue had been printed, which, though no copy is known, there is reason to believe was not sufficiently full or accurate to satisfy the expert. We cannot doubt that Michael must have visited Knowsley, probably more than once, in the course of purchasing and removing the books.

It is possible that this major transaction may have been the cause, or one of the causes, of that burden of debt he acquired in early (or early married) life, and carried ever afterwards, to the constant detriment of his fortunes.

CHAPTER II

EARLY CHILDHOOD
1709-1716

WITH a wife, and possible hopes of a family, Michael Johnson's thoughts turned to the question of house accommodation, which in his bachelor state would not seem of such great importance. The house he had occupied in Market Street did not accord with his new status, and the social improvement his marriage had brought. He did not need to look far : at the corner of Market Street and Breadmarket Street, and actually in the Market Place, was a house to be sold, which he had himself formerly occupied, and which, though not in its existing state sufficient to meet his needs, provided an excellent and commanding site. At the end of March 1707 he bought it, for £80, from Nathaniel Barton, a London silkman, who had inherited it from his mother in 1689. Complete demolition was necessary, for the house Michael had planned was to occupy considerably more ground. Building was at once commenced, and presently all Lichfield was able to see, rising phoenix-like from the ashes, and much as we see it today, the tall, four-storeyed house which was to become the birthplace of his famous son and, in due course, a place of pilgrimage for all those that profess and call themselves Johnsonians. In June 1708 the Corporation granted him a lease of the land in both streets on which he had encroached—for it having no garden or yard and being hemmed in by buildings on his back boundaries he could not encroach except forwards.

Michael would be a proud man as he stepped back from his shop door and gazed at the ambitious creation of his architectural fancy, with its formidable rows of windows above the sturdy pillars that carried the " overjetted " portion of the house on the Breadmarket Street front and gave shelter to the main entrance. Inside, the space must have seemed prodigious to a man probably used to confined quarters. The ground floor consisted of an excellent shop about twenty-two feet by twelve, with a small parlour for use on Sundays, and a kitchen. The first floor had a large bedroom over the shop, and two smaller bedrooms, all with fireplaces. The second floor provided four more bedrooms, with fireplaces, and in the attic, lit by dormer windows in the roof, were four more rooms again that would have been considered quite good enough for servants or apprentices. Actually, during the week, the family lived modestly in the kitchen in the basement, the whole house being cellared. Altogether there were eleven available bedchambers (some of which may have been used as stockrooms), two kitchens, a fine shop, a parlour, and a scullery, in addition to storage spaces. The running of such a house would provide plenty of work for his wife.

But his pride as a house-owner must have been tempered by some anxiety as to his financial position. His undertaking to pay £100 to the trustees of the marriage settlement, within nine months, had not been carried out, and was not carried out for many a long day, and then only in a modified form. His father-in-law, old Cornelius Ford, did better, and in thirteen months, instead of nine, assigned to the trustees two mortgages on his estate at Walsall, which next year, 1708, brought them a sum of £210. The intention was that the money should be put into property, but actually it remained in the hands of Joseph Ford, Richard Pyott having for some unknown reason resigned his trusteeship. Dr. Ford continued to pay the interest to Michael Johnson.

The matter of the parchment factory, built as we have seen on the Moggs, the low-lying land by Stowe Pool, remained unsettled until December 1707, when the Corporation granted a lease of Michael Johnson's encroachment to Sir Michael Biddulph, to enable the local baronet to secure his fishing rights. This involved Michael Johnson's becoming his under-tenant, at a rent of ten shillings an acre.

Cornelius Ford, now an aged widower, whose seven children had all married and dispersed, did not live many years after his removal to Packwood. Four months before the birth of his famous grandson, in May 1709, he died at the age of seventy-seven. A week or ten days earlier, feeling the weakness of approaching dissolution, he made his will, in which he indicated a wish to be taken back to Curdworth to be buried near his wife, a wish respected by his family. He made bequests to the poor of Packwood, Knowle and Curdworth, and left a noble each to his domestic servants. Legacies to the various members of his family included £5 to Michael Johnson, and £25 to Mrs. Michael. It is probable that most of his property had already been distributed : his Kings Norton estate he had turned over to his eldest son,

Dr. Joseph Ford, in 1707. The books he had valued so much were all allocated, but none went to Michael Johnson, who had no taste for evangelical literature, or to Michael's wife.

A friend of Johnson's gathered in conversation that his grandfather was "a little Warwickshire gentleman," and another pictured him as possessed of a hundred-or-two a year in land, on which he was content to live without making an effort to increase it. He certainly had sufficient means to be comfortably independent, and to give seven children a decent start in life. But probably he continued to farm the land in the various places where he settled, until old age made him content to let a son carry on.

Some two months after his father-in-law's death, Michael Johnson, on 25 July 1709, was elected Sheriff of Lichfield, and, despite the fervency of his Jacobite sympathies, took the necessary oath of allegiance to Queen Anne, and abjuration of the Stuart claim. Like a sensible man, he had his conscience well under control, and time and time again he required to exercise this useful faculty when his private convictions, if allowed free play, would have been a bar to the holding of public office.

For the first two years or more of his married life Michael Johnson must have felt it extremely likely that the husband was not destined to blossom into the father. But by this time he can hardly have been left unaware by his wife that there was going to be a change in his life, and still more in her own. It was a time for anxiety: to delay one's first experience of motherhood till the age of forty is always a dangerous proceeding. And so it proved in this case. On Wednesday, 7 September *old style*, or 18 September *new style*, 1709, about four o'clock in the afternoon, she was delivered of a son. Lying in the big bedroom over the shop she had "a very difficult and dangerous labour." George Hector, whom Johnson described as "a man-midwife of great reputation," and who was also, like his father before him, in large practice as a surgeon in Lichfield, while as parish doctor he attended to such various ills as broken legs and ribs, dog bites, scrofulous tumours, foul ulcers and scalds, gave him his best professional assistance. But the child was almost dead, and unable even to cry for some time. "Here is a brave boy," cried the doctor, as he took him in his arms, perhaps to conceal an anxiety which is reflected in the fact that "Samuel, son of

Michael Johnson, gentleman" (this designation in recognition of his civic office) was baptized the very same day. The Vicar of St. Mary's Church opposite, the Rev. William Baker, no doubt performed the ceremony privately in the house.

Michael's anxiety for his wife and son was not allowed to interfere with the performance of his civic duties. Next day, by a curious chance, fell an annual occasion of great importance, when the representatives of the city, with all pomp and ceremony, made the official perambulation of the boundaries, involving a sixteen mile ride. Mrs. Johnson was sufficiently recovered to enquire whom he would invite, and he was so elevated by parental importance that he replied proudly, "All the town, *now*." And "he feasted the citizens with uncommon magnificence," said the one-day-old baby in after years, "and was the last but one that maintained the splendour of the Riding."

Two godfathers were found for the child who were men of considerable standing. One was Dr. Samuel Swynfen, of Swynfen, the ancient family seat a couple of miles outside the town, which he inherited himself in 1726, on the death of his elder brother Richard, M.P. for Tamworth. He had taken lodgings in Michael Johnson's new house, for use as it suited him in the conduct of his practice. Grandson of Pepys's "great Mr. Swinfen, the Parliament man," he had graduated at Pembroke College, Oxford, ten years before, had proceeded M.A., and served as lecturer in grammar to the University. His medical degree he had taken only in 1706, but medicine became his profession. The other godfather, Richard Wakefield, a much older man, had been coroner and town-clerk of Lichfield since 1688. Dr. Swynfen, liberally educated, joined a liberal mind with a liberal character; while Richard Wakefield, a childless widower of easy means, added antiquarian tastes to professional capacity. It was no small advantage to little Samuel, handicapped in so many ways, to start life with such sponsors, men of culture and wide interests, in place of a brace of local tradesmen; and in their selection we see evidence that Michael's standards were not those of the ordinary shopkeeper. Whether he derived his name from Dr. Swynfen, or from his uncle, Samuel Ford, we do not know, but his younger brother, Nathaniel, was certainly called after an uncle. Probably his parents aimed at killing two birds with one stone.

Samuel Johnson's medical history was a long and difficult one. The first exciting chapter in it, after his birth, relates how, a few weeks later, an inflammation was found on his buttock, which was first taken to be a burn, but presently revealed itself as symptomatic of a natural disorder, and "swelled, broke, and healed." Soon after this, by his father's persuasion, he was put out to nurse with a Mrs. Marklew (*alias* Bellison, as the name was popularly distinguished), in George Lane, then lined with trees, about four hundred yards from their house. Mrs. Marklew, before her marriage, as Joan Winckley, had been a servant with Michael's Market Street neighbour, William Robinson, grandfather of Matthew Boulton's two wives. In 1707 she had espoused a young local brickmaker, John Marklew, recently made a widower, who worked for Michael Johnson—perhaps helped to build his house—and in February 1708 had a son born, to whose milk, over eighteen months later, Samuel Johnson succeeded. This son suffered from some disorder of the blood which showed itself in scrofulous sores, and in impaired vision, which in later years prevented him from earning a living. As Johnson himself developed both these symptoms, with a certain amount of facial disfigurement, it was thought by Dr. Swynfen that he must have got them from his foster mother's milk. His mother blamed her own family for the inheritance, and, as the buttock trouble preceded his nursing by Mrs. Marklew, Dr. Swynfen may have jumped to a wrong conclusion. The defect in his eyes was discovered while he was with Mrs. Marklew; and an issue in his left arm was cut there. With his "little hand in a custard" he took no notice of the operation, though he mistakenly grew to think he remembered it, placing the scene in the wrong house. The issue was left open for six years. The later operation he underwent—an operation which was bungled—for ulcers on his neck, would be in relation to the same physical weakness, and on it particularly was laid the blame for his almost losing the sight of his left eye, and never hearing with his left ear.

His mother visited him every day while he was at Mrs. Marklew's, and the neighbours were so inclined to ridicule her anxious attentions that at one time she would go by Tamworth Street and at another by Lombard Street. Not quite trusting the nurse, she resorted to the stratagem of leaving behind her fan, or a glove, and returning for it unexpectedly; but Mrs. Marklew always stood the test.

After ten weeks at George Lane, about the end of November, little Samuel was brought home, in his own words, "a poor, diseased infant, almost blind." His aunt, Mrs. Nathaniel Ford, whose husband, after apprenticeship to a mercer at Stourbridge, had settled as a clothier at Sutton Coldfield, where he was this year Warden of the Corporation, told him afterwards, with rare delicacy of feeling, that "she would not have picked such a poor creature up in the street." Even Dr. Swynfen said he had never known a child reared with so much difficulty. At least Johnson was encouraged in no grudge against the Marklews, for when a boy he used to call at their house and eat plentifully of the fruit that grew in the garden. While he was thus put out to nurse, his aunt Harrison, who lived nearby, had a child Phoebe born, afterwards Mrs. Herne, whose lunatic daughter, Elizabeth Herne, he helped to support in the days of his prosperity. Mrs. Herne, no doubt out of gratitude for this kindness, bequeathed to her distinguished cousin and "best friend," in 1781, the residue of her little estate.

The eye trouble continued. Lichfield, though far from negligible in medicine, boasted no specialist to deal with it, and the Johnsons were not in a position to wander far afield and incur heavy fees. But fortunately the "rich relation," for whom we often look in vain in times of trouble, on this occasion actually materialised. Over fifty years before, Mrs. Johnson's aunt, Elizabeth Ford, at that time the widow Tomkis, had married one William Barnesley, the squire of Trysull, near Wolverhampton. Mrs. Barnesley, whose signature alone confers dignity upon the Ford family, had long been dead, as also had her husband, a "good old gentleman" of scientific inclinations, who on an occasion in 1675 left his study and his books to ride round the district with Robert Plot, the famous naturalist, on a search for materials for his *Natural History of the County of Stafford*. But their only surviving child, Mrs. Harriotts, a childless widow some eight years older than Mrs. Johnson, lived on in the comfortable old Manor House, and in spite of her comparative wealth, evidenced by her jewels and dress as well as by the establishment she maintained, and of her different social position, did not ignore her humbler cousin at Lichfield.

In 1710 or 1711, before he had gained the slightest power of storing up recollections, little Samuel was taken by his mother to stay with this Mrs. Harriotts, so that a young Roman Catholic physician from Worcester, Dr. Thomas Attwood, a relative of Lord Petre, and something of an oculist, could come over to examine his eyes. Mrs. Harriotts must have been the prime mover in this affair, and have footed the bill. Dr. Attwood's report we do not know, but at least any definite opinion from a qualified man would help to set the parents' minds at ease. Poor Michael, however, was not properly grateful. He knew no relatives of his own capable of entertaining them in such style, and always cherished a jealous antipathy to Mrs. Harriotts ; and when she stayed with them at Lichfield, which she did not disdain to do, and he could not possibly avoid her, he took a malicious delight, as has already been mentioned, in outraging her ideas of Sabbath observance. She was a very strict churchwoman, but Michael too was ordinarily a pillar of the establishment.

There are few incidents in Johnson's childhood more generally familiar than that of his being taken to hear the great Henry Sacheverell. Richard Hammond, the Lichfield apothecary, father of the caustic-tongued Moll Cobb of Johnson's later years, was in the Cathedral at the time, and saw, among the great crowd, a familiar infant, "perched upon his father's shoulders, listening and gaping at the much celebrated preacher," as portrayed by the sculptor on one of the three illustrative panels to the monument in the Market Square. Old Michael explained to Mr. Hammond that the child had caught the prevalent zeal for Sacheverell so strongly that he could not be restrained from coming, and scarcely induced to go home. Boswell was somewhat sceptical of the story, but could not omit anything "so curiously characteristick." Hammond's granddaughter placed the incident just before Johnson's third birthday, but as he himself does not seem to have recollected it (and his memory for such things was extraordinarily retentive) the date must have been earlier. Sacheverell visited Lichfield on 16 June 1710, on his way to take up a living in Shropshire, when he had an enthusiastic reception from the Corporation, who were as keen as all the other Midland towns to do him honour—indeed keener, for the official wine cellar was opened, the church bells set a-ringing, and the celebration carried to such an excess as to make even the popular preacher himself uneasy, who not many years later, by the way, was to marry a Lichfield-born woman connected with the Howards and other prominent families in the town and even perhaps distantly with the Johnsons. Only a few months earlier he had suffered the three years ban on his preaching; but he was at liberty to take services, and ladies especially flocked to hear him read the prayers. This may have been the occasion of the incident, when Samuel was nine months old: one may "listen and gape" at a preacher without hearing him preach, and Michael's vanity may have supplied the gloss to the story.

Fate determined that Samuel's infant wanderings were all to be dictated by the question of his health. Trysull had been something of a journey, but nothing to what was to come. A year or so after that, in the March of 1712, his mother took him all the way to London, that he might benefit by the supposed healing power of the royal touch. It may astonish us now, when such things appear as dictated by the rankest and crudest superstition, that this tremendous expedition, and one so costly to a modest purse, was undertaken on the recommendation of Sir John Floyer, who, though remaining in the provinces, had a national reputation, and was recognized as one of the most enlightened and truly speculative physicians of the day. It certainly leaves us with no ground for condemning Mrs. Johnson, that she also should yield to a popular belief of the kind. Perhaps Lichfield, where, on an August day in 1687, James II. had "touched" a number of duly certificated people for the "king's evil," in the Cathedral, was especially prone to such a superstition, but its continued prevalence throughout the country is evidenced by Queen Anne, who publicly invited her scrofulous subjects to avail themselves of her healing powers, having "touched" as many as 200 persons at one time in 1714. A man from the adjoining village of Alrewas was so completely cured of the "king's evil" by the touch of Charles II., that he is said to have reached the respectable age of 110.

Samuel was now thirty months old, and he always carried faint memories of the journey, which at that time took two or three days. His mother, pregnant with another son, had, with true if a little short-sighted mother love, concealed her condition from those who would certainly have delayed her visit if they had known the facts. They were unpopular in the stage-coach by which they travelled: a boy who was sick under such confined conditions, thus adding to the numerous discomforts of this kind of travel, was scarcely likely to be appreciated, though one woman passenger certainly embraced him, to balance the disgust of the other.

At the Palace, Queen Anne, with her diamonds, and her long black hood, left an awe-inspiring if rather confused impression on his mind, childishly linked with the trivial recollection of a boy crying in the Royal precincts. That he himself never escaped from some vague superstition about the amulet with which she presented him—an angel of gold, with St. Michael the Archangel impressed on one side and a ship in full sail on the other—we can infer from his continuing to wear it suspended round his neck by a ribbon, where the Queen had placed it.

Their lodging in London, no doubt all arranged for them beforehand, was in that favourite street of booksellers, Little Britain, where John Nicholson, an honest and enterprising leader in the trade, gave them shelter under his sign of the King's Arms. He and Michael Johnson were probably known to one another through business dealings. Samuel's mind retained memories of his stay there: how the counter was on the left as he entered; how there was a dark little room behind the kitchen, with a hole in the floor for the jack-weight to fall through, into which he slipped his own leg; how there was a cat with a white collar, and a dog, queerly named "Chops," which jumped over a stick; and how he played with a string and a bell given him by his cousin, Isaac Johnson. Such is the child's world we have all known, without developing into Johnsons.

There was another reason for choosing Little Britain. Mrs. Johnson's elder aunt, Mary Ford, sister to Mrs. Barnesley of Trysull, had in 1643 married George Jesson, of a very substantial yeoman family long settled at West Bromwich. Their youngest son, Cornelius Jesson, had adventured to London, graduating through tallow-chandlery to ironmongering. In 1703, out of sixteen candidates, he was elected Steward of Christ's Hospital, an office which carried considerable responsibility in regard to the schoolboys, their clothing, their provisions, and their behaviour out of class. Mrs. Johnson only required to walk round the corner to call on this cousin, who could give her all the guidance she needed in the great city.

Before she left Lichfield Mrs. Johnson had wisely sewed up a couple of guineas in her petticoat—a kind of financial "iron ration"—in case she was robbed of her purse. In London she made several purchases. For herself she bought two silver spoons, having none at home, and for Samuel a speckled linen frock, always distinguished afterwards as his "London frock," as well as a small silver cup and spoon marked "SAM. I.," for a mere "S. I." would not have made it clearly recognizable as one of his own possessions at her death. Probably these little extravagances had necessitated the unstitching of her petticoat, for on the return journey to Lichfield they exposed themselves to public contempt, and the chance of the innkeepers refusing them even bed or victuals, by travelling with the poor people in a stage-wagon. His violent cough was the excuse his mother offered for this humiliation, but he ascribed it, perhaps a little unfairly, rather to the timid thrift of one little accustomed to handle money.

Soon after this London adventure Michael Johnson's business activity and public service were further recognized by his election, on 19 July 1712, as a magistrate for the city. There is no pleasure without pain: six days later the ardent Jacobite gravely declared before his brother magistrates that the "Solemn League and Covenant" was an oath unlawfully imposed upon the subjects of the realm, while the "zealous high-churchman" expressed his entire disbelief in transubstantiation. As his son told the ever-questioning Boswell, Michael "was to settle *that* with himself," and he evidently did so, as do all except the impracticable martyr, by one of those compromises which give the necessary suppleness to our consciences.

It was in this year, as near as he could recollect, that his mother, anxious no less for his spiritual than his bodily welfare, endeavoured one morning in bed to explain to him simply the mysteries of the future state, and the difference between Heaven, "a fine place filled with happiness," and Hell, "a *sad* place." His imagination was not much affected, though he satisfied her desire that he should repeat his lesson to Thomas Jackson, their man-servant. The mildness of her theology was perhaps to blame: the conventional Hell of the period, a vast incinerator with an unlimited supply of fuel and toasting forks, would have impressed him more than a Hell where one was allowed any opportunity of feeling *sad*. He strongly contended that children should be encouraged to tell their dreams to their mothers, for the first "corruption" that entered his heart came from a dream, though he would not divulge its nature.

Nathaniel, the younger brother of Samuel, with whom Mrs. Johnson was pregnant on the trip to London, was baptized on 14 October 1712: perhaps the ceremony had in his case been delayed. Samuel, now past his third birthday, was an interested spectator, and remembered all the circumstances. His mother taught him to spell and pronounce "Little Natty," as an evening entertainment for their guests, who must have been somewhat easily impressed.

It was to Samuel's fourth year, also, that was ascribed the composition of the verse about the duck on which, while still in petticoats, he trod with such careless violence as to cause its death. As a matter of fact, the epitaph was composed by his father, and the four variants of it we possess, all equally feeble and futile, suggest that old Michael, in his vain anxiety to have it attributed to his little boy, perhaps underrated the poetical capacities even of a clever child of three.

Little Samuel's precocity brought him much misery, for his father's foolish desire to make him "show off," whenever friends came in, deeply wounded the sensitive pride of the child. He so resented being treated as if he were a species of performing dog, that visits from neighbours were the signal for him to run away and climb a tree, where at least he was safe from such humiliation. He grew to loathe his father's caresses, knowing them to be the prelude to a forced display of his childish abilities. An old man's child, he afterwards said, became the plaything of dotage, and his bitter memories of suffered indignities made him condemn late marriages on that account. True to his feelings on the subject, in after life he would not hesitate to cause deep offence by refusing to listen to deliberate displays of childish precocity, where the audience may suffer even more acutely than the young performer.

A genuine instance of his early powers of memory, just after he had begun to read, and while he still remained in the petticoat stage, was provided one morning when his mother put the prayer-book into his hands and told him he must learn the collect for the day by heart. She then went upstairs, but had not reached the second floor when she heard him running after her to say that he could already repeat it, as he did to her astonishment.

One account says that he was taught to read by his mother, and by her maid, in whose lap he listened to the story of St. George and the Dragon. But his first real lessons in the language were extra-domestic.

In Dam Street, not two minutes walk away, lived Anne, the widow of Peter Oliver, a shoemaker in the Market Square, who had died in 1704, leaving her poor, and sometimes glad of assistance from local charities. "Dame" Oliver she was called, and ability to read the black letter, in which characters she borrowed a Bible from Michael Johnson, entitled her to the respect of her small charges. He must have been very young when he began to attend her little school, for he required to be escorted there and back. And he had no first hand recollection of an incident of which his mother told him. One day, and for the first time, his escort failed to turn up punctually to take him home, and though he was so blind that he required to go down on all fours to cross the channel in the road, he started back by himself. The good Dame Oliver, concerned for his safety, followed at a discreet distance, but on rounding a street corner he espied her following, and, as he was getting along quite well, his masculine spirit of independence was so outraged, and his temper so roused, that he turned about and attacked her with impetuous fury, and with all the physical violence of which he was then capable. However, Dame Oliver rightly discounted this childish outburst on the part of a pupil who she admitted was the best she ever had under her charge.

Shoemakers have always been advised to stick to their lasts, even if their widows have not been so strictly confined. But Thomas Browne, an old friend of Peter Oliver's, and like him once a shoemaker in Dam Street, defied the old adage by turning schoolmaster. His school was in a nine-roomed house, and when the young Johnson had learned all that Dame Oliver could teach him he was sent there to be under Tom Browne, as he was familiarly called. This would probably be about 1715, when Tom Browne was a man of near sixty, and Johnson about six. No one has ever discovered the spelling book he published, with its bold dedication "to the Universe"; but we know that he wrote a neat hand, and had a little property. His single schoolroom was furnished with one table, one chair, and a few old books: the pupils no doubt stood to receive their instruction, and the necessary chastisement with which it was punctuated. Tom Browne was not only intimate with the Olivers but also connected with the Rutters, who helped Michael Johnson with the tanning, so we see in what a small circle their affairs revolved.

In 1715 the Corporation of Lichfield, in view of the recent disorders in the county, presented a humble address to the King, explaining how their zeal for his person and government had preserved the peace in the city; and Michael, let us hope with inward reservations, duly signed the oath of fidelity and allegiance on 30 August.

When Michael Johnson married, in 1706, one of his first acts had been to acquire an extra sitting at St. Mary's church for his wife, which cost him another shilling. We can picture the couple every Sunday crossing the street for the ritual of church attendance, and, in due course, adding their two boys to the party. And we can picture their alarm, shared with the whole congregation, when on the Easter Sunday of 1716, April the first, in the middle of the sermon, a small avalanche of stones and mortar suddenly descended from the spire upon the roof of the church, with an ominous clatter. A general stampede followed, and numbers provided work for the glaziers by making a hurried exit through windows not intended for the purpose. It was by no means mere senseless panic, for the steeple was known to be in an unsafe condition, and this startling incident was naturally considered to herald its complete collapse.

To a small boy, the pleasureable excitement of being involved in a minor catastrophe of this kind would amply compensate for the first feeling of fear. And it served a useful purpose with little Samuel. For some time the precocious youngster had been developing a distaste for religion, more especially that aspect of it represented by attendance at church. So when, a few weeks later, the parishioners held a meeting and decided to take down the spire and use the stone for repairing the main fabric, his opportunity came. The church was perforce closed, and little Samuel, refusing to accompany his parents to St. John's Chapel, over a quarter of a mile away, whither the seats and pews had been removed, used to wander off into the fields, where he could read undisturbed, and escape from the feeling of inferiority that his "bad eyes" encouraged.

But even without church to go to, his Sundays were gloomy enough. His mother, cruel only to be kind, used to shut him up to read *The Whole Duty of Man*, and it is not to be wondered at that the book failed to influence him in any way. Even the chapter on theft did not convince him that it was wrong, though he thought that had such books been given to him for their literary excellence the moral lessons they sought to inculcate might have been unconsciously absorbed. If he did not read the *Apocrypha* it was read to him, though never at any time right through. His mind was in an unsettled state as regards his religious beliefs, and when he first felt able to reason he used deliberately to adopt the sceptical point of view in argument with his mother, and she did not flatter his vanity by any stern reproof. But, however far he may have strayed from orthodoxy, his conscience always functioned vigorously, and from the earliest time he could remember he had been forming schemes for a better life.

Michael Johnson continued to do a little publishing from time to time. In 1710 he had joined with a London man in issuing a sermon entitled *The Christian Synagogue: or the Original Use and Benefit of Parochial Churches*, preached in Birmingham by William Binckes, who had succeeded Lancelot Addison, father of Joseph the essayist, as Dean of Lichfield; and in 1712, in conjunction with a bookseller at Stafford, had published another sermon, *Evil Communications*, preached before the Assize Judges there by Dr. Richard Bynns. But, generally speaking, his business was of a nature that kept him constantly on the road: attending sales, and holding sales of his own, looking after his market-day stalls in surrounding towns, and dealing in all manner of things that today would not be handled by a bookseller and stationer. In addition, there was all the travelling entailed by his parchment and tanning activities. Indeed he was very rarely at home, or not for long at a time, though probably he did not ordinarily get further away than a day's ride.

In June 1716 he was at Trentham, in North Staffordshire, where Lord Gower had his seat. The great Tory nobleman boasted a fine library there, and the Rev. George Plaxton, a Yorkshire antiquary-rector, who, with a natural business aptitude not common to his cloth, acted as his unofficial man of affairs, spent many hours among its treasures. Michael Johnson was naturally well known to Mr. Plaxton, whose letter on this occasion, to the Rev. Francis Skrymsher, a kinsman of the Dr. Gerard Skrymsher with whom Michael was so closely associated, has become classic as a tribute to the old bookseller's acquirements and capabilities:—

> Johnson, the Litchfield Librarian, is now here; he propagates learning all over this diocese, and advanceth knowledge to its just height; all the Clergy here are his Pupils, and suck all they have from him; Allen cannot make a warrant without his precedent, nor our quondam John Evans draw a recognizance *sine directione Michaelis.*

We see from this what a familiar figure Michael Johnson was among the local clergy and all those persons who cared for learning (or wanted cheap help in their legal affairs). But "Parson Plaxton," beloved by Thoresby and other friends of kindred tastes, and whom Defoe claimed to have "turned inside out," was an inveterate wag, who could not write or speak without introducing quip or jest. We must not read the letter of such a man, old, sick, yet still irrepressible, too seriously, but rather as a piece of light raillery, in which playful exaggeration of Michael's scholarship was probably intended as a sly reflection on the shortcomings of the clergy who found it necessary to besiege him with their various requests. Still, a local bookseller who could, on his son's word, read Latin, had some claim to be termed "learned."

CHAPTER III.

AT LICHFIELD GRAMMAR SCHOOL
THE LOWER SCHOOL
1717-1719

THE reputation of the ancient Grammar School of Lichfield was not entirely made by Samuel Johnson and David Garrick, whom it sent forth to astonish the world in such very different ways. It could claim some famous pupils before their time. Elias Ashmole, the antiquary, and founder of the great Museum that bears his name at Oxford; William Wollaston, the philosopher; Gregory King, a Herald only eclipsed by his master, Dugdale; George Smalridge, a notable Bishop of Bristol; John Colson, the mathematician; John Rowley, an instrument maker of high repute, praised by Steele; and above all, Joseph Addison, the essayist—these men were various enough in their gifts and accomplishments to shed enviable distinction on any country grammar school. And preceding Johnson by not so many years had been some notable judges, Sir John Willes, Chief Justice of the Common Pleas; William Noel, also a Justice of the Common Pleas; and Sir Thomas Parker, Chief Baron, who carried the school's fame into the courts of law.

When Johnson, therefore, left the care of simple Tom Browne, now near his end, and entered the Grammar School, at the beginning of 1717 (perhaps following his father there), he became one of the heirs to its considerable traditions. These probably did not weigh much with a boy of seven, especially one whose physical handicaps gave him more than enough to think about. Though his health had improved, his appearance, to the common eye, was little better than that of an idiot; and one Lichfield gentleman reproved his sons for bringing to the house such a "disagreeable driveller." It was a hard fight for a poor boy, labouring under such disadvantages, to overcome them by any display of mental superiority. Perhaps it was just as well that his parents could not afford to send him to a boarding school, where his handicaps might have involved him in much more humiliation. He thought himself that it was a mistake to send boys away to school before they were twelve, for there were much more important things to be learned at home than Latin and Greek.

The actual schoolhouse, during Johnson's pupilage, was a detached building consisting of one large room, panelled in oak, with massive oak desks for the boys and loftier eyries at the end for the masters. It stood in St. John Street, opposite the Hart's Horn Inn. Discipline, with the result of its infraction, was never allowed to be forgotten, for the three-legged stool on which the boys were flogged stood before their eyes as a permanent piece of furniture in the schoolroom.

The junior usher at this time was Humphrey Hawkins, a man of about fifty, who had been appointed as far back as 1684. Not a university graduate, he received at first an annual "gratuity" of £5 for teaching the poor boys, which in 1705 was raised to £10. He also had permission to teach writing, and the casting of accounts, in the schoolroom, but out of school hours ; and augmented his income to the extent of another £5 a year by acting as clerk of St. Mary's church, where he entered up the accounts in his beautifully clear, "copperplate" hand. With a large and increasing family he needed every penny of his small stipends, and in later years he was granted assistance from a local charity.

Johnson, of course, with other town boys, rich and poor, entered the lower school, and thus came immediately under the tuition of Hawkins, whom he described as "very skilful in his little way." Neither Dame Oliver nor Tom Browne had been qualified to teach Latin, and Mr. Hawkins had to set to work to repair the deficiency. The "Exercises" principally relied upon were the well-tried works of John Garretson, William Walker and Charles Hoole, and the more recent one of William Willymot. Learned merely under discipline, and not providing food for conversation or serving any intellectual end, his "exercises" were soon forgotten after leaving school. With his constitutional indolence, he always looked forward to Thursdays, when instruction gave place to general examination, for no preparation was required and the questions were very little varied from week to week. Saturday, too, was devoted to examination, and he was much astonished on one occasion to find that George Hector, son of the doctor who had ushered him into the world, had never been taught his Catechism, on which they were sometimes questioned. In the scheme which he himself drew up later in life for the conduct of a grammar school, Thursdays and Saturdays were similarly set apart for examination.

He, for his part, found the conjugation of verbs difficult at these weekly tests, and one evening, depressed by previous failures, he felt particularly apprehensive as to his performance next day, though, as it turned out, quite unnecessarily. "We often," his mother remarked to him, "come off best, when we are most afraid." She confessed her pride to have so young "a boy who was forming verbs," when he told her, almost before he could speak plainly, that at least he "did not form them in an ugly shape."

On Thursday night the boys used to learn passages from their Latin *Æsop*, or from *Corderius*, to repeat on Friday morning, but not from *Helvicus*. A passage in one of the "morals," dealing with a man who vented his hatred on another by making him rich, he recited to his mother with mischievous emphasis, for the poor soul had never had a chance of discovering that any evil could result from the possession of money: the idea, she confessed, was beyond her comprehension. In his own scheme of teaching, just referred to, *Corderius* in John Clarke's edition of 1718 was the first Latin book to be studied, followed by the same editor's *Erasmus* of 1720, with an English translation.

Friday afternoon was devoted to the grammar book. They learned "*Quae Genus*," which he liked, while "*As in Praesenti*," for some reason, he heartily disliked. As a new boy, with no Latin, he had to read the "Accidence" through twice before learning it by heart. When they read the third section, "*Propria quae Maribus*," it was in the accidence they were examined, parsing it also sometimes with the help of Hoole's *Terminations*. He learned the whole chapter so thoroughly that he used easily to repeat it to his mother, and to his cousin Tom, son of Andrew Johnson, who had come over from Birmingham to live with them, probably to learn his trade of a currier at his uncle Michael's parchment factory. He even repeated it once in a dream, up to a point.

The week before they broke up, and the part of the week in which they actually broke up, was devoted entirely to examination, a respite from the usual routine enjoyed by masters and pupils alike, and their last two nights they even rejoiced in no "home-work." But there were holiday tasks to perform, an exaction which he always remembered with resentment. He felt that in the ideal education there should be no "home-work," but only "home-instruction."

Hawkins thought highly of his odd-looking pupil, and indulged him affectionately, for he recognized his real superiority over the rest of the boys. Johnson's mind was in a state of rapid formation, and particularly sensitive to the influence of his excellent master. With constant fresh impressions, his powers of observation developed also, and though he was little more than two years under Hawkins the period in retrospect seemed very much longer, as is always the case with children.

It is said to have been when he was about eight years old that an incident occurred which he was wont to relate to all his friends. While sitting in the basement kitchen, which the family occupied during the week, reading *Hamlet* (and few boys at that date had Shakespeare's works accessible), the ghost scene became so vividly alive to him that he had to rush up into the street to reconnect himself with reality. He had the normal child's love for romance: giants and castles he found more interesting to read about than everyday life.

Somewhere about nine months after Samuel's entering the Grammar School his father's tanning activities involved him in rather serious legal proceedings. On 10 October 1717 he was indicted at the Lichfield Quarter Sessions for practising the trade, when he had not been apprenticed to it for the requisite seven years, under an old act which also forbade employment of anyone so disqualified except as a journeyman or as hired by the year. But the man whose help in their legal affairs had been so eagerly sought, only a year or so ago, by the Staffordshire parsons, was at no loss in such a predicament. He drafted "The Defendents Case" fluently in his own hand, in legal form, the clauses duly numbered, and though he wrote it in the first person he afterwards corrected it to the formal third. That finished, he turned over the paper and wrote a more concise version of it on the other side, and handed it to his attorney, Joseph Adey, who as a young man had been with Samuel's godfather, Richard Wakefield, and who in this case was opposed by Theophilus Levett, the Town Clerk.

The formal brief prepared by Mr. Adey for the counsel, Mr. Moreton, followed Michael Johnson's draft very closely, even including some of the graphic expressions he had employed. His case was that, though, as a stationer, he had for full twenty years bought hides and skins for the manufacture of vellum and parchment, and had had the rejected ones tanned, he was committing no legal offence, for he had nothing to do with the actual process ; while John Barton, the principal witness, who undertook the work, was not his servant but rented a tanyard of his own, where " any countrey man that has a sterk Cow or Horse that dies " might bring the hide to be tanned. John Barton, who was a freeman of Lichfield, and the year before had been Warden of the local Company of Tanners, was certainly paid a weekly sum for subsistence by Michael Johnson, but he also received further payment, varying with the amount and quality of the work done. John Rutter, who had continued to tan for Michael after his mother's death, had only recently been passed over in favour of John Barton, and it was insinuated that he was at the back of the prosecution, for there was half of any fine inflicted to attract him as well as the hope of revenge. In Michael's own vivid words, he had " ungratefully now forgot the Bread he eat." Jonathan Mallett, who long ago had married the Johnson's maidservant, and was last year's Sheriff, was to witness that vellum and parchment makers in other places sent their unsuitable skins out to be tanned, just as Michael had done, and suffered no molestation.

It was a very representative court that sat in the Guildhall to hear the case against Michael Johnson, a court in which he was as well known to all the representatives of local authority as they were familiar to him. The presiding magistrates were the Senior and Junior Bailiffs of the year, in addition to those of the year before, with William Fettiplace Nott, Serjeant-at-Law, the Steward of the city, and son-in-law to Thomas Hammond, of Edial Hall, to be mentioned later. The Grand Jury of thirteen, all well known local men, returned a true bill against their bookseller neighbour, and he was ordered to appear at the next Quarter Sessions on 16 January 1718. But at that appearance Michael asked for a further adjournment, and this being granted he came up again on 24 April 1718, when he declared himself not guilty, and " put himself upon the country," as also did Richard Wakefield, Samuel's godfather, who prosecuted as coroner.

The Sheriff was now ordered to empanel a petty jury to try the case at the next Quarter Sessions, but once more delay ensued, and it was probably not till the October Sessions that the case actually came up before the jury. We know the personnel of the panel, and the twelve good men and true selected, thanks to Michael's handy pen, though their verdict is lost to history. But that his fellow citizens and fellow members of the Corporation did not condemn him in their own minds, on evidence which was familiar to them all, is clear from the fact that on 25 July 1718, while the case was still *sub judice*, he was elected Junior Bailiff of the city. On the actual day of the election he was away at Bristol Fair, and the unpalatable oaths that he was continually being forced to swallow were postponed till August. He performed his duties as Bailiff conscientiously, attending all the meetings of the Brethren of the Corporation and signing the minutes. It may be mentioned that John Rutter, held up as the evil genius of the case, married into a good family, and himself served as Sheriff of Lichfield in 1731.

Edmund Hector told Boswell that the decline in Michael Johnson's fortunes was due to his engaging in the parchment manufacture, which his continual absences from home did not allow him to superintend as closely as was necessary. But as he continued it for fully thirty years, and stoutly resisted all attempts to stop him, it can hardly have been consistently unprofitable. It must have been the parchment house by Stowe Pool that old Michael used to lock up so carefully after half of it had fallen down from neglect, an act which his son did not hesitate to describe as one of madness.

His main business was not neglected during these conflicts with the law. Early in 1718 he held auction sales at Gloucester, Tewkesbury and Evesham, and at other places in their neighbourhood. On 21 March 1718 he held one at The Talbot, in Worcester, at six o'clock in the evening. Shop books, pocket books, fine French prints, and maps of various sizes, were included with general literature, and the ladies were tempted by "fine pictures and paper hangings." The pictures were to be on view from noon, for daylight was necessary for their inspection, and the policy was to begin each day's sale with small and common books, to give time for the room to fill, "persons of address and business seldom coming first." Catalogues were to be obtained at the Lichfield shop, or the place of sale ; and the circular, with a true appreciation of social niceties, was addressed "To all Gentlemen, Ladies, *and others*, in and near Worcester."

These long journeys, taken on horseback, were of benefit to Michael's physical health, and provided a welcome means of escape when things went badly, or when Mrs. Johnson grew too querulous. Long stays at home drove him almost to the point of insanity, and what would have happened to him without the refuge of the saddle we can only guess. It was probably more accident than design which caused him to be at Chester Fair at some unrecorded date when little Samuel had the small-pox.

Neither Michael Johnson nor his wife was at all methodical, and if they had only had the good sense to keep accounts it would at least have helped them to see how they stood, and how things might be improved. Always industrious and hard working, as he was in his way enterprising and ambitious, Michael should have made a much greater success of his life than he did, for he was a well-informed man, of honest and independent character, with a vigorous and shrewd intelligence, as well as much more education than the ordinary tradesman. He wrote easily, in a hand bearing considerable resemblance to his son's, and if his grammar and spelling were a little wild there were plenty of gentlefolk in his day who, without his vigour, no more conformed to rule in such things than he did. Lichfield, respectable enough in its way, scarcely offered a sufficiently wide field for his abilities, so that although he won general respect there his financial position never accorded with his reputation in trade or his status as a public man in the town. The wide range of country he continually traversed in search of business shows how sparse learning was at that time, in relation to the square mile, when books were the luxury of the few, and even the ordinary wares of the stationer required only by a small fraction of the population. Modest receipts, offset by bad debts, reduced him sometimes to a state of practical insolvency, and on one occasion he had to seek substantial help from William Innys, the well known bookseller of St. Paul's Churchyard.

Though he was always a great favourite with the boys of the town, and almost alone in never suffering from their vexatious tricks, his son could only describe him as "wrong-headed, positive, and afflicted with melancholy." His "large and robust body," and his "strong and active mind," did not secure him from a species of acute hypochondriacal depression that often bordered on madness, and left him with no appetite for life and subject to a gloomy dejection of spirits. If it had not been for his active habits, and the absence of money or leisure to allow liberty for luxurious introspection, his mind might well have lost its equilibrium altogether. Though he was a man of pious character and carefully controlled speech, whom grief or joy never betrayed into loose or impious expressions, there was yet a strong strain of perversity in him. With all his gloom, he had a large share of vanity, though his circumstances gave him little opportunity of displaying it.

If Mrs. Johnson had been more literate, and possessed of some knowledge of books, her husband's life at home might not have been so miserable. Intelligent conversation can make even husband and wife agreeable company to one another. But, lacking any larger interests, her talk ran entirely in a narrow groove of domestic trivialities, and to a man whose business provides him with daily worries quite sufficient to try his temper and nerves the constant complaints and criticisms of a wife whose mind is ever concentrated on the petty irritations of the day are exasperating beyond measure. The most blameless character does not atone for nagging, and Mrs. Johnson, despite her many excellences, must be put down as a nagger. She never encouraged him by intelligent criticism, but merely kept harping on his want of success, and as she had no real conception of the nature of business her never-ending complaints and suspicions led to the inevitable result that he refused altogether to discuss his affairs with her. Naturally reserved, he sat moody and silent, hoping at the best for occasional respite from the unwelcome topic. As she kept no accounts of her own domestic expenditure she was less in a position to tease him about his lack of method, and about some branches of the business being run at a loss. She was for ever saying that they must not spend more than they could afford, but, womanlike, never attempted to find out what that amount was. Moreover, she had "married beneath her," and did not let him forget it, while he was too proud to argue such a delicate point. Little wonder it was that "they had not much happiness from each other." Yet there was never any actual breach between them, and to the world they probably appeared, as some might even say they were, an ordinarily happy couple.

An ill-matched pair are apt to display their worst qualities towards one another, and Mrs. Johnson's defects in her relations with her husband must not blind us to the fact that in all her other social relations she was conspicuously amiable. She won the complete affection of her children, and her neighbours held her in such high esteem that when an attempt was made to deprive her of a field in her possession no attorney would come forward to take up the case against her. She is said to have been blessed with a "good understanding," as well as much good sense, though, with little education, these qualities can only have been exercised in a very narrow field. She realised her son's value, but without any vanity. Great men are usually supposed to owe their character to their mothers, but we look in vain for signs of mental or moral distinction in Mrs. Johnson. She had no clear idea of how to bring up her children, and though she was continually telling them to "behave," she never explained how it was to be done, and when Samuel asked for more particular instructions she was completely at a loss. He said that the children of poor parents paid them no respect, and that although he loved his mother he yet was rude enough once, when she angrily called him a puppy, to ask if she knew what a puppy's mother was called.

As a small boy Samuel had a curious liking for dry oatmeal, and when a little older he always took porridge for breakfast. He was so fond of the coffee his mother gave him from her narrow store, that the memory of it helped to increase his affection for her in after life. Her one extravagance was tea, and Michael thought it so expensive that he succeeded in dissuading her from exchanging calls with the neighbours, who would have to be entertained with the precious beverage. But she resented such an unsocial injunction, and was afterwards sorry she had obeyed it.

About the end of May 1719, Samuel, aged nine, was despatched by his mother with Nathaniel, aged six, to Birmingham, sixteen miles away, to stay with her relatives. He wondered why people should be plagued with strange children, but Mrs. Johnson had the good sense to see that "changing the mode of life" (no doubt she meant for the better) was an advantageous experience, whatever her relatives may have thought. Most of the fortnight or so was spent with her brother, probably Nathaniel Ford, the clothier at Sutton Coldfield, whose wife's brusque tongue would be likely to call Samuel to account for such a grave offence as eating too much of a boiled leg of mutton, which Mrs. Johnson, impressed as usual by trifles, told him would hardly ever be forgotten.

Mrs. Ford, in spite of this act of gluttony, treated him with lavish affection, her rough ways and quick tongue being joined to a kind heart. The rest of this Whitsuntide holiday was spent with his saddler uncle, John Harrison, who had left his native Lichfield for Birmingham some years before. A widower, his household was run by Samuel's cousin, Sally Ford, daughter of his uncle Cornelius, whose sweetness of temper left an impression almost of perfection on the boy. There was a daughter of his own age, the Phoebe Harrison born while he was nursing at Mrs. Marklew's, whose elder brother, Cornelius Harrison, had entered Pembroke Hall, Cambridge, the year before. Unfortunately, John Harrison himself was a most detestable man, easily—and every night—affected by drink, mean, peevish, vain and fond of show: indeed his nephew only rejoiced that lack of means prevented him from developing his objectionable traits to a higher point of unpleasantness. The Castle Inn, next door to his shop, may have helped to his undoing. Directly opposite in the High Street was the bookseller's shop of Andrew Johnson. Poor Andrew had not prospered, and—ever the strong man in the woman's toils—his position was not made easier by a third wife who came to him cured of various physical ailments but owing money right and left to the doctors and surgeons who had effected the cure, one of whom hotly denounced her as an "ungrateful slut" to young William Priest, the Birmingham attorney, whose main interest was to save Andrew from imprisonment for his wife's debts.

There was little love lost between the two boys and their uncle Harrison, and the prolongation of their holiday for a few days after the vacation cannot have given either side much pleasure, though the rattle Samuel got for his whip delighted him. He wrote home to his mother about it, and asked in grown-up style that the horses should not be sent for them until the Thursday of the first school week. Michael Johnson himself brought the horses over, and mightily offended Samuel, who was feeling so important, by telling the ostler that he had "two boys under his care." Michael was then in the proud position of having a watch, on probation, which he sensibly returned to the maker when payment became due.

CHAPTER IV.

AT LICHFIELD GRAMMAR SCHOOL
THE UPPER SCHOOL
1719-1725

THE journey back to Lichfield safely accomplished, Samuel had to return to school, where he found a considerable change being effected. It had been the practice of the headmaster, the Rev. John Hunter, to keep back the town boys in the lower school as long as he possibly could, for the boarders were not only more profitable to him financially, but were also probably better bred youths and better scholars on the average. Things got to such a pass that Richard Wakefield, the Town Clerk, Samuel's godfather, decided that he must reprove Hunter and have the injustice redressed. There were eleven boys in Samuel's class, which was, as a result of the reproof, moved up bodily into the upper school, when, as he recollected it, his exercise in *Garretson* was about the gerunds : how far he got in *Æsop* and *Helvicus* passed out of his mind. Samuel, devoted to Mr. Hawkins, wept at the change, but the rest of the boys were less sensitive and did not worry. It was a serious matter for Mr. Hawkins, who evidently received some sort of capitation fee, and he complained that half his profits had gone.

"Johnson's schoolmaster" always suggests the figure of John Hunter, whose pupils have conferred upon him a distinction that falls to few heads of small country schools. Born at St. Albans, about 1674, he went to University College, Oxford, where he took his B.A. in 1695 and his M.A. in 1700. After a short time as second master at Birmingham School he went on to take charge at Solihull (which had robbed Birmingham of many of its pupils), and nine or ten years later, in 1704, was appointed headmaster at Lichfield, in succession to the Rev. Robert Shaw, who had taught Addison. To take the headmastership required his immediate ordination, and in 1709 his position in the church was consolidated by his appointment to a prebendal stall in the Cathedral. He was the typical "head" of the period, a very severe disciplinarian, delighting in the arbitrary exercise of authority, who thrashed the boys without mercy, and without considering whether the fault was due to excusable ignorance or deliberate negligence. The whip, in his opinion, was the best encouragement to learning. He would spring out-of-the-way questions upon them, the answers to which they could not reasonably be expected to know, with the birch ever ready to reward the unlucky. Johnson really hated him, thinking him not only brutal, but actually cruel, and often unjust ; yet he admitted his great scholarship and his quality as a teacher. If his brutalities reached such a point as to prevent any of his old pupils from sending their own sons to him, it was certainly immediately effective, as Johnson admitted it was with him personally, overcoming his disinclination to learn, and not causing him in later life to lose faith in the virtues of the rod. Hunter's grim joke, as he belaboured his pupils, that he did it to save them from the gallows, was not altogether unjustified, however it may conflict with modern educational theory. He worked, and worked successfully, with the tools of his period, but fashion has changed and they are not our tools. He had one solid merit from Johnson's point of view : he was an ardent Jacobite.

Hunter well maintained the dignity of his office in externals, and "never entered the school without his gown and cassock, and his wig full dressed." His imposing presence, and his exceptionally stern appearance, made him a most awe-inspiring figure, whose mere memory almost caused Johnson to tremble, even in manhood. But there was another side to this tremendous man, if the stories can be believed. So keen a sportsman was he, that a boy culprit could always hope to escape the rod if fortunate enough to be able tactfully to communicate the whereabouts of a covey of partridges. And according to Miss Seward, his granddaughter, he devoted his leisure hours to music and singing, and performed creditably upon the bass-viol.

But Johnson, though now in the upper school, did not come into much immediate contact with the dreaded Hunter, for his whole class was put under the care of the Rev. Edward Holbrooke, the senior usher. Johnson described his new instructor as "peevish and ill-tempered," and cited several instances of his ignorance of Latin, which got them into unmerited trouble with Hunter, to whom, when sent up for punishment a second time, they protested by telling how Mr. Holbrooke would not explain the particular passage in *Phaedrus* which had caused the trouble. John Taylor, however, who also was his pupil, said he was "one of the most ingenious men, best scholars, and best preachers of his age." So we must suspend judgment.

Holbrooke, the son of a Wolverhampton lawyer, was quite a young man, who had taken his B.A. from Corpus Christi College, Cambridge, in 1716, but did not proceed M.A. until 1721. His first ushership had been at Stafford.

Johnson had never realised the power of concentration on a mental task until once when he was sitting in the kitchen at home, in front of the window, thinking himself alone, and doing his first exercise for Mr. Holbrooke. So absorbed was he that, though he turned his head and saw his charming cousin, Sally Ford, who must have come over from Birmingham, dancing away in the room, he went on with his work quite oblivious of her presence, and regardless of time. He could hardly ever remember having achieved such concentration again. We have already seen how the Johnsons lived during the week in the kitchen : to light the parlour fire except on Sundays was an act of high social significance and meant a radical change in the mode of life, as momentous as nowadays to change from " high tea " to late dinner.

The easy Thursdays and Saturdays enjoyed by the lower school were now to seek. Instead of perfunctory examination, an ordinary lesson occupied Thursday morning, while the afternoon was devoted to syntax, as also was Saturday morning. *Æsop* soon gave place to *Phaedrus*, the only book they actually finished (for it was short), and the lines they learned, which latterly ran to thirty, had to be repeated to Hunter himself on Friday afternoon. The marginal " interpretations " to the fables they found of little help, and the notes at the foot they ignored altogether. Johnson thought that the masters really enjoyed "tasking," and that it reconciled them to long lessons. Masters and pupils are always to some extent at war, and the boys at Lichfield, faced with inimical authority on every side, enjoyed the malicious satisfaction of having a secret cache in a corner of the schoolroom where lay translations of the books they were reading.

Helvicus, which occupied Monday and Wednesday afternoons, they spent much time over, but found it so difficult that they made slow progress. Mr. Hawkins, who still took them sometimes, told them to omit " *Vestitus*," for it was one of the hardest dialogues in the book, and others, on food and fruits, they also dropped for the same reason. At noon each day they were required to punctuate their exercises, a refinement disregarded in the lower school. At the Whitsuntide when he entered the upper school, one Mrs. Longworth gave him a copy of *Hermes Garretsoni*, but he found it of so little use that its being lost, or stolen, at school, did not trouble him. Once, when they were set twenty-five exercises, he did them all, against the other boys' sixteen, but he kept some back, and five lay for a long time in a drawer in the shop. The first he had done quickly and shown proudly to his mother, who rightly opined that he would not get on so fast with the rest.

His great friend at school was Edmund Hector, nephew to George Hector the surgeon. A year or two senior to Johnson, he was yet his constant companion, in school and out of school. With many kindred tastes, and the still greater bond of affection, they would wander abroad together in the fields on holidays, Johnson talking as much to himself as to Hector ; or they would go to Dame Read's to buy tarts. To Hector he was ever a hero : his mental superiority over the other boys, which even impelled three of them by turns to carry him (no light load) to school, sitting on the shoulders of one boy, with another each side for support, that they might gain his assistance with their lessons, or, in winter time, to draw him along on the ice by a garter fixed round his middle, and held by a barefoot boy, was as marked as in later life was his dominance over the distinguished men who formed his intellectual circle.

Reserved and even saturnine in his manner, he did not mix easily with the generality of his schoolfellows. He was unable, through his bad sight, to join in the ordinary games, and jested afterwards that he had managed to be idle without them. He desired to excel at his work, but with such superiority of talents, such constant intellectual curiosity, and a memory so retentive that he seemed never to forget anything he had heard or read, his end could be achieved without great exertions, so that his companions rarely saw him studying. He would dictate verses to some of them, but not trouble to write them down himself. His sluggish inertness of temperament, and his disinclination for ordered effort, caused him to procrastinate, and his exercises were apt to be put off till the last moment. On one occasion the considerable tasks he should have accomplished during a long vacation were performed by his returning to school an hour earlier in the morning, and deliberately leaving mistakes in the first exercise, so as to gain time. He was never corrected in his actual work, but his fondness for talking, and distracting the other boys' attention in class, brought him occasional reproof and perhaps punishment from Hunter. Even his private reading, where he followed his own inclination, was only desultory, as far as his friends could see. To Hunter, with his studied deportment, the sight of Johnson, a great overgrown boy, rolling clumsily about on his form, as his body, in some peculiar way, responded to his mental efforts, must have been really distressing.

Hector remembered that he once recited eighteen verses to Johnson, who immediately repeated them word for word, except for a slight improvement in one place. His scholarship formed the standard for comparison at school, and other pupils were judged according to it. There was only one boy—and a "town boy" at that—Theophilus Lowe, son of a local plumber, whose scholarship was considered equal to his. But he was over eighteen months older, and in any case Johnson did not agree with the verdict. Though Theophilus Lowe won a fellowship at St. John's, Cambridge, tutored the celebrated Charles Townshend, and died a Canon of Windsor as well as a most estimable man (while his elder brother, Christopher Lowe, became one of the Principal Clerks of the Treasury), he did nothing to challenge Johnson's judgment of him. A prize of a guinea for some original Latin verses, given to Johnson by his noble neighbour at Elford, the Earl of Berkshire, himself a keen classical scholar who used to carry a *Horace* in his pocket, and then Deputy-Earl-Marshal, must have made him a very proud boy.

Though we must not build too much upon Johnson's pronouncement—echoed so wearyingly at prize distributions—that "a boy at school was the happiest of human beings," everything points to his having enjoyed his time there. In spite of his handicaps, he did join in some of the boyish activities of his friends, leaping easily the rail in Levett's Field, behind the School, where they played, climbing gates, and indulging a taste for impromptu gambols that he rather absurdly retained even in his days of greatest weight and dignity. He could scarcely hope to rival the performance of his uncle, Cornelius Ford, who, while on a journey, perhaps into Lincolnshire, came to an inscription by the roadside recording some remarkable leap that had been accomplished nearby, and, exclaiming that he could leap it in his boots, promptly proved as good as his word. Samuel had one athletic accomplishment of his own: he became a powerful swimmer. His first lessons were from his father, who used often to take him as a boy to bathe in the clear stream that branched off from Curborough Brook and flowed through the mill at Stowe till it emerged in the meadows beyond to rejoin the Brook. Old Michael encouraged him to persevere till he accustomed his limbs to the strange movements. In those days the lower part of the stream was heavily shaded by the overhanging branches of trees, which kept it quite secluded, but when these were afterwards cut down, and the stream, with its bathing pools, exposed even to distant view, it rather lost its charm for Johnson.

With the object of combatting his natural awkwardness he even went so far as to submit to a few lessons from a dancing master as well as from a dancing mistress, but his weak sight, which he said would not have enabled him so much as to get food if living in a savage state, soon made him desist. An old custom in the school which pleased him was the preparation of "furmenty"—wheat boiled in milk—for consumption on Mid-Lent Sunday and Christmas Eve. He came to occupy a position among the boys that mere scholarship would not have won him, for they accepted him as their natural leader, and acquiesced in his judgments as of a final authority.

We have seen how the closing of St. Mary's church, after the accident in 1716, had given him an excuse for avoiding attendance at services. But its re-opening on 30 December 1721, when Mr. Baker, the dignified Vicar, preached from a text in *Nehemiah* appropriate to the occasion, deprived him of this excuse. His absence from Pew Number 35, allotted to the Johnsons a month before, would have been very noticeable, so, if rather reluctantly, he came back, physically at least, to the fold. But he continued, in his own heart, unconvinced and apathetic towards religion, and quite ready to talk even more laxly than he felt against the beliefs which as a man he was always so eager to defend. Near the end of his life he dated his youthful disregard for religion as from the age of ten, say 1719–20. He had never really confided his scruples to anyone, being, as he said, sullen and reserved by nature in his childhood. His conscience pricked him, and he searched without success for evidences of the truth. Eventually he remembered having seen a book, in his father's shop, the *De Veritate Religionis* of Grotius, and blamed himself for not having consulted it. However, when he did refer to it, he found the Latin beyond his comprehension, and so felt relieved of guilt. In later days he sometimes carried the work in his pocket.

Almost the same age as himself at the School was John Eardley Wilmot, who went on to Westminster in 1723, and eventually became Chief Justice of the Common Pleas. Sir John, who could recall Johnson as a "long, lank, lounging boy," contended that the power to discipline was the greatest desideratum in a headmaster, so Hunter's severity had evidently not earned his resentment. "Tom" Newton, afterwards Bishop of Bristol, whom Johnson did not love, also went on to Westminster, in 1717: son of a prosperous Lichfield wine-merchant he was nearly six years Johnson's senior. Isaac Hawkins Browne, the poet, was only a year younger than Newton, and, like him, joined the trek to Westminster: it would be a later association which caused Johnson to describe him as the most delightful converser he had ever met. A schoolfellow with whom Johnson was very intimate and always maintained friendship was Robert James, who was six years older than himself, and whose father lived at Shenstone, near Lichfield: he left for Oxford in 1722, not yet dreaming of the "fever powders" that were to make him famous.

After Edmund Hector, probably Johnson's most intimate school friend was John Taylor. It is a little difficult to understand how they became drawn to one another, and what kept them in such close communion to the very end, for they had little in common. Son of a well-to-do lawyer at Ashburne, in Derbyshire, Taylor had good average abilities, but he valued the things of the mind much less than the flesh-pots he was so anxious to fill, and the qualities which made an unblushing office-seeker of the wealthy parson cannot have been completely concealed in the schoolboy. The love Johnson gave to Hector can hardly have been extended to Taylor, though he treated him with great confidence, crediting him with better capacities and intentions than did most of those in a position to judge.

Another notable schoolfellow was Charles Congreve. Descended from an ancient Staffordshire family, his father first cousin to William Congreve the dramatist, he was a year or so older than Johnson, and left for Magdalen Hall, Oxford, in March 1726. He was in the same form, but in later life, when Archdeacon of Armagh and almost comatose from his addiction to port, he could not be aroused to any interest in their former association, or in his other old schoolfellows. Very different were Johnson's relations with Charles's brother, Richard Congreve, who also went into the church. Though five or six years younger than Charles, he enjoyed Johnson's early confidences, in a friendship freed from all forms and ceremonies, and Johnson never lost his affectionate regard for this companion of his youth.

Another scholar much of an age with Richard Congreve was Gilbert Repington, son of a country gentleman at Tamworth, who, like his brother John, also known to Johnson, went up to Oxford, though only after an eight years spell at Charterhouse. Then there was Andrew Corbet, his own age, who has been credited later on with influencing Johnson's decision to go to Oxford himself. He was another representative of the squirearchy : his father, who died in 1715, had left him an estate in Shropshire. Andrew Corbet's uncle, the Rev. Dryden Piggott, had been at the school with Addison. Yet another cadet of an old Staffordshire house at school with Johnson was Bowyer Sneyd, who was, however, eight years older and left for Cambridge at the end of 1719 : he was uncle to the beautiful Honora Sneyd, who occupies such a romantic place in Lichfield's later annals. And William Bailye, the apothecary, grandson of Michael Johnson's bookseller rival, was his classmate under Hunter : his father, Richard Bailye, was, like the much younger Samuel Johnson, a godson of Richard Wakefield.

It will be seen that Johnson's schoolfellows included a number of distinguished men, and that even at this very beginning of his career he was able to establish friendly relations with many boys who had enjoyed all the social advantages of those who are now to be found only at the great public schools. These contacts would not only enlarge his outlook, but also help to give him that confidence and poise he always displayed in his dealings with people of rank.

Of Johnson's humbler schoolfellows, whom he continued to care for and visit long after he had become famous, we naturally do not know much. There was Harry Jackson, a man of little education or polish, who failed as a cutler in Birmingham and came back to live in poor circumstances in Lichfield. There were other unsuccessful companions of his childhood, like Sedgwick and Brodhurst, who no doubt were schoolfellows as well.

A very old friend of Johnson's who there is reason to suspect must have been at school with him was Caleb Hardinge, brother to Nicholas Hardinge, the classical scholar, and of a Derbyshire family. Caleb himself was a man of many parts, scholar, wit and Royal Physician, whose social connexions were supposed to excuse in him a licence of speech and conduct that made him the subject of many anecdotes.

While Johnson was making such headway at the Grammar School his father continued to play his part in civic affairs. But it was some time before he achieved his ambition of becoming the Senior Bailiff, or virtual mayor, of the town. The names of two members of the Corporation eligible for the high office had to be submitted each year to the Bishop. In 1722 and again in 1724 Michael Johnson's name was one of those put forward, but on each occasion he was the second nominee, and his lordship, the learned Edward Chandler, followed precedent in selecting the first, in the one case Richard Dyott, esquire, and in the other William Cary. In 1725, however, Michael Johnson, as senior nominee, was approved by the Bishop, and duly elected Senior Bailiff on 25 July. During his term of office he attended all the twelve meetings of the brethren.

It was in or about the year 1724 that Catherine Chambers, a girl of his own age, joined the household as maid to Mrs. Johnson, to remain with her, or with Lucy Porter, until her own death in 1767. Devoted to all the family, and they to her, the beloved "Kitty" of Johnson's letters, her last illness saw him deeply moved and praying by her bedside.

Business continued as usual. We know of only one book published by Michael at this period, *An Exposition of the Revelations*, in 1719, by Sir John Floyer, who had momentarily turned aside from medicine to theology. In spite of all attempts to stop him Michael persisted in the tanning that had brought him into collision with the law. Early in 1725 he was prosecuted by the Commissioners of Excise, but the local justices would not convict. The Commissioners accused them of acting in defiance of the clearest evidence, and in July instructed their local officer, on the occasion of the next offence, to send them an affidavit, so that the Exchequer could prosecute direct. What happened further we do not know, but at least Michael remained tenant of the land by the Pool until the end of his life.

Here again we see how local opinion favoured him, his election to office once more following immediately on his arraignment by the law, almost as if a deliberate affront were intended. Even the worthy Bishop may be said to have connived at it. That the defendant's son was heartily in sympathy with his father we find when we open the *Dictionary*, and read that "Excise is a hateful tax," adjudged by "wretches hired by those to whom Excise is paid"; or turn to *The Idler* to discover how a Commissioner of Excise is one of "the two lowest of all human beings."

CHAPTER V.

AT STOURBRIDGE GRAMMAR SCHOOL AND AN IDLE SPELL AT HOME 1725-1728

MICHAEL Johnson's undertaking, in 1706, to pay £100 to the trustees of his marriage settlement within nine months, had not been honoured through all these years. But on 16 September 1725 a deed was executed which to some extent straightened out the tangle of his affairs. By it he conveyed his house in the Market Square—valued at £200—to trustees, in favour of himself, his wife, and their children, he at the same time receiving £100 in cash for his own use out of the £200 that had been placed in the hands of his brother-in-law, Joseph Ford, as a trustee of the marriage settlement. So that he was an immediate gainer by the transaction.

Joseph Ford, the eldest brother of Mrs. Johnson, had, as we have seen, been educated to medicine. He was at Queens' College, Cambridge, but where he obtained his degree of M.D. (if he did obtain it) is not known. However, as soon as he was qualified, he settled in practice at Stourbridge, in Worcestershire, where he remained all his life, gaining high reputation as a doctor, making solid money, and becoming a leading figure locally. At the very outset he had strengthened his position by a prudent marriage. There had long been settled in the town a prosperous family of clothiers, the Hickmans, a younger son of which, Henry Hickman, fortified with Oxford and Cambridge degrees, had become quite famous as a fierce controversialist in the cause of Nonconformity, had married an aristocratic Strode from Somersetshire, and had even crept into the pages of Pepys's diary. This Henry's nephew, Gregory Hickman, who carried on the family business at Stourbridge, died a youngish man in March 1690, leaving a widow (whom, as Jane, daughter of Thomas Launder, a capital burgess of Kidderminster, he had married when she was a girl of eighteen in 1675), with a growing family; and this widow, before the year was out, remarried their friend, Dr. Joseph Ford, who was some five years her junior. Connexion with the Hickmans added to his importance, and a wife with some means would be a direct help to a young doctor.

Dr. Ford, after a long and successful professional career, died in March 1721, following a two months illness, from a gangrenous affection of the feet probably due to his gouty condition. His will was a lengthy and detailed one, and he would be the uncle of whom Johnson spoke in 1773 as having left his affairs in such perfect order, with nothing unconsidered. His own and his wife's portraits by the Verelsts, the plated sword that he wore as one of the symbols of his profession, his "study of books," and various personal articles he valued, were all carefully allocated ; and there were numerous financial provisions, one of which ordered his son within six months to pay £200 to his wife and executrix, without, however, specifying that it was the money held in trust for the Johnsons.

Now the principal party to the deed just mentioned, with Michael Johnson, was that son, "the Reverend Cornelius Ford, of the parish of Pedmore, in the county of Worcester, clerk," who had become his father's legal representative. Under the will of his mother, who had died in September 1722, he was again instructed to pay the £200 due to Michael Johnson and his wife. But the instructions, as before, had not been carried out, and the deed of 1725 was evidently in the nature of a compromise.

Cornelius was the only surviving son of Dr. Ford by his marriage to Mrs. Hickman. Born in 1694, and educated at Mansfield School (apparently after some time at Nottingham, under that celebrated grammarian, Richard Johnson), he went on to St. John's College, Cambridge, where he took his B.A. in 1713, later migrating to Peterhouse, proceeding M.A. in 1720 and being elected to a Fellowship in the same year. A man of brilliant natural gifts, easily displayed by his wit and versatility, his friends at Cambridge included such men as William Broome, the poet (whom he considered too coated with "scholastic rust "), the Hon. Charles Cornwallis, and Philip Stanhope, the famous Earl of Chesterfield. Of a naturally extravagant disposition, always inclined to society, and unsympathetic to mere scholasticism, association with rich young scions of the aristocracy would hardly tend to give him balance, or encourage application to any kind of serious work such as would have been required if he were to make good in a profession. With his Fellowship he stayed on at Cambridge, where he became an excellent classical scholar, for some years, but by 1723 he was living at Pedmore, close to Stourbridge, where his father had left him property. In June 1724, when himself only thirty, he vacated his Fellowship and married a mature spinster of forty-three, Judith Crowley, one of the large family of a successful Quaker ironmaster at Stourbridge, and half-sister to Sir Ambrose Crowley, Addison's "Jack Anvil" of *The Spectator*, who had applied such great business acumen and powers of organisation to his father's trade that his works at Greenwich, and on the Tees, had already made him rich and famous, and helped his family to begin a series of alliances with the aristocracy. The ironmaster who instructed William Penn how to develop the mineral wealth of his Sylvania is sure of a small niche in history.

If to marry an elderly woman with means is a crime, Johnson himself committed it not so very many years later. But knowing of Cornelius Ford's habits, and his genius for contracting debts, we cannot but suspect him in this affair of deliberate fortune-hunting. True that the Fords and the Crowleys were on terms of friendship, and that Judith, though possessed of £1200 in money, as well as her personal belongings, could not accurately be described as rich. Yet there seems something so ludicrously incongruous in the elderly provincial spinster, of Quaker upbringing, as the bride of the clever and highly sophisticated young man from the university, known a little even to such a man as Pope, and who had matched himself against wit and fashion, that we can hardly be persuaded to accept their marriage as one of natural affection, especially when we find that almost immediately it enabled the bridegroom to pay off one of the substantial mortgages he had effected on the properties he had inherited. At the time of the marriage Cornelius was a "gentleman," not the "clerk" of the deed fifteen months later, for he was only ordained deacon, on 1 January 1725, to fit himself for his new and more sober state.

There had probably not been much communion between the Fords at Stourbridge and the Johnsons at Lichfield, though there was a further tie between them through Dr. Ford's stepdaughter, Jane Hickman, having in 1701 married his own brother, Nathaniel Ford; she was the aunt who tempered her kindness to little Samuel with caustic comments on his behaviour. Their lot in life was so different, and they lived so far apart, that Cornelius Ford, at any rate, who had been away for long periods at school and college, is likely to have seen little of his uncle and aunt and their two sons. But the arrangements in connexion with the deed would bring them into touch, and probably involve actual meetings. As a man of education Cornelius would be greatly interested to find that he had a young cousin who was able to meet him more as an intellectual equal than were his other relatives.

The result was what might easily have been expected. Cornelius Ford, struck by the boy's unusual abilities, invited him, in the autumn of 1725, to stay at Pedmore. It was intended that the visit should run only to a few days, but the two cousins, though so unequal in age, and in the opportunities they had enjoyed, found such satisfaction in the friendly intercourse that the days soon became weeks. Cornelius, seeing how he could help Samuel in his classical studies, persuaded him to stay on, and became his temporary tutor, assisting him also in other subjects, anxious at least that he should not suffer by absence from Mr. Hunter's disciplinary establishment.

Cornelius, said to have been the original of the punch-bowl-presiding parson of Hogarth's *Midnight Modern Conversation*, and so accepted by his cousin, has come down to us as a rather disgraceful figure, typical of the worldly and dissipated cleric. Johnson himself said that his "abilities, instead of furnishing convivial merriment to the voluptuous and dissolute, might have enabled him to excel among the virtuous and the wise." But he had a warm corner in his heart for him nevertheless, and there is no reason to think that at the time of this Pedmore visit Cornelius Ford was indulging in profligacy or doing anything to disgrace the cloth he had only recently begun to wear. Even as a layman he had recently shown some interest in the parish affairs, and to the end of his short but chequered life he was a stickler for orthodoxy and respect to the clergy. If his conduct had really been as suggested, or if he had been separated from the wife he had married only the year before, Mr. and Mrs. Johnson, naturally conventional in their views on such matters, would hardly have allowed their young son to stay with one who might have corrupted him by example if not by precept.

It was all to Samuel's advantage that his cousin, though now a cleric, should be a man who had seen the world, including its frailties, through the eyes of a layman, and who, though a good scholar, was no pedant. His "acquaintance with life and manners," his wit, his good sense, his wide knowledge, and his finely-tempered judgment, made a deep impression on Samuel, which all the varied experiences of his own life left undimmed. As one who eschewed such dry subjects as philosophy and metaphysics, Cornelius particularly persuaded him to aim at all-round culture, rather than what would then have been considered high specialism : himself a man of the world he wanted his cousin to fit himself to shine in general educated society, and not to become so wedded to some narrow study as to win no welcome there. He seems, also, to have detected one of his cousin's weaknesses, and to have warned him against aiming too much at controversial victory, which would not help his progress in the world or encourage others to appreciate his worth. These fresh points of view must have been something in the nature of a revelation to a boy who, however great his capacities, or even his ambitions, had probably never approached the problem of his future career from such sophisticated angles.

The intellectual stimulus provided by this close association with Cornelius Ford must be regarded as having had a very vital effect on the development of the young Johnson's mental capacities, and as having given a definite trend to his scholarly outlook. There seems no doubt that Cornelius deliberately exerted an influence on his cousin in the direction of the humaner sides of learning that persisted through life, and as deliberately set himself to encourage that constant ambition to perfect himself as a conversationalist which eventually made Johnson perhaps the greatest talker of all time. Even forty-five years afterwards he longed to revisit the neighbourhood of Pedmore to review his conversations with cousin Cornelius, or 'Neely' as he familiarly called him.

Whatever the faults of "Parson" Ford, as he is usually known, the kindly interest he showed on this occasion in his young cousin, and the trouble he took to instruct him and guide his studies, evidences his possession of some excellent qualities of heart as well as of head. The days that had lengthened into weeks now lengthened into months, leaving Samuel Johnson still happily enjoying his cousin's hospitality at Pedmore, with all that it meant of fresh mental experience. It was only at the Whitsuntide of 1726 that he returned to his parents' house at Lichfield, full of new ideas through association with his brilliant kinsman.

It was not to be expected that such a flagrant piece of truancy would appeal to Mr. Hunter. It would be a poor headmaster who did not insist inexorably upon obedience to the rules of his school, and it was no more than justice that he should refuse to take back a boy who had not only absented himself for two terms but had during that time preferred a quite unprofessional kind of tutoring to the strictly disciplined instruction of the Grammar School. On the point of taking a second wife, in the person of Lucy Porter the elder, he could hardly have visualised the great, awkward schoolboy of sixteen, son of the local bookseller, as a future brother-in-law of sorts.

The Johnsons were therefore in a quandary, with the local Grammar School closed against their son, who was just requiring the finishing touches to his education. An effort was made by his father to get him admitted into the Grammar School at Newport, in Shropshire, not far from where his Skrymsher relatives lived, as a kind of pupil teacher. But the excellent headmaster, the Rev. Samuel Lea, would not accept him : the rejected of other schools are not often welcome elsewhere. Mr. Lea, who lived and held his post till 1773, afterwards became aware of the chance he had missed, and could only boast how near he had been to vicarious fame.

And now the experiences of the visit to Pedmore were to bear fruit. The Rev. Cornelius Ford, hearing of the difficulty in which his cousin was placed, and feeling himself to be in a measure responsible, advised that he be sent to Stourbridge Grammar School. As son of the leading physician in the town, Cornelius would have some inherited influence there, in addition to that earned by his own scholastic achievements. His half-brother, too, a younger Gregory Hickman, was one of the principal merchants there, whose youngest sister was married to Daniel Scott, a governor of the School, and whose eldest sister was wife to Clement Acton, a local ironmaster, grandson of the Shropshire baronet who ancestored Lord Acton the historian.

The suggestion was acted upon without much delay, and Johnson duly went to Stourbridge after the Whitsuntide vacation of 1726. Gregory Hickman had himself been one of the Governors, but it was probably Daniel Scott who gave formal consent, as required by the rules of the School, to the admission of a "stranger" like Johnson. If the headmaster, the Rev. John Wentworth, had raised any more serious objections they must have been smoothed over by Johnson's local friends. Wentworth was a middle-aged bachelor, a graduate of Oxford, who had been in charge since 1704 : a very able man but inclined to idleness, to absenting himself too long from the School, and to extending the holidays at his own discretion. Johnson entered on the terms that had been unsuccessfully proposed at Newport : he paid no fees, and in return gave some of his time to teaching the boys in the lower form. He made no pretence of paying court to Wentworth, who, seeing little likelihood of being credited with any success his big pupil-assistant might achieve, was especially severe to him. But, while at Lichfield he had learnt much in the school, and little directly from its famous head, at Stourbridge he admitted to learning much from Wentworth himself, and little in class. On balance, however, he did not make as much progress there as had been expected.

While at Stourbridge he would be able to keep in touch with his cousin near by at Pedmore. He probably lived with the ordinary boarders in the headmaster's house, where he was only separated by an inn from Green Close, the home of Gregory Hickman, who having first married a Moseley, a cousin of the Acton baronets, was now supplied with a second wife. These local family connexions, which probably included his uncle, and Gregory's brother-in-law, Nathaniel Ford, must have helped to make his abilities known to a much wider social circle than might have received him without them. He " was admitted into the best company of the place," indeed, and his powers of conversation made such an impression as left memories behind for many years to come. His natural position would be very different there from that of the tradesman's son at Lichfield.

And there was beauty to try his heart. Always impressionable to the attractions of the other sex, his " first love " had been Ann Hector, his friend Edmund's sister, a year or two younger than himself, the " genteel woman, very agreeable, and well-bred," with whom Boswell and he took tea in 1776 : she married the Rev. Walter Carless, whose mother, Ann Moseley, was a sister of Gregory Hickman's first wife. Here at Stourbridge he conceived a great admiration for Olivia Lloyd, a niece of Mrs. Cornelius Ford's, and indited verses to her. Olivia was a Quaker girl a year or two his senior, of the banking family, with a love for the classics that she passed on to her nephew, Charles Lloyd, the philanthropist, whose son again was the friend of Lamb. Another nephew, Sampson Lloyd, entertained Johnson and Boswell at Birmingham in 1776. At Stourbridge Johnson even had "colloquial disputes" with George, afterwards the celebrated Lord Lyttelton, a youth barely a year older than himself, who at Hagley was near neighbour to Cornelius Ford. While still a schoolboy Johnson used to try his dialectical skill by always choosing the wrong side in a controversy, as it allowed of greater ingenuity of argument.

There was one feature at Stourbridge Grammar School which must have delighted him, for Henry Hickman, of whom we have heard as the great-uncle of Gregory, had shown his interest in it by presenting a library of fine folios, including Greek and Latin classics, as well as books on general subjects. In Johnson's spare moments, as also in his exercises, he gave "proofs of his poetical genius," a number of which were even preserved by Wentworth himself, some original and some translations from the classics; while certain verses he planned then were not put into finished form until over fifty years later, when he dictated them to Mrs. Thrale. It was here probably that he translated Addison's "Battle of the Cranes and Pygmies" from the Latin. The School still shows the initials "S.J." carved on the wainscoting, to vouch for the authenticity of its most famous "old-boy."

It is probable that the total period of Johnson's stay at Pedmore and Stourbridge did not much exceed a year, and that he returned to Lichfield in the autumn of 1726, when his father was again having to swear allegiance to the Crown before his brother magistrates, and to repudiate the Pretender's claims so thoroughly that he was not allowed even the loophole of "mental evasion." The *Latin Dictionary* Johnson acquired on 27 August 1726, by Adam Littleton, who had been a local man, may have come from a Stourbridge shop: it is interesting as showing how, on 7 September 1726, his birthday (O.S.), he calculated his age correctly as seventeen. Evidently he was beginning to realise how rapidly he was ceasing to be a boy, and that it was time to take stock of himself and his prospects.

He was now to suffer a severe check to his career. It had always been his parents' ambition that, with his exceptional abilities, he should go on to the university when he had finished his schooling, with the church as his natural goal. But it was not to be. For some reason, after returning from Stourbridge, he stayed on at home, living a life that seems tragically out of accord with his intellectual possibilities. Whether it was the want of money alone which barred his path may be doubted, for in the case of notably clever boys ways and means are generally found to give them an education by which society stands to gain even more than themselves. Michael himself was certainly hard up at the time, for in February 1727 we find him borrowing £10 10 0 from Richard Rider, the future Chancellor of the Diocese and a friend of Samuel's godfathers ; but the Johnsons had many relatives and friends able, and one would have thought willing, to come forward with help at such a critical point in their son's life. We are tempted to suspect that there were other reasons for this sidetracking of his career, the most obvious being that of his health, which, physically as well as mentally, had always given cause for some anxiety. He himself often expressed a wish to adopt the law as a profession, but the expense was too great to make this possible, a fact he always regretted.

Idle though nominally he was during this stay at home, in the sense of having no definite occupation, he could not avoid taking some part in the conduct of his father's business. He confessed to having been bred a bookseller ; and he had mastered the art and practice of bookbinding, for which his bad sight and general awkwardness scarcely fitted him. He had, too, a thorough knowledge of all the processes of tanning, probably acquired at this period by helping with that most troublesome side-line of the business. But the routine of the shop was very distasteful to him, and he would get so absorbed in the books he was supposed to sell that the customers were lost sight of, his father's rebuke only drawing from him an admission that to place the conduct of business before the pleasure of reading was a task quite beyond him. On one occasion he thought that Nathaniel had hidden some apples behind a large folio, on a high shelf in the shop. When he climbed up there were no apples, but the folio turned out to be *Petrarch*, one of the restorers of learning, as he had heard him described, and his curiosity was so excited and his interest so held that he sat down then and there and read the book nearly through, for at school he would make no acquaintance with the medieval Latinists. Probably the historic occasion when he refused to accompany his father to Uttoxeter market belonged to this period, a refusal for which he did such humble penance there fifty years later.

Conscious of his purposeless existence, living but from day to day, and scolded by his father for lack of application, it must have been a depressing time for a boy who knew his powers. But there was one consolation, as we have seen. He was at least surrounded by books, and books on all manner of subjects. Never a consistent reader, constitutionally indolent, lethargic in mind as well as in body, and always following his own inclination, he yet roved over a very wide field of literature, and if his choice was desultory he took care to confine himself to standard works. What he read was " all literature, all ancient writers, all manly," but not much Greek except for parts of *Anacreon* and *Hesiod*. Indeed it was during this time of " idleness " that he acquired a large part of that immense knowledge of classical literature which stood him in such good stead in after life, but which, like all his other knowledge, was by the very method of its acquirement unsystematic.

Unlike the college student, who is mostly confined to what his tutor recommends, he was quite unrestrained except by his own inclination, by his instinctive taste for what was best, and by the chance of what books happened to be lying on his father's shelves. A copy of the *Satyricon* of Petronius bears his signature and the date 1727. Travel and voyages he almost entirely avoided, with " works of mere amusement," in spite of his lack of any conscious scheme. Yet he never relinquished reading tales of chivalry, which he afterwards considered had helped to unsettle his mind and prevent him applying himself to a profession. Though he loved poetry, he could rarely finish any actual poem ; indeed few people can ever have read so much with so little discipline beyond that enforced by personal taste. He professed to have known almost as much at eighteen as he did in the days of his literary dictatorship—only his judgment had improved since. His greatest period of study he put as from twelve to eighteen. Years later he said that a young man should read five hours a day to acquire much knowledge, so probably that was his own average. His lack of plan certainly saved him from the arid specialism against which his cousin Cornelius had warned him.

There was another side, also, to his desultory life at this time. We have seen that he had formed several strong friendships at School, and made a number of acquaintances among boys living in better and more cultured homes than the one Mr. and Mrs. Michael Johnson could offer him. Lichfield, though a small place, gained importance through its ecclesiastical, military and official activities, and could boast a circle of well educated persons, not rich but of easy means, who lived under conditions that favoured general cultivation of the mind and the growth of some intellectual ideals. It is from friendly association with people of balanced views that the truest education largely comes, and Johnson gained quite as much from the easy interchanges of educated society as from the regimented instruction of the schools. Indeed, looking forward at the distinguishing qualities of his mind when fully formed, we may say that what we most value in his attitude towards life and literature was born of a rich social experience to which specialised knowledge provided only a running commentary.

Preeminent in the Lichfield of Johnson's youth as a man of liberal and cultivated mind was Gilbert Walmesley, Registrar of the Ecclesiastical Court, and nearly thirty years his senior, who won the affectionate regard of rich and poor alike. He was the old-fashioned "gentleman and scholar," a true amateur of learning. Son of a former Chancellor of the Diocese who had also been Member for the city, he had enjoyed every advantage of upbringing and education, and after leaving Oxford had been called to the Bar at the Inner Temple. Extraordinarily widely read, and no less devout, he was yet a man of the world, who had seen the follies of fashionable life as well as its more admirable side. This man it was, settled then in bachelor luxury at the Bishop's Palace in the Close (the Bishop himself always living at Eccleshall Castle, well out of the way), and moving in the most exclusive of local circles, who, before all his early friends, helped to shape Johnson's life. As a lover of books there would be no shop in Lichfield holding so much of attraction for him as Michael Johnson's, where he was among the regular customers, and it would not require much converse with the bookseller's son to discover the boy's quality. It was later on, however, in Johnson's early manhood, that, as we shall see, their association became more particularly intimate and fruitful.

Another local gentleman who befriended Johnson, and invited him to his house, was Theophilus Levett, who had succeeded Richard Wakefield as Coroner and Town Clerk in 1721. A Cheshire bred man, born to good social connexions, and his wife of the Staffordshire Babingtons, he derived his baptismal name from Theophilus, Earl of Huntingdon, whose Countess was his godmother and lived in Lichfield during her widowhood of 1701 to 1706. Blessed with ample means, he did old Michael many acts of kindness. Samuel and his mother afterwards had business dealings with him, and with his son, John Levett, the kindness being continued. Then there were his godfathers, Richard Wakefield, now in retirement after trouble over some unknown irregularities, and Dr. Swynfen, who in 1727 followed many ambitious local people in moving to Birmingham. Other houses which welcomed him were those of Stephen Simpson, the lawyer, whose wife was sister to Joseph Adey, Town Clerk of Lichfield after Theophilus Levett, and John Marten, the apothecary, who had married the widowed Mrs. Howard in 1722 : his stepson, Charles Howard, afterwards the father-in-law of Erasmus Darwin, was only three years older than Johnson. John Marten, brother of Michael's old apprentice, Simon Marten, was a man of notable piety and moral worth (as befitted an ancestor of her who created *The Fairchild Family*), who is said to have kept open house for the cultivated society of Lichfield.

William Butt, the father of Cary Butt, who grew up to become a leading surgeon in Lichfield and to marry John Marten's daughter, used to welcome Johnson to his house in the holidays, and had to reprove his children for speaking slightingly of him as "the great boy." "You call him the great boy," he exclaimed, "but take my word for it, he will one day prove a great man." Johnson had a pleasanter memory of Cary Butt than is suggested by this story, how (at a time that must have fallen within the compass of this volume) he used on a week-day, before starting on his professional round, to lead his father-in-law into the church, and leave him in his seat. And John Marten is thus seen fully to have earned Johnson's commendation as a "pious man."

Lichfield society, he claimed, was the politest of any similar town in the country, spoke the purest English, and (greatest virtue of all) was the most orthodox in its religion. He always regretted that this stronghold of toryism had never (in his time) found its historian. Defoe, in his *Tour Through Great Britain*, published in 1724–6, described Lichfield as " a place of good conversation and good company, above all the towns in this county or the next," the " next " being Warwickshire and Derbyshire, incidentally alluding to its " fine school." So that Johnson's local pride had some real justification.

It was fortunate in many ways for Johnson, poor as he was and lacking in almost all the superficial graces that often assist advancement in life, to have opportunities at his very door of mixing with refined and educated people. But the settled character of such a society, highly typical in its way of an established order of things that it never thought of questioning, would tend to influence his own attitude towards the problems of human existence, and to assist in the building up within him of such a solid structure of conservatism as would suffice for over half-a-century to repel those revolutionary (and some would say more enlightened) ideas that often floated in the very air he breathed. Whether this was to his advantage or not it were profitless to discuss, but at least it helped him that he should gain assurance in meeting well-bred people. However at times he may have failed in some of the minor aspects of social observance, his easy complaisance of manner in the company of persons of birth and position was remarkable from his earliest manhood.

That family which, after Johnson's, became the most famous connected with Lichfield, remains to be mentioned. David Garrick, whose name is so closely associated with his, was seven-and-a-half years his junior, but seems to have entered Lichfield Grammar School before he had left, for Mrs. Garrick once asked him how little David did at school, and received the reply that her son would either be hanged or become a great man. Peter Garrick, Captain in the army, and his wife, daughter to a vicar-choral of the Cathedral, were poor enough, but as things are, or perhaps were, they moved by right in a social circle to which Johnson could only gain admission by his special talents. Yet friendship between the sons of the two houses must have begun early. Indeed, it is said to have been in 1727 that Johnson spoilt little David's first appearance as actor-manager, in Farquhar's *Recruiting Officer*, at the Garricks' house, by failing to write the prologue. The Garricks lived in Beacon Street, opposite the entrance to the Cathedral Close. The

Close, boasting but a couple of hundred inhabitants, formed almost a separate community, with its social superiority and its physical barrier from the town in the shape of the beautiful Minster Pool.

Apart from all these local families, there were, too, plenty of uncles and aunts and cousins of varying degree within a short ride, or even, to one so accustomed to long and lonely tramps, within a day's walk. The clannish spirit that was so strong in those days among people not absorbed into great centres of population made kinship a real social influence. His father's relatives, indeed, or those of whom they knew, were but humble folk, who were frankly looked down upon by Mrs. Johnson, and except for uncle Andrew Johnson, the impecunious bookseller at Birmingham, they scarcely appear in the story. But the Fords, with all their connexions, were a numerous breed, who could offer pleasant hospitality to their cousin from Lichfield, whenever inclination, or business, took him their way. There was the rich Mrs. Harriotts at Trysull, the uncrowned queen of the whole clan, whose interest in them all must have helped to weld it together, and whom he evidently visited again when he was grown up, for he preserved a vivid memory of the exceptionally regular way in which she ran her household. The Vicar of Wombourne-cum-Trysull from 1725 was Johnson's second cousin, the Rev. Cornelius Jesson, a Balliol man a generation older than himself.

There was the circle of Fords and Hickmans at Stourbridge, which had already played its part in the story. There were his uncles at Birmingham, and a few miles from Trysull there was Mrs. Johnson's sister, Mrs. Hardwicke, at Great Moor, Pattingham, where the Hardwickes had been settled as small gentry for many generations. Some of the Abnets, grandchildren of Mrs. Johnson's uncle, Henry Ford of Clifford's Inn, still lived on at The Manwoods, the house he had built at Handsworth. The Jessons, sprung from her aunt, were a prolific stock in and around West Bromwich, where their beautifully panelled house, built on ancestral Ford property, and now a public amenity, no doubt sometimes echoed to Johnson's footsteps. Of two of them we have already heard, Cornelius Jesson, the Steward of Christ's Hospital, and his nephew and namesake, the parson just alluded to. Johnson's uncle, Dr. Joseph Ford, attended his cousin Thomas Jesson, at Sutton Coldfield, in his last illness in 1703.

There were two of Johnson's uncles who strayed for a time right out of the Midland area which ordinarily contained almost all his near kinsfolk. Samuel Ford and Cornelius Ford both lived for some years at Stroxton, a tiny agricultural parish in Lincolnshire, where Samuel was churchwarden in 1714 and 1718, and Cornelius in 1700, 1707 and 1710. The cause of this rather surprising migration probably lay in the fact that the Hackets, whose seat was at Moxhull in Warwickshire, in the Fords' own country, also had an estate at Stroxton, and the Fords were just following in their wake. It was Cornelius Ford's youngest daughter, Phoebe, who for many years was the trusted housekeeper of Edward Gibbon, "author of the Roman Hisstorry," as she described him, and the historian's rather difficult relations with Johnson may have been partly due to this innocent but perhaps awkward situation. Phoebe's eldest sister was the Sally Ford of whom Johnson had such happy recollections. Strangely enough, an eminent but inimical scholar, a northerner, accused Johnson of speaking in the Lincolnshire dialect, but his uncles had probably both left the county while he was still a small boy, and there is no reason to think that he ever visited it till long afterwards, when he was the guest of Bennet Langton at Langton.

Johnson, we know, never freed himself altogether from the local accent of Lichfield, and "woonse" when he was "theer" asked his friends which of them wanted "poonch." But Staffordshire and Lincolnshire, with Derbyshire, Leicestershire and Nottinghamshire, have several dialectical features in common, so that anyone only superficially acquainted with the speech of Lincolnshire might easily imagine a Staffordshire man to be from the more easterly county, where people of some education are also inclined to the pronunciations "woonse" and "theer." Actual "dialect," in the shape of local colloquialisms or methods of expression, and words not widely current, can have entered very little into the speech of one who from his early youth had strictly trained himself always to express his thoughts as perfectly in conversation as if he were writing, though his occasional use of such words as "wench" in familiar talk perhaps betrayed him not a southerner.

CHAPTER VI.

AT PEMBROKE COLLEGE, OXFORD 1728-1729

WE never know what is best for us, and Johnson probably deplored as much as we are apt to do that he should be held up at home all this time, unable to proceed to the university for professional equipment, and making no serious attempt to qualify himself for his father's trade. It must have been his parents' hope, as well as his own, through all these long and seemingly abortive months, that eventually he would be able to resume the intellectual training that leaving school had interrupted, and this must have made it more trying for them all than if his future had been frankly accepted as unlikely to be more than that of a mere bookseller's assistant. But providence is often more far-seeing than we who grumble at its apparent caprices, and during this long and anxious time he was really, if unconsciously, equipping himself by his omniverous reading to be the essential Johnson we know. He grew to realize it a little himself, asking Boswell not to assume that he was " doing nothing then."

After two years existence under these backwater conditions, Johnson was at last to get the chance that had been waited for so long. What the circumstances were that eventually led to his entering the University of Oxford we do not know, but so far as the difficulty had been a financial one an explanation can be suggested. In February 1728 old Mrs. Harriotts, the head of the Ford clan, died at Trysull, and not only did she remember her cousin Mrs. Johnson to the extent of a pair of her best flaxen sheets and pillow cases, as well as a large pewter dish and a dozen pewter plates, but she also left her £40 for her own use. By the time her will had been proved, in March, and Michael had given his bond not to touch the legacy himself, some months had probably elapsed, and Mrs. Johnson may have found it hard to decide what to do with the money. She would not like to spend it on herself, with her husband, now in his seventy-second year, sufficiently humbled by distress to call the lady he had appreciated so little in her lifetime " our good cousin Harriotts." But there was one object to which she could devote it that would be to his pleasure and benefit as much as her own—the further education of the son whose great abilities they must have thought were running to waste. Forty pounds, as values went then, was about enough to pay his college expenses for a year, and the hope of scholarships, or of better times at home, may have tempted them to take the plunge. The suggestion that local gentlemen subscribed to help him does not seem likely : if they had felt so inclined it would have been earlier, while his school record was familiar to them and he was in disciplined mental training for competitive study. His departure from Lichfield was sweetened by a visit from his old schoolmistress, Dame Oliver, to say good-bye. She was running a small confectionery business, and delighted him with a present of gingerbread.

At any rate, on 31 October 1728, seven weeks or so after his nineteenth birthday, Samuel Johnson entered the University of Oxford, Pembroke being chosen for his College. His mother's cousin, Henry Jesson, had been at Pembroke sixty years before, while Richard Chambers, a connexion of hers, afterwards Prebendary of Hereford, had followed only a dozen years back. And William Vyse, a future Archdeacon of Salop, who was Johnson's own age and had probably known him at home, was then at the College. But much more to the point is it that Dr. Swynfen, Johnson's godfather, was a Pembrochian, whose elder brother, Richard, had contributed to the building scheme carried out at the College nearly thirty years earlier, while Richard Pyott, the county gentleman who so unaccountably became a trustee under the marriage settlement of Michael Johnson and Sarah Ford, had entered there in 1679. John Hall, Bishop of Bristol, who had been Master of Pembroke from 1664 to 1710, was a Worcestershire man, whose uncle, Thomas Hall, had given the little library to Kings Norton, of which we have heard in connexion with Johnson's grandfather, Cornelius Ford, who treasured his religious writings.

The biographers insist that Johnson's decision to go up to Oxford was largely due to his old schoolfellow, Andrew Corbet, or his father, having made some promise to support him there in the capacity of a companion. They err in stating that Corbet, who was a gentleman-commoner, entered with Johnson, for he had gone up eighteen months earlier, and his widowed mother, the daughter of a Shropshire baronet, had died early in 1728. Though he had been in residence up to the time of Johnson's arrival, he left almost immediately afterwards, the same week in fact, and never returned in person. The tale, however, is so categorically told that it must have some foundation in fact, and Corbet's immediate departure home may be taken as corroborating to a degree one would hardly anticipate the accusation that he left Johnson in the lurch.

Johnson was actually entered as a commoner at Pembroke College on 31 October 1728, and he paid the usual caution money of £7, to be repaid on leaving the College, less any outstanding charges. His father, despite his age, had anxiously travelled with him all the way from Lichfield, to see him through the opening stages of his university career. This was rather trying for Samuel, the father being so full of his son's scholarship, his poetry, and his Latin verses, that he held forth on the subject to the company at the College. Samuel, who sat modestly silent and uncomfortable, must once again have felt in the position of the performing dog, and that this was not a very auspicious introduction. His appearance and manner seemed strange to his new associates, but his shyness and their critical attitude vanished when a turn in the conversation suddenly caused him to break his silence with a quotation from *Macrobius*, and to make them realize that here was a youth whose reading had gone far beyond that of the ordinary undergraduate. William Adams, one of the Fellows, and afterwards Master of the College, was present at this curious interview, and recollected how old Michael managed to secure his son's introduction to William Jorden, another Fellow and Adams's own cousin, who was to be the boy's tutor. William Adams was a Shrewsbury man, and Jorden of Staffordshire origin, both being of Founder's kin at Pembroke through their Wightwick descent; and probably Michael knew something of their families. It was Adams who said of Johnson that he was "the best qualified for the University that he had ever known come there."

Though his father's departure may in some ways have been rather a relief, it would leave him feeling very much alone in a world that was new and strange to him. But he was not at all overcome by any feeling of awe for the authority under which he was now placed. He attended Mr. Jorden's lecture the day after his arrival, but, failing to be impressed, stayed away the next four days. On the sixth day Mr. Jorden, not having seen Johnson at his lecture on logic, called him to his room after dinner and asked for an explanation. Johnson, "starkly insensible" to the insult he was offering, said nonchalantly that he had spent the morning sliding on the ice in Christ Church meadow—for this was a winter of very early and severe frost. Mr. Jorden, admitted to be a very worthy man, but rather "heavy," was at least no mean psychologist, for instead of censuring his pupil, as an ordinary man would have done, he disclaimed any angry feeling, and asked Johnson to drink a glass of sherry with him, afterwards inviting some more undergraduates to join them and spend a pleasant afternoon in his room. Johnson, shamed by Mr. Jorden's magnanimity, felt the incident far more than if he had been actually reprimanded, and ever afterwards entertained the greatest personal regard for his first tutor, whom he described as a father to his pupils, and ready to defend them to the last. A contemporary rather unkindly spoke of Jorden as "a noted pupil monger," which at least indicates his success.

It was the custom for undergraduates at Pembroke, on 5 November, to declaim verses of their own composition, appropriate to the day, of which two copies were required, onc to hand to the tutor on entering the hall, and the other to retain for their own use. Johnson, still the victim of his procrastinating nature, is said in one account not only to have left the composition of the verses till the very morning they were required, but also to have failed to make the second copy, so that after he had handed the original to the tutor he had only his memory, aided by his powers of improvisation, to rely upon for his declamation, claiming no more courage for his act than is displayed by the man who, knowing himself to be a powerful swimmer, plunges straight into deep water. He said that he drafted his first exercise twice, but never again. Another account says that on this Gunpowder Plot anniversary, a day of "great solemnity" at Pembroke, he failed altogether to perform his appropriate exercise, and in lieu of it handed in a short set of verses entitled *Somnium*, in which he related how "the Muse had come to him in his sleep, and whispered, that it did not become him to write on such subjects as politicks; he should confine himself to humbler themes."

In spite of their hurried composition, his verses are said to have been "truly Virgilian," and to have made such an impression that Mr. Jorden asked him to furnish a translation into Latin of Pope's *Messiah*, in the Christmas vacation. Johnson denied the story that this task was either set him as an exercise, or inflicted upon him as a punishment, for he said the common exercises at Pembroke were all in prose, while such a punishment he would not have brooked. It was done of his own free will, following a very civil request from Mr. Jorden, to show the tutors what his powers were, and that if they had the weapons of arbitrary authority to wield against him, he was as surely armed with the sharp sword of satire, which in those days they dreaded to a curious extent, to use in his defence. At any rate, however we decide to reconcile the various versions of the story, the translation, and the speed of its composition, won Johnson high praise, and raised him very much in the estimation, not only of those within the College walls, but throughout the University. He also translated some of Dryden into Latin.

Johnson, no doubt because he was too poor to spend money on journeys, had stayed in College through the Christmas vacation after his arrival in Oxford, so that Mr. Jorden, who was also in residence as Vicegerent, would know how long his translation of Pope's *Messiah* had taken. All the gentlemen-commoners had gone home, and of the commoners only three beside himself remained. He had to continue thus to curb his desire to see his parents, and his "home town," as long as he was at Oxford. This would not contribute to his peace of mind, though he afterwards professed to think the system a bad one under which students at English universities were always having to re-adjust themselves to the differing conditions of life at home and in college. On one occasion when he turned the key of his room he imagined he heard his mother "distinctly call *Sam*"; but she was far away at Lichfield.

Everything in connexion with Johnson's career at College is beset with problems. One arises at the very outset, for, contrary to the University statutes, it was nearly seven weeks before he faced the Vice-Chancellor to be matriculated, on 16 December 1728. There is, however, no mystery about the room he occupied, for it was on the second floor, then the top of the tower, and directly over the College gateway. It was while Johnson was sitting in this room that that stout Jacobite, Dr. Matthew Panting, who had been Master since 1714, heard him soliloquise, in a voice not suitable for soliloquy: "Well, I have a mind to see what is done in other places of learning. I'll go see the Universities abroad. I'll go to France and Italy. I'll go to Padua and I'll mind my business—For an Athenian blockhead is the worst of all Blockheads." These intellectual excursions were never achieved, but he was able to avoid being an intellectual prig without them.

Whatever virtues Johnson displayed at College, regular work and close attention to his studies were not among them, any more than they had been at school, or during his two years at home. His constitutional indolence still prevailed over his intellectual activity. He seemed incapable of steady, sustained effort, and Dr. Panting recollected how he used to see him idling his time away in the quadrangle. Sometimes, no doubt, he would indulge in the ever fascinating hobby of watching the British workman's stolid mode of progression as the stones of the new College Chapel rose and took form. Slothful and irregular, without any guiding impulse, all his efforts were fitful, however excellent ultimately in result. His dislike of external discipline was as marked as his unwillingness to discipline himself. He paid as little regard as possible to the rules of the College, and was at times grossly rude even to those he respected. "Sir, you have sconced me two-pence for non-attendance at a lecture not worth a penny," he burst out to Mr. Jorden on one occasion ; for he still thought his tutor's abilities in no way comparable with his qualities of heart.

It is hard to condone such rudeness (indeed it should not be condoned), but he was bitterly conscious of his poverty, and short-sightedly thought that he would win a position by his literature and wit, by vexing the tutors and fellows, by disregarding hours, and by open contempt for all authority. His defiance of rules and regulations often had the appearance of high spirits, and the young students who surrounded him as he lounged by the College gate, entertained by his wit and distracted thereby from their own work, thought him quite a gay and amusing companion. Even then, he was "delicate in language," and his fellow-undergraduates, who respected his literary attainments, rather dreaded the reproofs he administered for careless speech, or the inappropriate use of such words as "prodigious." With the College servants he was evidently on good terms, for he delighted to meet them all again in 1754, including old John Hopkins, the butler. The only outdoor game he claimed to have played at College was cricket.

There was one practice in College which especially enraged the refractory young man. A servitor, on the instructions of the Master, was sent round to the undergraduates' rooms, at ten o'clock at night, to knock at their doors, and, in the case of no answer being given, to report them absent. He could not endure what he considered an attack on his privacy, when he was very likely engaged in study, and would often rather run the risk of being punished for late hours than conform to rule by answering the call. Sometimes, forgetting his sympathy for the poor servitor, he became more than a passive resister, and with some of his friends would join in chasing the innocent instrument of discipline round the College, the "field" inspiriting themselves by singing an old hunting song, to a jangling accompaniment of pots and candlesticks. Whitefield, who entered the College a few years after Johnson had left, found this one of his duties as a servitor, but the "hunting," which sometimes actually endangered the servitor's person, seems then fortunately to have ceased.

If it be thought that Johnson was prone to exaggerate when he dwelt upon his past misdemeanours and shortcomings—as indeed he was—there is yet considerable evidence to corroborate his admissions of slackness, unruliness and even insolence at College. William Adams, always his true friend, was moved to expostulate with him about his conduct, and the calm and considered reproof of such a man, as gentle as he was learned, induced a sense of shame that he was too proud to admit. But it did not completely cure him, and even Mr. Jorden, for whom, in spite of his lack of learning, he developed increasing love and respect, so much so that in after life he said that he would have wished no other tutor for his own sons if he had had any, suffered through this intractable spirit.

It is only human nature that, when he had long escaped from it, Johnson should have extolled the rigorous discipline and regular routine of university life, as beneficial to the student. Even the ill-observance of the rules, or failure in duty on the part of individuals, left the merits of the system unaffected. He praised the spirit of "progressive emulation" which caused the students to wish to please their tutors, the tutors their colleges, and the colleges the university. Possibly he was more affected by the discipline than he would have cared to admit at the time, or than his wayward conduct would suggest. There was certainly one influence in the College life that he could not resist. The regular practice of religion, and the constant inculcation of orthodox ideas on the subject, quite cured him of his clever-boyish inclination towards heretical argument, the exercise of which would not indeed have been tolerated, and in which he was probably never altogether sincere. If his inherent defects of temper remained unaffected—and how many of us ever overcome those ?—his principles of piety were greatly strengthened : the intellect at least conformed, if the spirit continued to rebel. His reading there of Law's *Serious Call to a Holy Life*, just published, had a decisive influence on him ; he found its arguments "quite an overmatch," and they turned his thoughts definitely towards religion as the greatest of all subjects for study and contemplation.

Theology, indeed, founded on a close study of the Fathers, accounted for much of that spasmodic—and extraordinarily rapid—reading in which at College, as elsewhere, he fiercely indulged when the mood seized him. And he was not now quite without a basic plan. He laid down a scheme for his reading, embracing classical literature and ethics as well as theology. He even planned to master a wide field of science, but did not go far in a subject so foreign to his genius. His solidest reading was in Greek, in *Homer* and *Euripides* rather than the historians. He enjoyed metaphysics most—not following his cousin, "Parson" Ford, here—but did not concentrate even on that. The great advantage of his fitful way of working lay in the fact that periods in which he would greedily devour the contents of a library were balanced by moods of corresponding indolence—or apparent indolence—when deep and brooding meditation enabled him thoroughly to assimilate the wisdom of the scholars, so that it blended with his own thought. He ran no risk of intellectual constipation.

Poverty was the thing that galled him most, and old shoes and shabby clothes, which by those who can at any time renew them are often worn with complete indifference, to him, who saw them only as hateful and inescapable signs of his own lack of pence, were a constant cause of shame. But it was his pride only, and not his belly, that suffered : the College accounts show that he fed as well as other commoners who came from comfortable and even wealthy homes. It is quite wrong to picture him as if he were in the position of a servitor, but he felt as deeply for what he thought the disgrace of the poor scholar who had to wait at table as he did the humiliations of a different kind to which poverty exposed him personally in the more privileged position of a commoner. Strongly as he held with the idea of subordination in the life of the outside world, he thought that an assemblage of scholars should shed all such distinctions and live on a plane of monastic equality.

John Taylor, Johnson's friend at Lichfield Grammar School, got his father's permission to follow him to Pembroke, where they could enjoy one another's company. But Johnson, scrupulous as ever when not contending with authority, discouraged the idea of his friend coming to a college where there was not a really able tutor. He made enquiries throughout the whole University, and found that the tutor with the highest reputation was Mr. Edmund Bateman, of Christ Church. So to Christ Church Taylor went, matriculating on 10 March 1729, immediately after going into residence at the College. Mr. Bateman, only five years older than Johnson, was a son of Sir Christopher Wren's deputy at St. Paul's Cathedral, and it is rather curious, considering this association with Johnson, that not long after he became a Prebendary of Lichfield Cathedral, and later Master of St. John's Hospital there, as well as son-in-law to Bishop Smalbroke and so brother-in-law to William Vyse.

Taylor's presence at the University would make things pleasanter for Johnson, though he carried the odium of Whiggery with him. But it led, quite innocently, to another humiliation. Mr. Bateman's lectures being so much superior to those of his own College tutors, Johnson used to go across to Christ Church to get them at second-hand from Taylor, till the exquisite young men there began to comment on his shoes, which had become so worn that his feet actually showed through the leather. Johnson, morbidly sensitive to his shabby appearance, promptly ceased his visits. A friend at Pembroke, one of the gentlemen-commoners, in whom we can recognize William Vyse just mentioned, moved by a spirit of genuine kindness uninformed by much tact, ordered a servitor to place a new pair of shoes at Johnson's door, which so infuriated him when he came out and saw them, that he hurled them away in a paroxysm of ungrateful indignation.

There was a happier incident in connexion with the Christ Church association. Charles Arbuthnot, son of the John Arbuthnot who combined medicine and literature with such distinction, had recently taken his degree there, and through Taylor, or perhaps some less personal medium, he became so interested in Johnson's translation of Pope's *Messiah* that he contrived for Pope himself to see it, his father being acquainted with the poet. Possibly Mr. Bateman had something to do with it, for his stepfather was Erasmus Lewis, the friend of Pope, and a near neighbour in London to John Arbuthnot. Pope, with a rare generosity that he, in common with most others of his kind, did not always display, commended it very warmly, and said that posterity would find it difficult to decide which was the original. Michael Johnson, ever the proud and equally untactful father, is said to have printed the verses on his own responsibility, without the knowledge of his son, who was greatly incensed. A year or two later, in 1731, they were printed under proper auspices, at Oxford, by John Husbands, a young Fellow of Pembroke, in his *Miscellany of Poems by Several Hands.* The preface described them (or misdescribed them, if we are to believe Johnson) as "deliver'd to his Tutor as a College Exercise, by Mr. *Johnson*, a Commoner of *Pembroke College* in *Oxford*," and they constitute the first item in any Johnsonian bibliography. Husbands' *Miscellany* had a list of some 500 subscribers, including about half of all Johnson's Pembrochian associates, yet the name of the most distinguished contributor is not among them. Poor Husbands, a man of worth and promise, got little credit from his book, and died the year after its publication.

Taylor, of course, was a friend of early days, and Johnson did not form any intimate ties with the undergraduates whose acquaintance he made only at Oxford, even those of his own College. But he admitted having played draughts, in the common-room, with "Phil Jones and Fludyer," though never for money. Philip Jones, an Oxford man by birth, had matriculated a year before Johnson: his alleged love of beer did not prevent him having an extraordinarily regular record in College, and his reputation there for being a bit of an ass and a coxcomb perhaps had some relation to his failure to become more than a very undistinguished parson. John Fludger (for so he spelt his name) was son to a Mayor of Abingdon, and entered only a week after Johnson, though of course considerably younger. He was a Wightwick foundation scholar, and a "scoundrel," according to the Johnsonian definition, in that he was a Whig. His politics, and even his contempt for his own University, helped to make him a more aggressive and successful man than his friend Jones, and his career in the Church included several excursions into polemical theology, one of great length.

Then there was John Meeke, his own age but two years his senior in College, whose superiority in classics excited his jealousy to such an extent that, on his own confession, at the lecture in hall he would sit as far away as possible from him, that he might not hear him construe. "Honest Jack Meek," as a fellow-undergraduate dubbed him, came of a family having modest connexions with the Court, and his grandfather had been Latin Secretary to Charles II., so classics were in his blood. He, too, took orders, but remained a resident fellow in College, and Johnson felt eventually that his own career, with all its trials and adversities, could give a few points to that of his friendly old antagonist, whose "excellent parts" left him immured all the time in an intellectual monastery.

Through all his failure in the matters of discipline and application, the College authorities could see his remarkable powers when he chose to exercise them. Probably he grew less rebellious in spirit after he had been some time in residence, for Dr. Adams on one occasion told Boswell that he had been regular in attending his tutor's lectures, as well as those in hall. He must have come to realise the folly of his conduct, and how little it could gain him the respect that he thought imperilled by his poverty. He had certainly one advantage over most of the undergraduates, who had to rely for their reading upon books lent by their tutors or borrowed from the library, for he possessed a collection of his own that could truthfully be described as remarkable for a first year student, even had he come from a prosperous home. We can only imagine that his father had supplied him with most of them, and some 115 volumes would be a pretty heavy load for the carrier from Lichfield. They were not mere booksellers' rubbish, and dated down to 1727. Such recent works as Pope's *Homer*, in eleven volumes, could not have been cheaply acquired. A good proportion of the books were in English literature, which officially was not then a subject for study at the University. There were the poems of Spenser, Milton,

Pope, Edmund Waller, Matthew Prior, Edward Young and Ambrose Philips, as well as of minor versifiers such as Edmund Smith, who had been a friend of Gilbert Walmesley's. But there was no Shakespeare. English prose was but poorly represented, except by Addison.

Most of the books, naturally, were editions of the classics, or classical translations, or works by Englishmen written in Latin. He claimed to have read Latin with as much ease when he entered Oxford as he did in his maturity. There was a decent collection of Latin writers, yet not including Plautus, Terence, Martial, Juvenal or Statius. For Macrobius, whose prose he quoted with such effect on his arrival in Oxford, we look in vain. There was Kennett's *Roman Antiquities*. The solid reading he did in Greek was not well reflected ; and while *Homer* was there *Euripides* was missing. Theology had a firm basis in the *Bible* and the *Prayer Book*, with the works of a few minor writers on the Scriptures. But Law's *Serious Call* he can only have borrowed. There were three works on geography and the use of the globes ; but his distaste for the science of mathematics finds no contradiction in the list. Physics, too, were unrepresented, for he learned no more of the subject than he could help. Locke's *On Education*, and, more particularly, Barecroft's *Advice to a Son in the University*, would be of some topical interest to him as a student. A book he picked up on the College stairs and read with interest, Jonathan Richardson's *Essay on Painting*, he did not add to his library. The most remarkable gap in the list is caused by the absence of any works in French or Italian. Modern languages had no place in the University curriculum, but his books were not a mere reflection of his academic needs, so it certainly looks as if he had not then much real acquaintance with them, though, as we shall see later, he had enough French to enable him to read Le Grand's version of Lobo's *Voyage to Abyssinia*. An old gentleman at Oxford advised him to read hard while there, as when he grew older the inclination would disappear and poring over books become irksome.

The man who is, perhaps, the most familiar to us of all Johnson's College friends did not come into residence until October 1729, though he had matriculated in June. This was Oliver Edwards, whose defeat in his attempt to become a philosopher, because " cheerfulness was always breaking in," has made him a figure of the truest Dickensian quality, whose words are quoted almost as often as those of any of the novelist's creations. Son to a substantial citizen of Devizes, in Wiltshire, and a year or so younger than Johnson, he took up the law and became a solid and respectable figure at The Six Clerks' Office in Chancery Lane, with a comfortable estate in Hertfordshire that his second wife had brought him. His only regret, when Johnson met him again in 1778, was that he had not remained to take his degree, gone into the church, and got a good living, like their fellow-collegian, Matthew Bloxam. The days when he and Johnson drank together at an alehouse near Pembroke Gate, discussing Latin verses the while, must then have come to seem very distant.

It was in the actual month of Oliver Edwards' entry that Johnson, feeling a mere register of it in his mind would be insufficient, definitely recorded a resolution to "bid farewell to sloth, being resolved henceforth not to listen to her syren strains," by writing it in Latin, on one of the loose sheets of his informal diary. When we consider his conduct while at College we must do so, not in the narrow spirit of the moralist or disciplinarian, but with some of the sympathy that comes from a more modern attitude of understanding towards his physical and mental condition. His tendency to depression was no mere superficial symptom of the mind, allied to lack of moral fibre, but a definite affliction that came to him with his father's blood and pursued him through the whole of his life, bringing him at times very near to the point where the reason ceases to exercise control over the thoughts and actions. The restless spirit which made him unable to settle down to regular work at Oxford, that made all authority so distasteful, and left him often utterly listless and melancholy, was more evidence of a physical condition requiring a doctor's diagnosis and treatment than any defect of character for which he could justly be censured. Even the particular quality of his religion, which always seemed more imbued with gloom, and awe, and fear, and the dread of punishment, than with any idea of joyful service, was probably to some extent a medical symptom.

Johnson told Hannah More that at Pembroke they were "a nest of singing birds." But he was the only "singing bird" in residence, and perhaps a less appropriate description of his own notes could scarcely be found. Shenstone did not appear till two or three years after he had left, and if that gentle pastoralist did not reach great heights of song, still more it can be said of others from the nest that they were " but of a small pipe." Of Johnson's actual associates in College it can without offence be said that they were not, for men of education, a distinguished company : there was less intellectual promise among them than among his youthful fellow-pupils at Lichfield Grammar School. The fellows in residence, including as we have seen, William Adams, William Jorden and John Husbands, none of them did anything original : they all took orders, and John Ratcliffe's Mastership of the College, and that of William Adams after him, were the highest honours they gained. Of his fellow-undergraduates none did more than get comfortable office in the church and elsewhere. John Fludger, Philip Jones, John Meeke, William Vyse and Oliver Edwards have already come into the story of his College life, and Walter Chapman, afterwards Prebendary of Bristol, kept up with him in later years. Many, of course, became country parsons, a few went to the bar, and one at least embraced medicine. Some, like Thomas Crawley, of Flaxley Abbey, or Nicholas Hyett, of Painswick House, both in Gloucestershire, were squires in embryo, and not called upon to make good otherwise. One of the rich young gentleman-commoners, James Hallett, could have claimed connexion with Johnson's family (if he had wished to do so, which is at least doubtful), for he was a grandson of Sir Ambrose Crowley, the brother-in-law of " Parson " Ford. But none of these men come into the story of Johnson's College life, as it is known to us.

William Jorden, for all the time he was Johnson's tutor, filled the office of Vicegerent, or deputy to the Master of the College, whose special duty it was to maintain discipline. In March 1729 he was elected by the University Rector of Odstock, in Wiltshire, but it turned out that the University had not the right to present, so the appointment fell through. However, on 8 November 1729 he was presented by his own pupil, William Vyse, to the Rectory of Standon, in Staffordshire, giving a bond to resign when William Vyse should himself claim the living. The induction did not take place till 12 December 1729, Jorden having in the meantime remained in College. On Jorden's actual departure his pupils, including Johnson, were transferred to his cousin, William Adams, but, as Johnson's own career at College ended on almost the same day, the relationship, in his case, never became more than nominal, though he did claim to have performed exercises under Adams. Adams, too, admitted afterwards that Johnson was above his mark, a confession characterised by Johnson as "liberal and noble." It is possible, however, that had he come under Adams's direct influence, even if he had not gained much intellectually from having a more competent tutor than Jorden, he might have acquired something of those smaller virtues of gentleness, consideration and equability of temper that distinguished the future Master of the College.

CHAPTER VII.

AT HOME AGAIN: VARIOUS ATTEMPTS TO BECOME AN USHER 1729-1732

THE sparest entry in a diary may be the most revealing. " 1729 *Dec. S. J. Oxonio rediit.*" The intensive brevity of the statement seems to invest it with an ominous significance. And rightly so, for the few words conceal one of those tragedies that require no comment, no emotional amplification, to bring home their completeness. In the second week of December 1729 Johnson did return home from Oxford. The great experiment, so long delayed, and entered upon eventually at so much sacrifice, yet from which such big things must have been expected, had come to an abrupt end. The youth of brilliant promise was again to lose the directing impulse provided by a definite goal, and to become like a rudderless vessel, blown hither and thither by the winds of circumstance. Had he not won distinction in after life his record at College would have been an absolute blank to us, except for his translation of Pope's *Messiah*.

Actually, it is probable that when he turned his back on Oxford it was with the hope at least that he might be able to come back. He left College in the usual way, at the end of the term, and did not send his books home but packed them in a case, with some personal papers of a particularly private nature, and left them in the care of his friend Taylor at Christ Church. It has generally been stated that his College career came to a premature end by the failure of money supplies, due to his father's dwindling fortunes, and to his own consequently increasing debts. He certainly owed a considerable sum for his board, at least equalling the £7 he had paid as his caution money, but a gilded youth like Andrew Corbet was in similar case. His weekly bill for board averaged about the normal figure of eight shillings, and the full amount for his 58 weeks in residence was £24 odd. There were also charges for chamber rent, for tutors' fees, for fuel and candles, for the servitor, for the bedmaker, and for other small requirements, which altogether would total about as much as his board, the account for everything being rendered quarterly.

Johnson always displayed an interest in the economics of life at any university, perhaps kept alive by the rather bitter memory of his own experience. But whatever it was which compelled him to leave Oxford, any unpleasant recollections he retained were associated with his own personal troubles and not directed against his College or University. Even had he completed the normal course, taken his degree, and won formal academic honours, he could not have cherished throughout his whole life a greater affection for the whole institution of Oxford.

We cannot rule out the money problem in considering the premature termination of his University career But there is another factor of perhaps even greater importance, which has already been stressed—that of his mental and bodily health. In this Christmas vacation, immediately after his return from Oxford, the symptoms of his malady became far more acute than ever before, and he "felt himself overwhelmed with an horrible hypochondria, with perpetual irritation, fretfulness, and impatience; and with a dejection, gloom, and despair, which made existence misery." Whether it was the onset of these symptoms that caused him to come home, or his coming home under the compulsion of circumstances that caused the onset of the symptoms, we do not know. But the reticence of those who must have known exactly under what circumstances he did leave Oxford—almost a conspiracy of silence—points to a condition of mind which their delicacy disinclined them to disclose to Boswell. The event marked an epoch in his medical history: never again did his mind and his body enjoy that feeling of balanced ease which accompanies normal good health. But it marked an epoch of a different kind in his spiritual development, for near the end of his life he said that his interest in religion was about this time revived by sickness, never to be lost again. It was his own bodily condition which caused him, from his early days, to be "a dabbler in physic."

When first attacked by this malady so acutely Johnson made what to a man muscularly strong, as he continued to be through all his vicissitudes of health, seems the most natural reply. He submitted his body to violent physical exertion, thinking that it would exorcise the demons of nervous irritability and melancholia which possessed him. He would walk to Birmingham and back, a distance of over thirty miles, or undertake some other severe form of bodily exercise. Years later, in *The Rambler*, he pointed out how "frequent and violent agitation of the body" provided an escape from misery to happiness. But such heroic measures this time proved quite ineffectual. His good friend Edmund Hector was shocked: immediately on Johnson's return from Oxford he could see that there was something radically wrong with his old schoolfellow, and began to fear for his mind, and even for his life. Johnson himself said that at that time he did not know "how to manage" such an attack: experience must have taught him a method of disciplining himself more effectually to preserve his mental and physical balance through these dreadful surges of depression. But he never overcame the dread of losing his reason.

There was one very unfortunate result of this particular spasm of illness. Driven almost to desperation by a condition he could find no means of alleviating, he wrote a close and reasoned account of it in Latin to submit to his godfather, Dr. Swynfen, showing at least that the purely intellectual side of his brain was as clear and sure in its action as ever. Dr. Swynfen was so impressed "with the extraordinary acuteness, research, and eloquence" of the statement that he was tempted by his admiration for his godson's abilities to show it to various friends. This, however innocently intended, was indeed a gross betrayal of confidence, on a subject of peculiar delicacy, for Dr. Swynfen himself thought the symptoms indicated a possible loss of reason in the future. It is small wonder that Johnson very deeply resented such a disclosure of his most intimate communications, and could never again feel really reconciled to a godfather who, apart from this one strange lapse, had discharged the pleasant duties of his position so admirably. But that he harboured no bitterness is shown by his long extended kindness, in the later years of his life, to Dr. Swynfen's daughter, Mrs. Desmoulins.

Even had Johnson been in the enjoyment of perfect health his circumstances would have been enough to make him feel wretched and miserable far beyond the ordinary. The cruel disappointment of seeing his career at College ended after only a year of residence, of realising that there was now no chance of his taking that degree without which he could scarcely hope to succeed in any profession or avocation of learning, and the ignominious return to his father's shop and failing business, might well have driven the sanest man almost to despair.

Twenty years old, without money, without credentials of any kind, without the taste or capacity for business, and with a wretchedly unstable constitution, what chance would he have even of earning a living, much less of winning any of that distinction which he must have felt was his due ? That he could not enter the Church had ceased to be a deprivation, for, in spite of his deep regard for religion, some delicacy of conscience had determined him not to follow the advice of his friends and take orders. But he never ceased to regret that he had been bred to no profession.

It is small wonder that of such a period in his life there should be no record. After his return from Oxford in December 1729 there is not known one single fact of his career until the autumn of 1731. We can only imagine how he spent those two years—helping once again in the shop, doing more irregular reading, and perhaps getting some teaching engagements, as health and opportunity allowed. It were idle to attempt to reconstruct a story for which we have no basis of facts, but this second spell at home must have held even more of misery and frustration than that preceding his year at Oxford. It would be at this period that he made the acquaintance of John Green, afterwards Bishop of Lincoln, who served for a time as usher at Lichfield Grammar School, when, according to Miss Seward, he and another embryo bishop, Thomas Newton, competed for the favours of the headmaster's young daughter, her own mother-to-be. Johnson's cousin Tom, the currier, son of old Andrew Johnson, after going back to his people in Birmingham, had returned to Lichfield in 1728, a young man of twenty, no doubt to help his uncle Michael in the tanning business : he married and remained on in Lichfield till at least 1742.

The curtain is not lifted until 30 October 1731, when he wrote from Lichfield the first letter of his that has ever been traced, only a few days before the death of his old schoolmistress, Dame Oliver. Addressed to Gregory Hickman, it reveals that some time before he had visited Stourbridge and received much kindness and help from that worthy connexion of his mother's, but that the object of his visit—which was to secure the ushership of the Grammar School there—had not been achieved. The disappointment of which he speaks, probably succeeding others of which we have no record, would account for his having to offer apologies for the long delay in acknowledging his kinsman's kindness, for which he expressed his warmest obligations, and his sincerest thanks, with an assurance that such delay did not spell "forgetfulness, disrespect, or ingratitude." He asked one favour, that Gregory Hickman should excuse the composition of the verses he had asked for, saying that to write them against personal inclination was "the most disagreeable thing in the world," and that "one's own disappointment is no inviting subject." If Gregory Hickman had really asked for a metrical celebration of Johnson's failure to gain an ushership it certainly suggests that his practical benevolence was accompanied by a lack of ordinary consideration for the feelings of one whose letter, in conclusion, confessed himself "yet unemployed." Johnson would seem to have made some attempt to satisfy his kind patron in the matter, but found the subject so barren as to afford no material for his muse.

Why Gregory Hickman should have thought of asking for verses needs little explanation. For it must have been on his recent visit to Stourbridge that Johnson had written the lines, "To Miss Hickman, Playing on the Spinnet." "Bright Stella, form'd for universal reign," whom he there apostrophises, was Dorothy, the seventeen-year-old daughter of Gregory Hickman by his first wife, and later to become the mother of the famous physician, John Turton, who had Edward Gibbon among his patients and attended Goldsmith in his last illness. Dorothy's mother we have seen was dead when Johnson attended Stourbridge Grammar School in 1726, and she had already acquired a stepmother, who, it is interesting to recall, was niece to John Bridgen, Professor of Divinity at Gresham College, London, and first cousin to Edward Bridgen, the cultured London merchant who long afterwards married Patty Richardson, daughter and amanuensis of the author of *Clarissa*.

It was on 22 August 1731, probably about the time of his visit to Stourbridge, that Johnson lost the only relative he had who bore any promise of distinction—his cousin Cornelius, or "Parson" Ford, the half-brother of Gregory Hickman. After the time of the stay with him at Pedmore, and the subsequent few terms at Stourbridge Grammar School, the cousins can have seen very little of one another. In January 1727, after having been ordained priest on the first day of the month, Cornelius was presented by Lord Chesterfield, his old College friend, to whom he is said to have acted as chaplain, to the Rectory of South Luffenham, in Rutland, purchasing the advowson with £840 from his wife's fortune. He held the living till his death, but spent little time in ministering to his parishioners, for his inclinations were all towards town life and the company of the wits. Latterly his ordinary residence was in the fashionable Piazza, facing Covent Garden Church, where at the Bedford Coffee House he could meet Pope and other famous men of letters. At this time he seems to have given some assistance to the notorious John Henley, who had been at College with him, in the conduct of his queer "Oratory" in Lincoln's Inn Fields.

But behind this life of easy indulgence there always lurked for "Parson" Ford the shadow, or indeed the substance, of debt. His tendency to extravagance and loose living increased very much in these last years, until, after borrowing money right and left, and mortgaging the family properties, including Haunch Hall, at Kings Norton, which his great-grandmother Ford had bought in 1649, we find him a prisoner in the Fleet in the early part of 1731. In May he regained his freedom, but only to engage in a series of writ-dodging expeditions between Pedmore, Luffenham and London. He died in his favourite Piazza, at the Hummums, an hotel which was run as a kind of bagnio. A few weeks after his death his uncle, Samuel Ford, was writing to William Priest, the Birmingham attorney, to ask how the Haunch Hall property now stood.

There is nothing that "Parson" Ford wrote by which we can judge his talents, save a Latin epitaph to his father's memory. But in his own circle, which comprised men of rank and fortune as well as men of wit and letters, he undoubtedly made a great reputation by his powers of conversation. It is remarkable that he should years earlier have anticipated his famous cousin's passion and capacity for talk in such a high degree. Indeed, this love of talk rather debauched his mind (as it might have done Johnson's had his circumstances been easier), and helped to prevent any serious application to study. His friends recognised, as did Johnson, that he had talents which might have advanced him far in any profession if he had had the will to succeed. But with his love of company, and a mind stored with the riches of such favourite authors as Garth and Prior, Congreve and Addison, he preferred to expound good-humoured wisdom from the tavern chair, in his easy and elegant English. His potations never flustered him, or (and this was a curious trait in his character) caused him to relax in his refusal to listen to irreligious conversation, or freethinking attacks on the clergy, showing the justice with which Johnson years afterwards defended him from the charge of impiety.

"Parson" Ford left two maiden sisters, who are said to have boarded for a time with the Michael Johnsons. It is not clear whether this was when Samuel returned from Oxford, or just after their brother's death, but whenever it was it made him feel at the time that there was not much room at home for him. If it was after their brother's death they did not stay long, for in ten weeks or so they were at Wolverhampton. And only a little later sorrow came to the tall house in the Market Square, when Michael Johnson, who had built it and made it a landmark familiar not only to the people of Lichfield but also to many scattered through the neighbouring counties, died in the first few days of December, in his seventy-fifth year. He was an old man, sorely tried by adversity, and pursued by a demon of despondency, who had been compelled to lead a life of hard and unceasing travel and toil and exposure, with a last year or two of real need, so that the "inflammatory fever" which is said to have been the actual cause of his death may have acted but as the last straw required to break down his power of physical resistance. Catherine Chambers, their valued servant and friend, made the arrangements for the funeral, which took place at St. Michael's, Lichfield, on 7 December, 1731.

It is an illustration of the dramatic irony that often passes unnoticed on the biographical stage that though we only see Michael as the father of the great Samuel Johnson he never so saw himself, for he died when his son's fortunes were at their lowest ebb, and when no one could possibly have seen the awkward youth in the bookseller's shop, against whom fate seemed to be in active conspiracy, as the future leader of English letters and one of the greatest of our national figures. We feel we should like to go behind the scenes and tell the old man such a story of struggle and eventual fame as would help him to realise that his own life had not been lived in vain.

When we come to consider the reasons for Michael Johnson's failure to achieve any solid success in life, we see it principally in lack of method and in loose financial control. With a number of irons in the fire, he made no attempt to co-ordinate his activities or calculate their relative expense and profit. It was a hand-to-mouth method he followed, entirely dependent on his own energy, a quality he possessed in a greater degree than judgment, and when that energy began to flag things naturally went from bad to worse. He had many of the qualities that win success—industry, intelligence, enterprise and resource—but there were defects in his equipment which rendered them more or less nugatory. No business can succeed without proper organisation, and that must always be interdependent with changing financial conditions that cannot be realised without an adequate system of accounts. Probably at no time in his life did he know exactly how he stood ; indeed he may always have felt in such a financial mess as even to dread the idea of an investigation that would make it all too painfully clear. His son recalled long afterwards how small were the profits of a country bookseller, and how troubled he was with bad debts. The difficulties he experienced in bargaining with his customers are illustrated by the story of one of them, who, after unsuccessfully pressing him to sell a book much below its proper price, sought to clinch the matter by pointing out that he " bought an almanac of him every year." Michael was never " bankrupt " in the legal sense, or he would have been deprived of the magistracy which even his burial entry allows him, but he failed to accumulate any reserve and was for long in difficulties. Mrs. Johnson was not the wife to help such a man on : her criticism, if frequently expressed, was quite unconstructive, irritating only where if more informed it might have stimulated and encouraged. But evidently Michael Johnson was a very " difficult " man, and a far wiser wife might have failed to influence him.

A trifle attached to some part of 1731 is the composition of " Verses to a Lady, on receiving from her a Sprig of Myrtle." The muse was Johnson's own, but the sentiment was vicarious. Morgan Graves, elder brother of the more celebrated Richard, wishing to make an adequate return to the young lady near Birmingham who had honoured him with this romantic gift, got Edmund Hector to seek the aid of Johnson, for in polite circles poetry was the proper language of gallantry. Johnson, as ever, procrastinated and forgot ; and it was not till Hector called again to remind him that he dashed off the verses in five minutes.

Probably it was after his return from Oxford that Johnson on one occasion met William Inge, of Thorpe Constantine, who died in July 1731. This great Staffordshire squire, scholar and antiquary, a distant uncle of the retired Dean of St. Paul's, had married, greatly to his financial advantage, a cousin of Ambrose Philips, and he illustrated the poet's extreme touchiness in regard to any criticism of his work by relating to Johnson a trivial incident that occurred when they met at table and Mr. Inge asked for an explanation of one of his lines.

Michael Johnson left no will, and there is no legal record of the disposal of his estate. The cheerful anticipations of the marriage settlement had not been fulfilled, and there was little remaining for the widow and children except the house and shop, and these followed the settlement. Mrs. Johnson's business capacities probably got no further than the ability to stand behind the counter and hand out anything that was asked for, but Nathaniel, the younger son, was now nineteen and able to help his mother, who had the house and the stock for her life. Samuel would have the best knowledge of the books, but these would naturally become less and less in evidence after Michael's death, or at any rate books of any value or consequence.

Three months after his father's death he at last received a definite appointment. In March 1732 he was offered the position of usher at the Grammar School of Market Bosworth, in Leicestershire, and very naturally accepted it, for, whatever qualms he may have suffered, his position was now too desperate to allow the indulgence of personal preferences. There were evidently private influences at work here, especially as Johnson was not the Bachelor of Arts he should have been under the statutes. The squire of Market Bosworth, and the ruler of all its affairs, was Sir Wolstan Dixie, fourth baronet, whose far-back predecessor and namesake, Lord Mayor of London in 1585, had founded the Grammar School. Sir Wolstan's widowed mother, Lady Dixie, was resident in the Bishop's Palace, at Lichfield, in 1727, while his brother, the Rev. Beaumont Dixie, Rector of Market Bosworth, had married in 1728 the sister of Andrew Corbet, Johnson's school friend, at Lichfield Cathedral. The Dixies were also connected with the Pyotts of Streethay, of whom the head had been a trustee of Michael Johnson's marriage settlement, as well as with the Astons.

Great as were Johnson's acquirements it is doubtful whether under any circumstances he would have made much of a success as a schoolmaster. In the first place, his physical handicaps, his bad sight, his nervous tricks, and his general awkwardness, would always have made him a butt for young boys, who are cruelly critical and pay little regard to scholarship if unaccompanied by other personal gifts and qualities that they can appreciate. At any rate, his new post only made him more miserable than before. He hated the drudgery of the school, and complained bitterly of it in his letters. The dull monotony of the life, day after day going through the same weary routine of trying to instil the rules of grammar into boys who disliked their share in the process as much as he did his, irked him almost beyond endurance. Yet in his leisure time at Bosworth he did much serious reading.

But the most trying feature of the life there was outside the hours of school. It was a condition of the engagement that he should live as one of Sir Wolstan's household, in his fine mansion not far from the School, to officiate as a kind of private chaplain and say grace at table. It is true that under the school statutes the usher, who was paid £20 a year by two instalments, had a house allotted to him in the School grounds, and was forbidden to undertake any other duties. But this would hardly trouble Sir Wolstan, who was not only the principal trustee but took upon himself practically the whole management of the School and the appointment of the masters. A young bachelor of about thirty, brutal, purseproud, domineering, boorish and with a very violent temper, he was not only ignorant himself but without any respect for learning in others. To be at the beck and call of such a bully, treated as roughly as if he were a servant, was an unspeakable humiliation to Johnson, who, however poor and unfortunate, always carried under his shabby coat the sensitive pride of the scholar.

The headmaster of Market Bosworth School at this time was the Rev. John Kilby, a man some years over sixty, educated at Lincoln College, Oxford, who for most of his life had been Vicar of St. Margaret's, in his native town of Leicester. It was only in 1730 that he was called to succeed that much more famous scholar and schoolmaster, Anthony Blackwall, who had died there in harness. We know nothing of Johnson's relations with Mr. Kilby, except that they resulted in his gleaning some reminiscences of Styan Thirlby, the theologian, whom Kilby had taught when usher at Leicester Free School early in the century.

By the time Johnson went home for the summer vacation his father's affairs were on the point of being settled, and on 15 July 1732 he received the share of the estate to which he was entitled, a modest twenty pounds, probably a third of the personalty. Until his mother's death he would be entitled to no share of the house and stock, and a brief diary entry records his realisation of the fact that he would have to make his own way in the world without help from anyone. He resolved to fight against the disintegrating effect of poverty, that it might not cause his mind to relax, or drive him into any kind of crime.

Eleven guineas of this sum were immediately laid by, for future emergencies. Next day he set out on his journey back to Market Bosworth, travelling the whole of the twenty-five miles on foot. It must have been with great misgiving that he tramped along the country lanes, getting nearer and nearer to the scene of last term's misery, knowing that the hateful and menacing figure of Sir Wolstan would soon confront him once again. But perhaps the consciousness that at last he had a little money in his pocket, over and above what was necessary for bare subsistence, gave him a new feeling of independence, and a new feeling of courage. At any rate, very soon after he had come back, things reached such a pitch that he could stand it no longer : he openly quarrelled with the brutal and truculent baronet, threw up his appointment, and within a week or so was once again in Lichfield. The whole incident remained to him like a horrid dream, which he dreaded to recall, and long afterwards the mere sight of a road leading to Bosworth agitated his mind.

It was not, however, a place unattractive to everyone, but a favourite resort of the county people in the district, who twice a week thronged the bowling green at the local inn. The greatest sportsman in the neighbourhood was that wealthy squire, Thomas Boothby, of Tooley Park six miles away, who in 1705 had married Hester Skrymsher, from High Offley, sister to Johnson's "very near relative", Charles Skrymsher. This seemingly close connexion with the celebrated fox-hunter, famed throughout England, of which we do not even know that he was aware, makes one of the most curious problems of his life, as it conflicts so entirely with all he tells us of his father having no relatives with which to confront his wife when she was letting him know the social superiority of her own kith and kin. Thomas Boothby, one would think, might very effectively have been introduced into the conversation as a counterblast to Mrs. Harriotts.

So once more the unfortunate Johnson was without employment. But almost immediately a chance presented itself of another ushership, and, in spite of his recent experience, he made haste to apply for it. His friend John Taylor had left Christ Church in September 1730, without taking a degree, returning to his house at Ashburne, and since his father's death in November 1731 had carried on the family practice as attorneys, marrying his first wife in the following April. It was at Ashburne that the vacancy had occurred which seemed to provide Johnson with another opportunity of trying to make good as a schoolmaster. Andrew Corbet, whose sister, Mrs. Rupert Browne, lived at Hungry Bentley, near Ashburne, was the first to write to him about it. The letter reached Lichfield on the night of 26 July 1732, and next day Johnson sent off a letter by messenger to Taylor, presuming without much question or ceremony that his old friend would do all he could to further his interests, and asking what steps he had better take, and whether he should come over in person.

The vacancy at Ashburne had arisen through the death, only a week before, of William Hardestee, who had been usher at the Grammar School since 1713, under the Rev. Samuel Burnett, and a successor was wanted at once. But Johnson had not enough local influence, or perhaps applied in person and did not make a favourable impression. The governors and assistants of the School, in all but full strength, attended a meeting on 1 August, and elected Thomas Bourne, of Leek in Staffordshire, as their usher. One of those who voted was Brooke Boothby, whose sister was to become such a very dear friend of Johnson's before many years were out. As a matter of fact Thomas Bourne, who only a few months before had made a second marriage, never took up his duties, and remained at Leek until his death in 1771. Possibly his new wife dissuaded him from going to Ashburne, where in September 1732 his place was filled by one Job Sowter, a candidate from Nottingham. Johnson was evidently not even in the running for the post, but hardly for lack of a university degree, his successful competitors not being graduates either.

CHAPTER VIII.

STAY IN BIRMINGHAM ENGAGEMENT TO MRS. PORTER 1732-1735

AFTER his wretched experience at Market Bosworth, followed immediately by his failure to secure the ushership at Ashburne, Johnson spent some more months at home without definite occupation. In the October of 1732 there died a man whose name is familiar in connexion with his, and whom he is likely to have encountered in the flesh—Charles Claudius Philips, the eccentric itinerant musician, sometime of Bridgnorth, whose monument in the church of St. Peter's at Wolverhampton, where he was buried, bears not only the "common-place funereal lines" written by Richard Wilkes, a local physician and antiquary of some note, but also the "exquisitely beautiful" verse that Johnson composed extempore to better them, at the instigation of David Garrick. "Claudy" Philips, as he was familiarly called, who is said to have been born in Wales, to have been brought up in comfortable circumstances, to have "made the tour of Europe," and to have experienced a serious reverse of fortune, used to traverse Staffordshire with his fiddle. When things went well, his laced clothes reflected his prosperity; when things went ill his shabby appearance bespoke his distress, and he would then steal into the inns and public houses of an evening and accept such modest reward as the company he had entertained by his playing were moved to contribute. He is said to have had an extraordinary "rapidity of execution," and to have extemporised largely under the sway of his own emotions, producing "a wild and plaintive melody" that conformed to no rules of musical composition but moved his hearers to an ecstacy of self-forgetfulness. He was the true artist, completely contemptuous of gain, living for his fiddle alone, and giving delight by his performance wherever he went.

There was no use in Johnson remaining at home indefinitely. Even if he helped in the shop, his presence there was not really necessary, nor did it hold any promise for himself. He had to take some steps towards carving out an independent career of his own, and about the end of the year 1732, after his few months at Lichfield, he accepted a generous offer from his old school friend, Edmund Hector, now settled in Birmingham as a surgeon, to go over there and stay with him for a time as his guest. Hector was lodging with Thomas Warren, the bookseller, in the house he had recently taken in the High Street, adjoining the Swan Tavern. It was a familiar neighbourhood to Johnson. The home of his disagreeable uncle, John Harrison, with whom he had stayed in 1719, was quite close ; and the bookseller's shop of his father's feckless brother, Andrew Johnson, who had died in June 1729, while Samuel was at Oxford, was also near-by.

When Johnson's own troubles were over, he told Boswell that the idleness of the Lichfield people was that of philosophers who used their heads to make "the Birmingham boobies" work for them with their hands, but quite a number of his contemporaries exchanged the quiet cathedral city for the bustling capital of the Midlands with much advantage to themselves, from Matthew Boulton downwards. Though still nominally only a market town it was already world-famous for the advances it had made in the use of metals for innumerable commercial objects.

Hector's idea, no doubt, was that it would be to Johnson's advantage to be brought into close personal contact with Warren, who was not only the leading bookseller in the town, but had now embarked on a more adventurous career as a printer. It is significant that the first number of his newspaper, *The Birmingham Journal*, appeared in November 1732. In the conduct of such a paper the help of a man with Johnson's knowledge and literary gifts would be very valuable. And so it proved. Warren became interested in the new boarder, and presently there appeared in its pages a series of essays from Johnson's pen which his bibliographers would rejoice to discover if a file of the paper were extant.

Edmund Hector was no ordinary friend, for he entertained Johnson as his guest for some six months, at the end of which time, towards the middle of 1733, Johnson, having as yet no very definite plans for a career, moved into lodgings in another part of the town, in the house of a man named Jarvis ; while Hector took a house of his own in the New Street neighbourhood. Johnson would miss very much the affectionate daily intercourse with Hector, and the meetings with Hector's friends, among whom were Harry Porter, the mercer, who would not see in the penniless young apprentice to literature his successor in Mrs. Porter's affections ; and John Taylor, a little younger than himself, whose great mechanical ingenuity, which, when he applied it to the gilding and japanning of metals, eventually made him one of Birmingham's greatest and richest citizens and benefactors, was already in evidence. Johnson, who was always immensely curious about trade processes and the like, would find much more in common with a practical man such as Taylor than with any mere dilettante of literature. But Birmingham people generally could not endure Johnson, who would seem a strange creature to men busily engaged in commercial pursuits. A man he is pretty sure to have met at that time was William Priest, an attorney some dozen years only older than himself, who was familiar with the affairs of his uncle, Andrew Johnson, acted for some of his mother's Ford relatives, and was professionally involved with the whole circle in which they moved.

Whatever Johnson lost by the move into Mr. Jarvis's lodgings, where he was settled by June 1733, it was while there that he accomplished his first literary task of any size of which we know. This was the translation of Father Jerome Lobo's *Voyage to Abyssinia*, from the French version of Joachim Le Grand, of 1728, the actual Portuguese original never having been printed, and remaining unprinted even to this day. He had read the work while at Oxford, and mentioned to Warren and Hector that he thought an abridged translation of it into English might be of interest and also of profit. The two friends were impressed, and urged him to undertake the task himself. Johnson agreed, and as the book was not to be had locally he borrowed it from Pembroke College, perhaps from a friend and not from the library. The reading of this book while at Oxford shows that he must even then have had a working knowledge of French ; and also that he cannot have rigidly maintained his earlier determination to eschew works of travel as bordering on the frivolous.

But Warren and Hector had not reckoned with Johnson's dilatory ways, and that procrastinating spirit which played havoc all his life with so many good intentions. He started off in fine style, so much so that Osborn, who was Warren's printer, was kept busy setting up the copy as it was supplied. But his promise to maintain the output was not kept, his spate of energy soon exhausted itself, and the work in consequence came to a standstill. This was very disconcerting for Warren, and Hector, who knew his friend, saw that there was but one way to overcome his "constitutional indolence." He pointed out to him that, lacking a supply of copy, the worthy Osborn was without employment, and that he and his family were suffering in consequence. This was an argument to appeal to Johnson's heart, and he set to work again, his mind exerted to the full while physically he was so inert that he lay all day in bed. The big quarto was placed before him on the counterpane, and he dictated his translation, while the faithful Hector wrote it down and carried the sheets to the printer, who was thus kept busy again. By these heroic means the work was quickly completed, though, as we shall see, it was not actually produced till 1735. The correcting for the press was done almost entirely by Hector, and Johnson himself saw few of the proof sheets. The translator's reward from Warren was five guineas, and though this may seem a small sum it must be remembered that it was equal to his quarter's salary as an usher.

It is clear from his own confession that Johnson at this time was again assailed by the melancholic tendency that had reached its height after his return from Oxford, and that never ceased to threaten his physical and mental well-being. Yet he retained many happy memories of the evenings he and Hector spent together in Warren's house, or in the genial atmosphere of the Swan Inn opposite. In 1733 Warren printed a volume of *Sermons*, by the Rev. Edward Brodhurst, a minister of the Old Meeting in Birmingham, who had possessed an excellent library, and some think that Johnson must have helped with the preface.

Though Johnson's old schoolmaster, John Hunter, had married Lucy Porter the elder in 1726, and he must therefore have met her when he visited at the schoolhouse, he did not meet her brother until this stay in Birmingham, when Hector, who bought his clothes from Harry Porter, introduced them, as we have seen, with eventual momentous consequences that can hardly have been foreseen by any of the parties concerned. Harry Porter's shop was in the High Street, not far from Warren's, and had been there at the time of Johnson's visit to the town in 1719.

While Johnson was in the Birmingham lodgings, his godfather, Richard Wakefield, died about the end of August. His will proved him a generous benefactor to Lichfield, as well as to his native Tutbury, and Johnson benefited to the extent of five pounds. This would be a useful help to him when money was very scarce, but would not maintain him for more than a month or two. With his translating job finished, and Warren evidently not in need of his regular services, he had not much reason to remain in Birmingham, so in the February of 1734 he returned once more to Lichfield. Every return to his native place must have advertised his failure, and depressed him accordingly.

However, it was no use brooding, and he looked about for some work to undertake. It struck him that he might print the Latin poems of Politian, in an annotated edition, with a life of the author. He remembered, as in the case of Lobo's *Voyage*, that Pembroke College had his works, and asked an old member of the College, the Rev. Robert Boyse, recently appointed the first minister of Smethwick, on the western side of Birmingham, to borrow the volume for him while on a visit to Oxford. Mr. Boyse duly drew the book out on 15 June 1734, Johnson's old rival, John Meeke, being then librarian and making the entry recording the loan. When Johnson got the book in his hands he was able to consider his scheme more carefully, and a few weeks later, in August, he issued his "Proposals" and appealed for subscriptions, which were to be sent to him, as editor, or to Nathaniel Johnson, bookseller in Lichfield, who was now conducting the business. The terms involved the payment of half-a-crown on subscription, and another half-crown on the delivery of the completed work in quires. It was to consist of more than thirty sheets, and the price was low. But Johnson was unknown, and the book of a limited appeal, so that subscriptions did not come in as they had hoped. The scheme had to be dropped, and the work was probably never really prepared. And, sad to relate, Pembroke College never got back its copy of *Politian*, which was found on Johnson's shelves after his death.

The evil demon of slothfulness still threatened to master him, and he was painfully conscious of the fact. A diary entry of 27 August 1734, made at ten o'clock at night, confesses that he had "trifled away" the day, except that he had "attended the school in the morning"—which suggests some temporary teaching job. And at night he had read some of John Rogers's *Sermons*, and "began the breakfast law anew," whatever that meant.

Just a week after this something happened which was vitally to affect his life, though even he probably did not realise it at the time. On 3 September 1734 Harry Porter, the Birmingham mercer whose friendship he had made while lodging in Warren's house with Edmund Hector early in the preceding year, died at his house in the High Street, at the early age of forty-three, so paving the way for one of those queer romances that men of letters are so prone to offer us.

Harry Porter, though a mercer and woollen-draper, and keeping a shop, occupied rather a different position from his fellow-tradesman of today, when the distinction between wholesale and retail trade has become so marked as ordinarily to carry certain social implications. He came from an old and well-to-do family, settled in the sixteenth century at Alvechurch in Warwickshire, about ten miles south of Birmingham. The real founder of the family fortunes was Harry's great-grandfather, Henry Porter, born at Alvechurch in 1570, who settled at Edgbaston, even then almost part of Birmingham, where he died about 1620. By his marriage in 1594 to a daughter of William Colmore, he became allied with one of the leading families in Birmingham, and his eldest son, who left no children, is described as an "esquire." His daughters, too, married into the small squire class, one to Waldyve Willington, who was appointed Governor of Tamworth Castle by the Parliamentarians. The second son, Thomas, was a mercer at Bromsgrove; the third son, Robert Porter, a sword cutler in Birmingham, was the Cromwellian captain whose letter describing Prince Rupert's attack on the town in 1643, when his own mill was destroyed, was first printed in that same year. Of Henry Porter, the fourth and youngest son, little is known, except that he must have been the father of yet another Henry Porter who was a mercer, like his uncle Thomas, but in Birmingham. This last Henry Porter, born about 1650, was a man of substance, long a governor of King Edward's School in Birmingham, who at his death in 1710 was buried with his grandfather and eldest uncle at Edgbaston. And this Henry's second surviving son, born in 1691, was Harry Porter, so christened to distinguish him from his father: he again was buried at Edgbaston.

Harry Porter was brought up to the trade which had comfortably supported his father, who left him £400 on condition that he was apprenticed to his elder brother Joseph. Almost immediately he was out of his time, in 1715, he married, his wife being Elizabeth Jervis, then living with her widowed mother at Warwick, but a native of Great Peatling in Leicestershire, where she came of a long line of small country squires. Thus enters the story "Tetty," the historic object of Johnson's affections. We know she was old enough to be Johnson's mother, and even Harry Porter was over two years her junior. She brought the young mercer a portion of £600 and upwards, but in spite of this and other advantages he did not prosper, and even when he died his widow had to make a resignation of his affairs to an attorney.

Miss Seward, who, of all the witnesses concerned, is the least to be relied upon, tells us that Johnson attended the sick bed of Harry Porter with great assiduity. We can believe that or not, as we like, but there can be no doubt that he must have begun to court the widow without much delay, an enterprise which would involve a good deal of travelling backward and forward between Lichfield and Birmingham. Indeed not many weeks after Harry Porter's death he appears to have been actually staying in Birmingham. For it was on 25 November 1734 that he wrote his well known letter to Edward Cave, founder and editor of *The Gentleman's Magazine*, offering to contribute to the paper, and concluding with a request for an answer to be "directed to *S. Smith*, to be left at the Castle in Birmingham, Warwickshire," where it would reach "your humble servant," who remained anonymous. It is not too tactful a letter, as it suggests that "the literary dissertations" he proposes, in Latin or English, would be more appreciated by the public than "low jests, aukward buffoonery, or the dull scurrilities of either party;" and also speaks critically of the poetry, and what passed for wit, in Cave's journal. He offers original contributions of literary interest, and generally recognises his own capacity to effect an improvement in the periodical, as well as to advise with regard to other kindred projects. He asks to be informed "in two posts" whether his suggestion is agreeable, and if so what the terms would be. Cave was evidently not offended by the rather complacent tone of the letter, and his reply, dated 2 December, is said to have accepted Johnson's offer. But this is very doubtful, as nothing resulted for some time.

Why Johnson wished to remain anonymous we do not know, or why to Cave, a complete stranger, "S. Smith" should appear a more desirable contributor than "S. Johnson." The Castle Inn stood in the Rothermarket, the continuation of High Street, and was kept by the widow of Henry Cambden, whose son succeeded to it after her death, and was known to Johnson's uncle, Nathaniel Ford. Widow Cambden's second daughter, Elizabeth, five years younger than Johnson, afterwards married Benjamin Roebuck, brother of the celebrated inventor, John Roebuck, and in 1777, after her death, Johnson regretted that he had not seen her in recent years. It is an extraordinary genealogical coincidence that Benjamin Roebuck, after choosing for his first wife this early friend of Johnson's, should for his second have selected a near cousin of Boswell's from Scotland with very different social connexions.

We are so accustomed to think of Johnson exclusively as he was in his later years, when he had grown very bulky, that we are apt to make the picture retrospective and in that relation false. For at this time he carried no spare flesh whatever: tall and of big physique he was yet lean to an uncommon degree, and his huge bones protruded in such a way as to make him look unpleasantly like an anatomical model. The scrofula, too, or King's evil, which Queen Anne's touch had so signally failed to cure, had left its marks deeply graven on his face. And he took no pains to remedy his natural defects by attention to his appearance: apart from his careless indifference to dress he was so unfashionable as to wear no wig, but to display his own hair, which was "straight and stiff, and separated behind." With all these disqualifications, added to the "convulsive starts and odd gesticulations" which had developed through his nervous troubles, he was rather a figure to excite unsympathetic ridicule than to capture the affections even of an elderly widow. But Mrs. Porter had the intelligence to form her judgment of him from deeper observation, and after he had first come to tea to pronounce him the most "sensible" man she had ever met in her life.

In the midst of his courtship the translation he had prepared of Lobo's *Voyage to Abyssinia*, in the winter of 1733-4, was at last published. It was noticed in *The Gentleman's Magazine* for January 1735, and the title page describes it as printed for A. Bettesworth and C. Hitch, at the Red Lyon in Paternoster Row. Arthur Bettesworth and his son-in-law Charles Hitch were leading London publishers, but the actual printing of the book was done in Birmingham. The dedication, obviously written by Johnson himself, was to John Warren, esquire, of Trewern in Pembrokeshire, a landed gentleman who had been High Sheriff of his county in 1712, as had his father before him in 1674, but who is not known to have had any literary interests, or any other suitable qualifications beyond his name. As it expresses not merely gratitude and respect, but also, more familiarly, "sincerest affection," some sort of kinship is rather suggested between the Birmingham printer and the South Wales squire. The "Johnsonian style," as we now understand it, was a gradual development, and not as pronounced in such early writings. He claimed to have modelled his style on that of Sir William Temple, who died in 1699, though the resemblance is not very apparent to others; and on "Proposals" by Ephraim Chambers for his *Cyclopaedia*, first published in 1728, which have not yet been discovered.

Harry Porter's business as a mercer was taken over by William Ward, and the widow vacated her house in the High Street to Thomas Warren himself, who moved in from a dozen doors away. So where exactly the courtship was conducted we cannot say. If, as Boswell avers, Johnson had kept himself so much in check that now his affections were released he became a more ardent lover than the average man, it would be wise to get her family out of the way, for to growing children the sight of their recently widowed mother, a middle-aged woman of forty-six, being wooed so vigorously by a strange figure of a man full twenty years her junior, might well be an actual humiliation. The eldest son, Jervis Henry Porter, was a boy of eighteen, training for the navy, who naturally fiercely resented his mother's ridiculous love affair with the penniless interloper: indeed he never forgave her or became reconciled to Johnson. Lucy, the only daughter, was nineteen, and the eldest child, but her nature was less stubborn and she would not have the instinctive male disgust for unnatural matings: she did not quarrel with her mother, and afterwards became the affectionate friend of her stepfather. Joseph Porter, the younger son, was only about ten or eleven, so did not feel it as keenly as Jervis, and proved not irreconcilable to Johnson in later years, when a prosperous merchant at Leghorn.

However, despite their difference in years, the displeasure of her children, and the natural opposition of all their relatives, Johnson and Mrs. Porter became engaged to be married. It was now more than ever necessary for him to find some regular occupation which would produce an income on which to support the married state. The fact that his wife would bring him a fortune of seven or eight hundred pounds made a great difference in the situation, as all his previous schemes had been those of a young man without any capital at all. To him it would seem almost like wealth, and it really was equal to a good many thousand pounds today. It would not be necessary for him now to be a servant: he could hope to do something in which he remained his own master. And so there formulated in his mind the idea, natural to one who had made several attempts at schoolmastering, to establish a select private "academy" of his own—not that he himself ever gave it that name.

The thought of setting up a home, especially if it were to be combined with a school, reminded him of the little private library that he had left in the charge of his friend John Taylor, at Christ Church, when he returned from Oxford in the December of 1729. The box in which they were packed had been locked by Johnson, who placed therein also some papers of a particularly private nature that he did not wish to be seen by the common eye. But Taylor disappointed him: he either opened the box and got the books out himself, or, when he also left Oxford in the following September, allowed it to get into the hands of someone who took similar liberties. The books, Johnson heard, had come into the care of John Spicer, a contemporary of Taylor's at Christ Church, and one of the Repingtons of Tamworth kindly offered to get his brother Gilbert, now a freshman at Christ Church, and Johnson's old schoolfellow, to see about them. So, on 18 May 1735, after some delay in waiting for the correct address, Johnson wrote from Lichfield to Gilbert Repington, asking him to collect the books, pack them in boxes, and despatch them to him at the Castle Inn, Birmingham, to which a carrier went once a week from Oxford. He undertook to pay all charges for the boxes, porterage and postage. He enclosed a complete list of the books, with very abbreviated titles, and was so eager to hear what their condition was that he begged a reply by return. Whatever indignity they may have suffered by being unpacked, and possibly used, not one volume seems to have gone astray out of the 115 odd, though what had happened to the private papers about which he was so anxious we do not know. It is very strange that he should have been content to be without his books for over five years.

Johnson asked Gilbert Repington to remember him to another old friend, Richard Congreve, to whom he would have written personally had he known his college, and to suggest a letter from him. He also spoke of "many other acquaintance in the University whom he remembered with pleasure," and the letter generally shows that any feeling of bitterness or humiliation that remained after the premature and miserable termination of his Oxford career over five years before had now worn away. Such acquaintances as were still at Oxford whom he remembered from his undergraduate days could only have been dons, or servants.

The scheme for his own school was brewing in Johnson's mind, but he could not give it effect until he married. There is many a slip 'twixt the cup and the lip, and he would hardly dare to undertake any considerable liabilities before he actually had a moneyed wife to share them. In the meantime he was open to outside employment, and through the agency of some good friends an opportunity came of a coaching engagement. The Rev. John Addenbrooke, Incumbent of St. Chad's at Lichfield, learned that Thomas Whitby, a county gentleman seated at Great Haywood, on the other side of Rugeley, and a former High Sheriff of Staffordshire, had a son he wished to be prepared for the university; and so he approached Theophilus Levett, the town clerk of Lichfield, asking if he would find out whether Johnson was prepared to undertake the responsibility, and mentioning the least sum that "could be offered to a gentleman of character for half a year's attendance." Mr. Levett wrote to Johnson, who replied favourably to the project, except that his "affairs" (how much the word covered!) would not allow him to stay so long. Johnson's letter was forwarded by Addenbrooke, on 10 May 1735, to Mr. Whitby, who was asked to name the sum he was prepared to pay for the shorter period proposed. Addenbrooke particularly impressed upon the boy's father how much he had to gain by engaging Johnson, who could (an he would) teach him more in a few weeks of private tuition than would ordinarily be learned in a year's work at the university. An immediate answer was requested by Mr. Addenbrooke, so that he could inform Mr. Levett, and get Johnson to present himself in person before his prospective employer.

On 18 May Johnson was still in Lichfield, when, as we have seen, he wrote to Gilbert Repington asking him to expedite the return of his private library from Oxford, which, by the way, might be useful to him in his coaching work. But he soon concluded the business with Mr. Whitby, and was installed as temporary tutor at Great Haywood. The family there consisted of the father and mother, with three sons and two daughters. It was the eldest son, John Whitby, aged nineteen, who required coaching: he must have suffered some check in his education, for it was usual then to go up to the university at a much earlier age. The full half year spoken of and more elapsed before he went to Oxford, where he matriculated from University College in March 1736. It is rather an extraordinary coincidence that his widow, who afterwards engaged in a tangled series of marriages, or supposed marriages, that brought her into much discredit, had for one of her "husbands" John Robins, M.P. for Stafford, who was directly descended from Johnson's great-uncle, Henry Ford, the Clifford's Inn attorney.

Johnson, in later life, told a friend that a private tutor "must expect insolence" in a position that was "a very disagreeable and mortifying one," owing to the treatment that it was traditional to accord the humble dependent. Let us hope that it was not his experience at the Whitbys which was the cause of these bitter remarks. When he was not busy improving the son's classics, he frequently took the younger daughter, Jane, a girl of thirteen, in English, a circumstance she long remembered. On Sunday he would walk over to their church at Colwich, a mile and a half away, where John Clements, an Oxford graduate of his own age, was vicar, and on his return astonish the family by his ability to repeat almost the whole sermon, as well as to criticise it and suggest improvements. John Clements can have been no fool, to engage Johnson's attention so closely, and we know that at his death in 1793 he was an F.S.A., which suggests extended interests. It is rather curious that latterly he held the living of Appleby in Leicestershire, whose Johnsonian associations will appear later. John Dunn, who at this time kept the inn at Wolseley Bridge, Colwich, had some connexion with Johnson's family, and towards the end of his life the Doctor interested himself in the affairs of his granddaughters, the Miss Colliers, whose stepfather, Thomas Flint, was Dr. Taylor's factotum at Ashburne.

Addenbrooke always had Johnson's regard for the help given him at this time. Forty years afterwards, when Addenbrooke was Dean of Lichfield, Johnson, in his *Journey to the Western Islands of Scotland*, had included a paragraph appearing to censure the Cathedral authorities for a projected act of vandalism, but recollecting that it might wound the Dean, to whom he owed this kindness, he realised its impropriety and had the leaf cancelled in time. This all points to his stay at Great Haywood not having left an unpleasant memory.

Gilbert Repington duly conveyed Johnson's message to Richard Congreve, at Christ Church, who wrote to him as desired in a few weeks.

But it was hardly the letter Johnson had looked for: it was much too formal in its expression to come appropriately from one with whom he had formerly lived on such terms of intimacy as dispensed with all ceremonious compliments. Johnson certainly acknowledged "a very important kindness"—perhaps concerned with the despatch of his books from Oxford—but did not like to think that the easy friendship they had enjoyed in the quiet seclusion of country life could by the air of Oxford be changed into mere formal acquaintance. So in his reply, written from Mr. Whitby's house on 25 June 1735, he invites Congreve to resume their friendship on the old terms, and to repay any pleasure he might have derived from Johnson's conversation in their early days by a frank communication of his thoughts and opinions, that they, in spite of the distance which separated them, could enjoy the equivalent of social intercourse. He remarks on the usual custom among friends when meeting after a long separation to begin by relating to each other all that has happened to them since their last intercourse, and he hopes Congreve will follow this practice. But for himself he says that, as so little has happened to him that it would give pleasure to relate, he will not trouble his correspondent "with an account of time not always very agreeably spent," but ignore the disappointments of the past in favour of his plans for the future. He announces his intention to "furnish a house in the country, and keep a private boarding-school for young gentlemen," and thinks he shows no vanity in believing that he can improve on the methods of teaching common at the time. But before actually drawing up his scheme of education he would study the methods used at the principal schools, and asks Congreve if he will kindly tell him the system employed at Charterhouse (where Congreve had been a pupil from 1728 to 1733, probably after a spell at Lichfield Grammar School), and get from some one else that of Westminister. All he wanted was a list of the classes, with the exercises and authors for each.

It is rather amusing to find that Johnson, while appealing to his friend for a frank interchange of confidences, fails to reveal the fact of his approaching marriage to Mrs. Porter, which was to take place in a fortnight's time. He knew very well that Congreve, in common with all their relatives and friends, would stand aghast at the idea of such an extraordinary union.

CHAPTER IX.

MARRIAGE TO MRS. PORTER
SETS UP SCHOOL AT EDIAL
1735-1737

"The Widow Porter," in connexion with Johnson, always suggests a figure rather comic or grotesque, and when we consider their respective ages, and the whole circumstances of their courtship, we must admit here was excellent material for ribald humour to those not nearly enough concerned to be angry. If, as Johnson gravely asserted, it was "a love-match on both sides", that only makes it more ludicrous. But now that we approach so closely the date of her marriage to Johnson it is time to take serious count of Elizabeth Jervis and her antecedents.

On both sides "Tetty" came of old and excellent stock, as such values are ordinarily appraised. Her father's family had been Leicestershire squires for unnumbered generations. Jervis of Thorpe Langton—or Jarvis, as it was commonly pronounced, and by Johnson spelt—was already an ancient family when about the middle of the sixteenth century it made a short move and fixed its habitation at Great Peatling, a small village some eight miles south from Leicester town. In 1618 the head of the family served the office of High Sheriff of the county. No member rose to any distinction, or even made a great match : the succession was of smallish landowners whose intermarriages were with families much of a parity with their own. Tetty's great-great-grandfather, George Jervis of Great Peatling, is identifiable with one of the name who matriculated from Merton College, Oxford, in 1579, after three or four years at Eton : while her grandfather, Samuel Jervis, entered Pembroke College, Cambridge, in 1646, as a fellow-commoner. But neither of these ancestors seems to have proceeded to a degree, and they are no evidence of any intellectual bent. It was Samuel's only surviving child, William Jervis, of Great Peatling, esquire, and lord of the manor, born in 1659, who fathered Tetty, but he died in 1695, nearly fifteen years before the birth of his distinguished son-in-law, and is little more than a name.

Her mother, daughter of Henry Darell, a barrister of the Middle Temple, came of another landed stock at least as old as that of the

Jervises, and with a much more interesting history. Long settled at East Chart, in Kent, the family later moved to Scotney, in the same county. Edward Darell, who died in 1573, left Scotney for Pagham, in Sussex, and changed the status of the family, as well as its geographical location, for he was not content simply to remain on the land but went out into the world and became Clerk of the Acatery to Queen Elizabeth, an office which put him in charge of the provisions for the Royal Household. His younger son, Sir Marmaduke Darell, followed in his father's footsteps, but rose higher : knighted in 1603, he served as Victualler of the Navy and Cofferer of the King's Household, buying the manor of Fulmer, in Buckinghamshire, as evidence of a prosperous career. Sir Marmaduke's son, Sir Sampson Darell, knighted in 1619, was a Gray's Inn man, like his father, but also took a degree at Queen's College, Oxford. Born about 1594, he succeeded his father at Fulmer Place, and died early in 1635. He had nine children, and the youngest son was Henry Darell, the grandfather of Tetty.

Henry Darell was born about 1633, but not till 1662 was he admitted to the Inner Temple, and only to migrate to the Middle Temple in 1664, where he was duly called to the bar in 1666. He was a married man when admitted to the Inner Temple, and a widower a few months later. For his first wife, a daughter of Robert Thomson, of Royton Manor, Kent, he had the greatest affection and regard, but when next year he made a second venture, with a widow, he found her so perverse and unkind that they had no happiness together. In 1672 he was in poor health, yet proposing very soon officially to accompany his friend, Lord Willoughby of Parham, to Barbadocs, where that peer was Governor. But the Governor did not go out till five months after this, and probably without Henry Darell, who died not more than a year or two later at Tangier. If the costliness of the monuments he desired to be erected to his own and his first wife's memory in Kentish churches is any index, Henry Darell must have been a man of pretty large means, and his property interests were considerable.

Anne Darell, who became the mother-in-law of Johnson, though she did not live to make the connexion a personal one, was a daughter of the first marriage to Anne Thomson, and through it was descended from some old Kentish families. A not very remote ancestress to be proud of was Mrs. Honywood, of Charing, who lived to see 367 descendants.

After her father's death Anne passed to the guardianship of her father's friend, Francis Eedes, of the Inner Temple, who belonged to a prominent Warwick family, and the association thus formed with that historic town had far-reaching results, for without it Johnson would never have met and married her daughter. Anne Darell married William Jervis about 1679, and though he was already the squire of Great Peatling the couple's eldest son and heir came into the world at Warwick. Their other children, however, were born at Great Peatling, where, after the father's early death in 1695, the family stayed on for some years.

Elizabeth, the daughter of William Jervis, esquire, and Mistress Anne his wife, was born on 4 February 1689, in the early morning, and baptized by the curate of Little Peatling on 16 February. "Tetty," the name by which Johnson afterwards affectionately called her, was a common provincial diminutive favoured by the middle and lower classes. Only six when her father died, he can have meant little to her. She had a younger as well as an elder sister, but both died in childhood. Her eldest brother, Richard Jervis, the heir to the estate, had in 1689 entered Rugby School, where the next brother, William, followed just after the father's death.

Richard Jervis, who had gone on to St. John's College, Cambridge, as a pensioner, in 1698, developed rather extravagant habits when he grew up, and the trustees had to sell some of the Peatling land. In 1703 a fresh settlement was effected, in order that Richard's debts might be cleared off, under which £600 was to be paid to Elizabeth, the only surviving daughter, as against the £400 named in her father's will. By 1707 Elizabeth's mother had gone to live at Warwick, but her grandmother Jervis remained at Great Peatling and died next year, leaving Elizabeth all her household goods and jewelry, as well as half the residue of her estate. Thus was made up Tetty's fortune of about £800.

On her twenty-sixth birthday, 4 February 1715, a licence was issued for the marriage of "Henry"—his legal name of Harry must have been frowned upon by the clerk—Porter, of Birmingham, bachelor, to Elizabeth Jervis, "of Warwick," showing that her mother had remained in the town. The couple's acquaintance probably came about through a branch of the Colmore family of Birmingham having settled at Warwick, where two Williams of the clan, father and son, barristers and Magdalen College men, were about this time successively Members for the town. The Porters, as we have seen, claimed cousinship with the Colmores, who at Warwick were closely associated with the Jervises and acted as their trustees.

For the daughter of the Leicestershire squire to marry the Birmingham mercer was not the "romance" a similar match might be considered today. All social values at that time were different, and trades which now are supposed to involve some measure of social ostracism in polite circles then carried no such disqualification. And the short account of the Porters has made it clear that they were themselves a family with some traditions, whose position was quite equal to that of well-to-do professional people today, as is shown by their marriages through a good number of generations.

And now, having learned all we need to know about Tetty and her origins, we can resume the story where it left off in the last chapter. Johnson, writing to his friend Congreve at Oxford, on 25 June 1735, asked that the reply be addressed to him at Mr. Whitby's at Great Haywood, so that he clearly had no intention of leaving immediately, although his marriage was to take place in a fortnight. Any arrangements he still required to make cannot have been of an elaborate character, and as the pair had planned a wedding at a distance, away from all disapproving relatives and friends, they had only themselves to consider. Speculation has been busy as to why Derby was chosen, and why St. Werburgh's there. The Rev. William Lockett, who had been Vicar at St. Werburgh's since 1722, was a Cheshire man, educated at Cambridge, who previously had been assistant master at Derby School under Anthony Blackwall before that notable head went on to Market Bosworth. It may be that schoolmastering associations had brought Johnson into touch with Lockett. At any rate, on 8 July 1735, Johnson presented himself before Mr. Lockett at Derby, and secured a licence for his marriage to Elizabeth Porter, of St Philip's parish, Birmingham, widow, the ceremony to be performed either at St. Werburgh's or St. Philip's, the surety being his childhood's friend, Charles Howard, now a proctor of the ecclesiastical court at Lichfield. And next morning Johnson was able to produce the Widow Porter and take her to St. Werburgh's to be married.

The couple had evidently ridden to Derby the day before, probably from Lichfield, some twenty-five miles away, and not from Birmingham, which is about forty. A good authority stated that Mrs. Porter herself lived in the Close at Lichfield during her widowhood, but if so she must have returned to Birmingham before her marriage. It was on this ride to Derby that Johnson resolutely defeated an outbreak of coquetry on the elderly Mrs. Porter's part. She, bred on romances in which women treated their lovers as subservient creatures, would keep on changing her pace, purely to tease him, till he felt compelled to assert himself by riding on ahead and leaving her to catch up with him as best she could, in tears but disciplined by his masculine defiance of her caprices.

Johnson's aging mother, whose consent he had dutifully sought to the marriage, was probably the only one of the relatives on either side who did not actively oppose it. Devoted to her son, and knowing his self-willed nature, she was too sensible to risk a break by trying to thwart him. The strongest opposition came from Harry Porter's eldest brother, Joseph. Joseph Porter had not been content just to follow in his father's footsteps, but had gone off to London to make his fortune. He became a prosperous Hamburg merchant in Ironmonger Lane, his portrait painted by Hogarth, with a country house at Mortlake: as a bachelor he was able to help the less fortunate members of the family, including his brother Harry's children, who owed their success in life largely to him. But when Harry's widow married "the literary cub"—we can accept Miss Seward as our authority here—he very naturally refused to have anything more to do with her, however ready he continued to be to help her children.

So much ridicule has been attached to Tetty's appearance, through Garrick having exercised his lively and mischievous wit at her expense, that it is rather hard to approach the subject unbiassed. According to him she was "very fat, with a bosom of more than ordinary protuberance, with swelled cheeks of a florid red, produced by thick painting, and increased by the liberal use of cordials; flaring and fantastic in her dress, and affected both in her speech and her general behaviour." And again, he said that "she was a little painted puppet, of no value at all, and quite disguised with affectation, full of odd airs of rural elegance." Miss Seward, who could only describe her at second hand, is no more complimentary, and such an accumulation of abuse is rather overwhelming. But it is probably much exaggerated, and her portrait, though perhaps taken earlier in life, shows a good looking and attractive woman. William Shaw, who relied upon Dr. Swynfen's daughter, Mrs. Desmoulins, for particulars of Johnson's early life, said she was still handsome when Johnson married her, so much so that his friends used to chaff him on her superiority over him in that respect. Johnson himself told Mrs. Thrale that his wife had beautiful hair, blonde as a baby's, which he wisely discouraged her from dying black.

We may conclude that Mrs. Johnson was naturally a well-favoured woman, even in middle age, but that her over-anxiety to appear as a suitable wife for a young man led to injudicious experiments in beauty culture. Her addiction to opium, or other drugs, was probably the result of ill health and domestic troubles in her later years. She is said to have possessed a shrewd judgment, with a satirical turn, and to have been quite competent to discuss literary matters with her husband, who said that she " read comedy better than anybody he had ever heard ; in tragedy she mouthed too much "—a tribute so refreshingly impartial in its expression as to carry conviction. To Johnson, always confident of being able to distinguish "the *born gentlewoman* " from the baser kind who had to rely merely upon " adventitious accomplishments," it must have been a satisfaction that his wife came of a family that could not be charged with the shameful offence of possessing " an estate newly acquired by trade."

We do not know where the strangely assorted couple went to live immediately after their marriage. The plan to start a boarding school had not yet taken a practical shape, and Johnson, though unwilling now, in his more independent financial position, to become an usher again, was still ready to forego the scheme if he could get a headmastership. An opening presented itself, at Solihull, some seven miles south-east from Birmingham, and close to the homes of his mother's forbears. This opening was due to a chain of circumstances following on from the death of the Rev. John Kilby, Headmaster of Market Bosworth Grammar School, under whom Johnson had served during those wretched months of usherdom in 1732. Kilby's death took place in August 1734, and the usual delay occurred over the appointment of a successor. But on the very last day of the year we find Sir Wolstan Dixie, the evil genius of Johnson's stay, writing in his usual brief and authoritative way to the Rev. John Crompton, who had been head at Solihull since 1704, offering him the vacancy at Market Bosworth. Sir Wolstan had had very good accounts of Crompton from some friends, and baited his offer of the post (which he said was in his own sole nomination) with the assurance that it was worth £103 clear annually in money, apart from the house and gardens. Crompton was not slow to accept, and a fortnight later was formally sworn on his appointment.

The sudden defection of their able head "huffed" the trustees, if relations had not already become strained, and even in the following August, when Johnson, through the kind agency of Gilbert Walmesley, was led to apply for a vacancy that had remained unfilled for over seven months, they were still sore about it. Probably the school was not in a very flourishing condition at the time, for the trustees, in writing to Walmesley declining to engage his nominee, sugared the pill with a suggestion that so excellent a scholar as they had found Mr. Johnson to be, by inquiry since the receipt of the application a fortnight before, "deserved much better than to be schoolmaster of Solihull." But if extremely civil, they were no less frank. The real reason for the refusal was that Johnson "had the character of being a very haughty, ill-natured gentleman, and that he has such a way of distorting his face (which though he can't help) the gentlemen think it may affect some young lads." By "haughty and ill-natured" they probably only meant that Johnson was independent and "difficult," and not that he was malevolent. It is quite in accordance with modern theories of neuropathy that they should have thought it dangerous to put young children, with their instinctive tendency to imitation, in the charge of a teacher evidently suffering from those convulsive twitchings of the face generally known as "tic." The successful candidate was the Rev. Richard Mashiter, whose son afterwards succeeded him.

Once the Solihull application was refused, Johnson was free to proceed with his plan for a private school. There was at the little hamlet of Edial (pronounced, and sometimes spelt, "Edjall"), two or three miles west of Lichfield, a large brick-built house called Edial Hall, enclosed by substantial walls, which had been erected soon after the Restoration by Thomas Hammond, an opulent citizen of

Lichfield, who had served pretty well all the public offices open to him locally, and whose nephew, Richard Hammond, the apothecary, has already come into the story. A magistrate, keeping his own coach, and connected with such considerable families as Pyott, Wollaston and Thacker, he required a house suitable to his dignity. And he must also have some eccentric feature to distinguish it. So he, or his architect, produced a very queer looking roof, the pyramidal form of which was interrupted about two thirds of the way up and a flat constructed, surrounded with an ornamental balustrade. In the centre of the flat rose a tall cupola or lantern, with an exit door from the stair or ladder which served for an approach. The whole conception was freakish, and however good a view such a peculiar feature provided over the surrounding country it quite spoilt the architectural effect of what otherwise would have appeared a plain dignified house of the period. The roof slopes below had dormer windows, and two tall chimneys, one a kind of miniature Cleopatra's Needle in effect.

Gilbert Walmesley, ever at his elbow with help and advice, encouraged Johnson in his scheme for the school, and recommended him to rent Edial Hall for the purpose. Thomas Hammond had died in 1702, and the only son had conveyed it in 1716 to his sister's husband, William Fettiplace Nott. At the time Johnson became interested in it (and no doubt it was the very " house in the country " he had in mind when he wrote to Congreve) the property was let in lots, and when he decided to follow Mr. Walmesley's advice he became simply a subtenant, probably just for the residence itself, which, without its attendant amenities, would be rather a drug in the market.

No one could pretend that Johnson was cut out for schoolmastering of any kind, and an ambitious venture of this nature would have needed someone with very special qualities to make it a success. Mr. Walmesley, no doubt, thought that his scholarship would attract pupils, but that scholarship was backed up by no degrees, and in any case can not have been known to a very wide circle. The kindly patron did all he could to give his young friend a start. He helped to secure a nucleus of pupils, first among whom will always be remembered David Garrick, now a young man of eighteen, whose education at Lichfield Grammar School had been interrupted by a spell under his wine-merchant uncle at Lisbon. Davy had not yet found the proper outlet for his lively talents, and his Latin and French both required improvement. There was also Davy's younger brother, George Garrick, a boy of twelve. And Mr. Walmesley, who in the April of 1736 gave up his bachelor state to marry Magdalen, daughter of Sir Thomas Aston, one of a family whose name was to become very closely associated with Johnson's, was instrumental in getting another pupil in her sixteen-year-old cousin, Lawrence Offley, whose father, a local squire, had been Member for Bewdley and a Gentleman of the Privy Chamber. But all the efforts of Mr. Walmesley, and of such of their relatives as had become sufficiently reconciled to the marriage to be willing to help them, could add no more than five or six pupils, and the total never exceeded eight, some of whom were only day boys.

The school could not possibly pay its way on such a basis, and its prospects grew rather bleak. Johnson's physical disabilities, as has already been stressed, were a heavy handicap to start with. Such "oddities of manner, and uncouth gesticulations," as afflicted him, made him a natural butt for the thoughtlessly cruel ridicule of the boys; and the tales of those who went a step further and peeped through the keyhole of the bedroom door in order to observe their master's "tumultuous and awkward fondness" (what a genius Boswell had for the graphic phrase!) for his elderly bride would not make for a spirit of gravity in the school. And quite apart from all such considerations, his own exceptional powers of mind, and the facility with which he could acquire knowledge, would not give him that sympathetic understanding of the capacities of the ordinary boy so necessary in the teacher. As we have seen, he was unmethodical in his habits, and by nature slothful. From his earliest youth he had wasted his time by lying late in bed in the morning, and almost the only occasions in his life, after leaving Oxford, when he rose early of his own free will, were one or two mornings at Edial. The education he had given himself in French and Italian, after leaving the University, was to his advantage, but offset by his modesty in making no claim to teach science or prepare young men for the Church. And he suffered from youth, a disease that at twenty-seven is but slowly cured.

The Edial school was probably not actually opened till the beginning of 1736, for after Johnson had failed at Solihull in August there would not be time enough to rent and furnish the house so as to be ready for the last quarter of the year. Hopes would wax high in the first days of the experiment, but as the summer approached and the additional pupils he needed did not appear, he felt he must make a special effort to attract some, and this effort took what was then the bold and unusual form of an advertisement in the *Gentleman's Magazine* he thought himself so well qualified to improve. "At Edial, near Litchfield in Staffordshire, Young Gentlemen are Boarded, and Taught the Latin and Greek Languages, by SAMUEL JOHNSON." This, printed on the last page of the numbers for June and July, was an appeal not to the local gentry, who had failed him, but to educated people throughout the country. And they too failed to respond, not having the slightest idea who Samuel Johnson was, or what were his qualifications.

In May 1736 Dr. Swynfen died at Birmingham, but with an encumbered estate, and a huge family, he was not able to leave his godson a legacy. Ten days before his death he had contracted to sell Swynfen to a kinsman for £19,000 odd. His house and practice were taken over by Dr. John Turton, who had married Dorothy Hickman of Stourbridge in 1734, as already mentioned.

It was in the early stages of the Edial experiment that Johnson was able to advise a young cousin of his who was shortly to proceed to the University. When his grandfather, old Cornelius Ford, had died at Packwood in 1709 he was followed there by his third son, Samuel. Samuel Ford married a daughter of Richard Chambers, of Kings Norton, and granddaughter of the Rev. Timothy White, Vicar of Northfield and Master of Leicester Hospital at Warwick. This uncle of Johnson's, as we have seen, afterwards lived for a time at Stroxton, in Lincolnshire, and while churchwarden there in 1717 he had a son Samuel born to him. Samuel Ford the younger was educated at Sutton Coldfield Grammar School, under Paul Lowe, and at the end of 1735 was almost ready to go up to Oxford, to prepare for the Church. So he applied to his cousin at Edial to advise him as to the best course of reading to follow in the meantime. Johnson felt rather at a loss, as he was not sure what particular study his cousin proposed to pursue, but he recommended him to confine himself to the languages till he entered the University, and gave him a list of the Greek and Latin authors best for him to read, so that he might become "tolerably skilled in all the dialects."

In regard to Latin Johnson advised a thorough grounding in the earlier authors first. He concluded with a characteristic piece of advice, largely revealing the secret of that extraordinary command of language which contributed so much to his own fame in after years. "The greatest and most necessary task still remains, to attain a habit of expression, without which knowledge is of little use. This is necessary in Latin, and more necessary in English; and can only be acquired by a daily imitation of the best and correctest authors." We see how he must have schooled himself on these lines from his earliest youth, and realise once again to what a large extent genius is often what tiresome moralists try to persuade us it is—an infinite capacity for taking pains. And it is interesting to observe how closely the trend of the advice to Samuel Ford follows, though in a rather less sophisticated form, what was impressed upon Johnson himself ten years before at Pedmore by their common cousin, Cornelius Ford—that the accumulation of knowledge can benefit no one but its possessor if there is lacking the art and power of expression. He might well have added his Pedmore mentor's further advice, to gain real wisdom by mastering the basic principles of every subject he studied.

Samuel Ford entered Trinity College, Oxford, in March 1736, and migrated to Emmanuel College, Cambridge, two years later, where he took his degree. He lived a long life as a pluralist parson in Herefordshire, surviving Johnson by over eight years: his mild facial resemblance to his celebrated cousin was not matched by any intellectual affinity, so far as we know. It is curious that there is no record of their having met as men.

After the advertisement in *The Gentleman's Magazine* had fallen quite flat, hopes for the school succeeding became very slight. So again he turned to the idea of taking a salaried post, his pride a little humbled by adversity. The locale this time was Brewood, in Staffordshire, about fifteen miles west from Lichfield, where the Rev. William Budworth, a very able pedagogue who never quite got his deserts, had succeeded the Rev. James Hillman in 1731 as headmaster of the Free Grammar School. Budworth had been head of Rugeley Grammar School for three years, and it is thoroughly in keeping with the extraordinarily irregular scholastic proceedings of the period that he should have remained on there two years longer while the schoolhouse at

Brewood was being made habitable for him. The famous Richard Hurd, afterwards successively Bishop of Lichfield and Worcester, whose brother married a daughter of George Hector, the "man midwife" who brought Johnson into the world, had been a pupil of Hillman's at Brewood, and was so anxious to have the advantage of Budworth's teaching that he changed over to Rugeley for the two years and then came back to Brewood with him to finish. Budworth had about 1715 been a pupil of Anthony Blackwall's at Market Bosworth, and his reputation was well known to Johnson, who now conceived an ambition to become his assistant.

But the usual difficulty arose, and although Budworth well knew Johnson's quality as a scholar, he felt compelled, very much to his own regret, to decline the services of anyone with such trying physical peculiarities. Like the trustees of Solihull School, the year before, he thought that Johnson's "convulsive motions might render him an object of imitation, and possibly of ridicule, with his pupils." Budworth was not correspondingly discreet in other directions. There was an element of scandal about his *ménage*, for the housekeeper he required as a widower had been the mistress of Viscount Lisburne, and her pretty daughter by that nobleman introduced a note of gaiety into the establishment that scandalised some of the parents. But the young lady achieved the highest respectability, marrying the Rev. Watson Hand, member of a prominent Lichfield family, and after his death Johnson's old schoolfellow, Thomas Newton, Bishop of Bristol. Hand was a cousin of Johnson's school rival, Theophilus Lowe, for whom Newton had a great admiration and regard.

There were many idle hours to be filled in at Edial during these last months of the school's existence. Burton's *Anatomy of Melancholy* helped to provide him with intellectual entertainment, and anxiety for the future made him turn his mind towards the possibility of earning a living for himself by literary composition. So he followed the fashion of the time and set himself to write a tragedy in blank verse, though probably conscious that he did not really possess the kind of imagination that nourishes dramatic art. *Irene*, if the first original literary work of any importance he attempted, is also the least regarded, for it is purely an artificial piece of construction in the classical tradition, which never kindles into life as a play. The story he derived from

Richard Knolles's big *General History of the Turks*, published in 1603, which was lent to him by David Garrick's elder brother Peter, then an officer in the Navy. The tale there is a very crude one, of a beautiful Greek, Irene, captured by the Turks in 1453 and taken as mistress by the Sultan, who remained so amorously enthralled by her for three years that his proper duties were neglected. Being warned of the disaffection of his subjects, he pulled himself together and made a great resolve. He summoned all the nobles and officers together, and after an appropriate speech, with Irene by his side, he proved that he was still at bottom a man of good principle, and the master of his passions, by striking off her head with his falchion.

This story was a least a century old in print when Knolles wrote, and had appeared in Italian, French and Latin works, as well as in English. And after Knolles there were at least three plays of *Irene* before Johnson began a fourth, so that the tale was rather hackneyed. Johnson had the highest opinion of Knolles's narrative skill, which later he eulogised in *The Rambler*, and which long after inspired Byron, but he was not inspired by it himself. He had the good sense merely to get the idea of the story from Knolles, and to work it out independently in his own way, and give it some moral purpose, but even allowing himself this freedom playwriting proved an uphill and laborious task to him. He began with an elaborate draft, describing each scene in detail, as well as the characters, including some afterwards omitted, and giving precise references to authorities, in a fashion as unlike that of the mature Johnson as well could be imagined. When he had completed this draft he began to write the actual play, regrouping the material, and dividing it into five acts. Before he left Edial he had sketched out the first three acts, and planned and partly written the conclusion. According to Shaw, his earliest biographer, his godfather, Dr. Swynfen, tried very hard to persuade Johnson to publish the play in the country, with a dedication to Bishop Edward Chandler, who had been translated from Lichfield to Durham : if this be correct the play must at least have been projected before Dr. Swynfen's death in May 1736. But Johnson disliked the idea of seeming to court Church patronage, and refused to be persuaded.

His twenty-seventh birthday, on 7 September (O.S.) 1736, was not celebrated under very auspicious conditions. He prayed that he should spend it " in such a manner that he might receive comfort from it at the hour of death, and in the day of judgment." We may wonder what he could possibly have done, in the quiet shades of Edial, and on this single day, to affect him at death or prejudice his position on the day of judgment, unless he had felt inclined to vent his general dissatisfaction on Charlie Bird, the sixteen-year-old boy who helped about the place. He intended " tomorrow to review the rules he had at any time laid down, in order to practise them." Our best intentions are always for tomorrow.

The miniature of Johnson, the earliest known portrait of him, is said to have been painted about 1736. It was probably done to please his wife, and it would only be in the early days of their married life that such an extravagance could have been considered. And if we calculate pedantically from his own spoken figures, it was in this same year that he fell in love with Mrs. Emmet, a strolling actress who was playing the part of Flora, in Cibber's *Hob ; or the Country Wake*, at the Lichfield theatre. But this was an innocent passion of which even his wife needed not to disapprove. Perhaps it was when so moved by Mrs. Emmet's charm that he performed the feat recorded by Garrick on a visit they paid in their young days to the theatre at Lichfield to watch some strolling players. The chair which Johnson occupied on the stage, between the side-scenes, was taken by a local innkeeper during his momentary absence, at the instigation of a Scots officer who was disaffected to Johnson, and when he rudely declined a civil invitation to quit it Johnson quickly seized both chair and man and hurled them away into the pit. Mr. Walmesley intervened in the cause of order, and Johnson, now at peace with the world, settled down comfortably to enjoy the play. It was in 1736, too, that his cousin Fisher Johnson, elder brother of Tom, went from Birmingham to Leicester, where he married and made his home.

CHAPTER X

FIRST VENTURE TO LONDON
1737

GILBERT WALMESLEY was a friend who never failed. His practical advice and help were ever at Johnson's service. For young men of promise he had a special kindness. At his hospitable board Johnson, with his friends Robert James and David Garrick, confessed to have "enjoyed many cheerful and instructive hours." He not only possessed an immense fund of humane learning, but he had to a quite remarkable degree that faculty for communicating it which Johnson had urged his cousin Samuel Ford to try to cultivate. There was scarcely a single day in Johnson's life in which he did not feel conscious of some benefit from Walmesley's conversation, however strongly he dissented from what he oddly described as "the virulence and malevolence" of his Whiggism.

Mr. Walmesley's belated marriage, in 1736, to Magdalen Aston, introduced an interesting and attractive figure into Johnson's life, or at any rate helped to cement an earlier acquaintance. Mary, or Molly Aston, as she was called, always filled a very special place in his affections. Daughter of a baronet and coming from a social world other than Johnson's, she carried its imprint in her appearance and demeanour, but with a well stored mind and quick intelligence she knew she was not stooping when she accepted the local bookseller's son as her friend. Very much better favoured than her younger sister Magdalen, at the time of whose marriage she was a woman of thirty, she had dignity and grace of bearing, while her face showed great intelligence and sensibility. With lovely auburn hair, and a fine complexion, it is no wonder that Johnson was so carried away by admiration as to declare that she was the loveliest creature he had ever seen, or that the whole evening he spent once with her, though hardly *tête-a-tête*, was not happiness but rapture, and sweetened the rest of the year. Perhaps it is not surprising that, with a keen wit allied to her physical attractions, she was not loved by her own sex. The Miss Aston who comes so much into Johnson's visits to Lichfield in the evening of his life was Elizabeth, whose place in the family was between Mary and Magdalen.

It was Mr. Walmesley's friendly counsel again which determined the next move in Johnson's life. The Edial school steadily declined, and eventually petered out altogether. George Garrick, one of the pupils, went on to Appleby School, in Leicestershire, in February 1737. Johnson was once more without employment : the capital his wife had brought into the partnership was much reduced by the cost of the furniture and equipment for the school (including the small deal escritoire now at Pembroke College, Oxford), and by running it all these months at a loss. His only personal asset was his half-written play *Irene*, and as Mr. Walmesley had high hopes for his success as a tragedy writer this literary effort was a serious consideration to him, when the question came to be discussed as to what it was best to try next, after such a variety of failures. It had been decided that David Garrick, who stood to him more in the relation of a friend than a pupil—if a friend who never quite lost the pupil's inferiority complex—should study for the bar, and as Captain Garrick, for whom Mr. Walmesley had a high regard, could not then afford to send him to the university, it was proposed, in the meantime, to enter him at the Temple and make up for the deficiencies in the future actor's education by some kind of private tutoring. Johnson had turned him into a competent classical scholar, but he still wanted instruction in mathematics, philosophy and humane learning generally.

It struck Mr. Walmesley that no better man for the purpose could be found than his old and dear friend of Oxford days, the Rev. John Colson, a noted mathematician, son to a former Vicar-Choral of the Cathedral at Lichfield, and an old boy of the Grammar School, now Upper Master of the Free School at Rochester in Kent, with whom he had lost touch for a few years. So on 5 February 1737 Mr. Walmesley wrote asking whether he would take in his agreeable and promising young friend, David Garrick, board him, and attend to the weak points in his education, explaining that he was a sensible fellow and a good scholar, who, after almost daily intercourse since childhood, had won his affectionate regard. Captain Garrick would pay what was required, so far as possible. Colson had an excellent house over and above his salary, and Garrick was to be his private pupil, the free education in the school itself being reserved for sons of Rochester freemen, with the intention of directing them towards maritime pursuits.

Colson wrote favourably to Mr. Walmesley in his reply, and agreed to take young Garrick. This gave the opportunity to embrace Johnson in the projected scheme. Mr. Walmesley had had *Irene* read to him by Johnson, in its unfinished state, and been so impressed that he encouraged the author to complete the play and try to get it produced on the stage. This meant a visit to London, and it occurred to them that, as Garrick had to go there on his way to Rochester, Johnson might accompany him as an older friend who could act as a check on Davy's natural tendency to exuberance. It would have been better if Johnson could have finished his play first, but Garrick's arrangements were made and he could not wait.

And so the historic venture came about. Johnson made what arrangements he could for his wife to remain behind in the country, on what was left of her fortune, with her faithful daughter Lucy, who had lived with them at Edial. On the morning of Wednesday, 2 March 1737, he set out with Garrick on their long journey to London, some 120 miles away. Economy was the order of the day: the luxury of the coach was not for young men with their fortunes yet to make, but that most frugal expedient of "riding and tying," by which one horse was made to serve two horsemen, each walking and riding alternately, the horse being tied up at regular intervals to await the pedestrian. It was a humble progression, though it led to a dual fame such as no other pair of adventuring companions to London have ever achieved.

As soon as he had seen them off, Mr. Walmesley sat down and wrote to Colson advising him of their departure. Davy Garrick was to travel straight through and arrive in Rochester early the next week, and Mr. Walmesley said that had he a son of his own it would be his ambition to deal with him thus rather than send him to the university. He hoped that Colson would come back with his pupil in the summer, and stay a few weeks in Lichfield. As regards his other neighbour, "one Mr. Johnson," it was the wish of that "good scholar and poet," whatever the fate of the tragedy, to get some translating to do, either from the Latin or the French, and he trusted that Colson would be ready to help his fellow-Lichfieldian in any way he could.

Nathaniel Johnson is a very obscure figure, and plays practically no part in his elder brother's story. He was actually trained to his father's business, and carried it on for his mother after the old bookseller's death. Following Samuel's marriage he made arrangements to open a shop at Stourbridge, but Samuel advised their mother, for whose affection they used to contend, against the scheme, which fell through. This left Nathaniel with rather bitter feelings towards his brother, who he complained would not even treat him with ordinary civility. He felt that the friends at Stourbridge who were ready to help him had been put to trouble and expense that he could not repay. Later he carried on a branch business at Burton-on-Trent, where he was in very low water, with no money and not sufficient credit to buy even a quire of paper. He had apparently been guilty of some dishonest practice in the business, for which his mother generously forgave him. He held her in much affection, yet even of her he complained that she had been disinclined to allow him a share of the working tools. Altogether he was in a very depressed state of mind, hardly caring what happened to him, and half decided to join the stream of unfortunates flowing into the new state of Georgia, which General Oglethorpe, Johnson's friend of later years, was engaged in settling. However, he remained in England, and probably was the "near relation" of Johnson's who went to Frome, in Somersetshire, as a bookbinder and stationer, in 1736, and stayed about a year—"a lively, noisy man, that loved company," and frequented the alehouse. Johnson said that Nathaniel had a "manly spirit," which he showed by refusing to admit the existence of a single bad road among all the wretched tracks on which he was accustomed to travel.

The first news for Johnson after his long journey was of the death, sudden it would seem, of the unfortunate Nathaniel, only twenty-four years old, who was actually buried at Lichfield, beside his father, before the two adventurers reached their destination. The thought of his old mother left alone to grapple with all the family affairs, aided only by Catherine Chambers, their faithful maid, who had arranged the funeral, was not one to cheer him in his new and strange surroundings. And Garrick, who did not go on to Rochester at once, as intended, was to have a still heavier blow dealt him, for a week after leaving Lichfield his father, the excellent Captain Garrick, also died there. This unexpected event threw all his family affairs into confusion, and the funds with which David expected to be supplied were not forthcoming. Under the will of his uncle David, the

Lisbon wine merchant, who had died at Carshalton only ten weeks earlier, he stood to inherit £1000 when he came of age next year. But his father was his trustee in the matter of this legacy, and had thought it fair under the circumstances to leave David junior one shilling only in his own will, as he had a large family to provide for. So that there would be no money available for some time, till the interlocked affairs of his father and uncle were settled. It was not possible for him to go on to Rochester, for he had not the means of paying Mr. Colson's charges. Almost immediately after his arrival in London he had entered himself at Lincoln's Inn, on 9 March, and that seems to have been his only move in the direction of the law.

Johnson and Garrick, both so suddenly bereaved, kept together therefore for a time in London, with nothing between them but the cash they had brought from Lichfield, and anything they could earn by odd jobs. In spite of careful living, the cash was soon exhausted, and they began to feel the pinch of want. But Garrick had some second-hand acquaintance with Thomas Wilcox, a bookseller of decent standing in the Strand, where he traded under the sign of Virgil's Head, so they went to him for financial assistance, telling him frankly of their situation. Wilcox's heart was moved, and as they modestly limited their request to five pounds he advanced them that amount, which was in due course repaid. Johnson would have been glad to get some literary employment from Wilcox, but that astute tradesman, noting the applicant's size and strength, and acquainted by long experience with the extremely precarious profits of authorship, told him bluntly he had "better buy a porter's knot." Johnson took the advice in good part, if he failed to act upon it, and came to look upon Wilcox as one of his best friends. It is no insult to a scholar to suggest that he has the physical capacities for heavy labour.

The two friends, with their different ambitions, soon went their own ways, and Garrick eventually found himself at Rochester as a private pupil in Mr. Colson's house. Garrick's talents were not only of quite another order than Johnson's, but were always meant by their owner to satisfy his desire for money as well as fame. Johnson did not benefit from Mr. Walmesley's recommendation of him to Mr. Colson, but that may have been the fault of his own independence. His thoughtful patron, however, had given him a letter of introduction to Henry Lintot, his own London bookseller, which brought the young adventurer a few literary commissions of which we have no trace. Johnson in later life used to associate his arrival in London with the tragedy of Eustace Budgell, cousin to his famous townsman Addison, who threw himself into the Thames in despair on 4 May 1737.

Johnson's first lodgings in London were in an upstairs room at a house in Exeter Street, a *cul-de-sac* blocked from the Strand by Exeter 'Change. His landlord was one Richard Norris, a staymaker, who had some remote Lichfield association with the Bailyes, who again were mixed up with the Garricks. The need for economical management was pressing. Fortunately he came armed with some sound ideas on the subject. A friend he made in Birmingham, an Irish painter who had spent some years in London, won Johnson's admiration by his thorough knowledge of the ordinary ways of life, gained by direct experience and " not strained through books." He had explained to Johnson how he devised a system by which he could live in London, and make a creditable show, on thirty pounds a year. He paid eighteenpence a week for a garret ; breakfasted on bread-and-milk for a penny ; met his friends only at a coffee house, where an expenditure of threepence ensured for him several hours a day in good company ; dined for sixpence ; and denied himself supper. On his clothes he spent ten pounds a year, and on the day when he changed his linen he went abroad and visited his friends. This left him about fourpence a day for extras. Though it involved rigid self-denial, such a plan of life did not spell any real hardship, or any risk to health, any more than for a young artist or author to live simply in London today on a few pounds a week.

But it is unlikely that Johnson would be able to follow his mentor's system very closely. He might reduce considerably the amount spent on dress, which was quite out of proportion to the whole, but when it came to the petty economies Johnson, for all his hard schooling, was not one to adhere to any rigid plan. He could not keep money : if he did not spend it on his own needs he gave it away on the spur of the moment to anyone who seemed worse off than himself. The dining place he chose was the Pine Apple, in New Street, not far from his lodging, where, like his mentor, he got a good cut of meat for sixpence. He met interesting people there, including a number who had travelled, and it struck him as curious that though they foregathered each day familiarly, as at a club, yet they did not even know one another's names. The company generally took wine, but Johnson simply paid an extra penny for bread, and gave the waiter a penny, making the bill eightpence only. And the tip ensured him better attention, so that he was not without guile. If he was not able to follow his friend's advice to the letter, at least he recognized the good sense of the method, used often to recall it when his own circumstances had grown easy, and would not allow that it was a matter for ridicule. He himself considered that thirty pounds a year should have enabled a single man of education to live decently at that period, if he were reasonably careful.

He formed no special friendships on this first stay in London, being too busy getting the lie of the land, and looking out for employment. He was as yet quite unknown, an obscure provincial who had done nothing to win his literary spurs. But, through his Lichfield connexions, there was one house where he was always welcome, and an exclusive one at that. Gilbert Walmesley's sister-in-law, Catherine Aston, had in 1730 married the Hon. Henry Hervey, then a soldier stationed at Lichfield, who was a younger son of the Earl of Bristol. "Harry" Hervey, who afterwards took most inappropriate orders, and in 1744 the additional name of Aston, was still an officer in Kerr's Dragoons when Johnson stayed in London, and moved in the most fashionable circles, but he did not hesitate to let the poor scholar from Lichfield mingle with his guests. He was in most respects a far from admirable character, a reckless little spendthrift, neglectful of his profession, and in his father's eyes fit only for gaol. But he had wit and charm, with something of the poet in him. Johnson was under no delusions as to his vicious habits, but loved the man who once secured his release from a sponging-house. A few acts of spontaneous kindness may atone for a host of serious failings, at least to those who experience the kindness. It may have been that David Garrick actually introduced him to the London house of Hervey, who had taken a great fancy to the embryo actor at Lichfield, and offered him the reversion of his brother-in-law's commission.

Not more than four months after his arrival in London Johnson found that under the conditions of life there he could get no quiet in which to work at his still unfinished tragedy. So he repaired to lodgings at Greenwich, next to the Golden Hart tavern, in Church Street. There, undisturbed by the bustle of the city, with its constant interruptions, he would walk in the beautiful Park, composing as he went. Sometimes, as he perambulated the town, he might see the great ironworks of the Crowleys, and his mind be carried back to the old days at Stourbridge, to his cousin "Parson" Ford, and the rest of the family circle there. We know that years afterwards he showed himself familiar with the economics of the Crowleys' business.

While at Greenwich, on 12 July, he wrote once again to Edward Cave, with whom he had failed before to get into touch. This time he made no foolish mystery about his identity: the sorry pretence of "S. Smith" was quietly dropped. There is no suggestion that Cave would know at all who he was: he writes as "a stranger in London," who has observed the generous offers made to men of letters in the papers run by Cave, and who has a scheme to submit. The scheme was to prepare for publication a translation from the Italian of Father Paul Sarpi's *History of the Council of Trent*, together with the notes added by Pierre Le Courayer to his French edition. He meets the possible objection that there was already an English translation by pointing out its defects of style, and offers to submit a specimen for examination of his own attempt to better it. But if he cannot improve on the style, he thinks that the addition of Le Courayer's notes will turn the balance against the existing translation. He asks for a speedy reply if Cave cannot consider the scheme, and for an appointment if he can. Cave did nothing definite for a time, being well supplied then with literary help, but eventually, as we shall see, adopted Johnson's suggestion.

Even the delightful seclusion of Greenwich did not enable him to finish *Irene*, which still required acts four and five completing, as well as general revision. The wretched tragedy seems to have been the one literary work in which Johnson's extraordinary facility of composition deserted him. He admitted afterwards that he only took to tragic poetry because he could not afford to study law. Deciding at last that it could only be completed where it had been begun, before the summer was over he returned to Lichfield with the manuscript in his pocket. There, re-united to his wife, he applied himself manfully to putting it into its final shape, a slow and painful process to one who ordinarily wrote without effort and almost without need for revision. It was only to be expected that a work produced in this way should lack inspiration, and bear signs of the difficult labour that gave it birth. When Walmesley first heard the play read he expressed some sympathy with the heroine in the accumulation of distresses that her creator had piled upon her, and asked how he could "possibly contrive to plunge her into deeper calamity." And Johnson, with ready wit at the expense of Walmesley in his professional capacity, promptly replied, "Sir, I can put her into the Spiritual Court!" At least the story shows on what easy terms Johnson stood with his patron.

It is rather remarkable that after these months in London, when a keen and receptive mind, interested in every aspect of human life, was first confronted with all the novel features of metropolitan activity, Johnson should have disappointed his townsmen by having nothing much to tell them. The London of that day, with its great river artery spanned by a single bridge, with its filthy cobbled streets, and its comparatively modest size, was very different from the London we now see, but it would be no less impressive to Johnson. Perhaps the reticence was induced by his own disappointment, for, though the trip had brought him experience, it had brought him no more tangible reward. His mother was curious to know whether he "gave the wall or took it," for when she had stayed there long before it was by this sign that the peaceable citizen was to be distinguished from his more quarrelsome neighbour. She probably reminded him how his great-uncle Henry Ford, the attorney, had had his chambers in Clifford's Inn, and been much in London.

CHAPTER XI.

RETURN TO LONDON
1737-1739

JOHNSON on this occasion stayed in Lichfield only for three months. Towards the end of the year 1737 he packed up his things and made off once more for London. This time it was not to be a mere prospecting journey, but a definite removal, and so his wife accompanied him, Lucy Porter being left behind with relatives. With Garrick he could " ride and tie "; with an elderly wife he would have to be more extravagant and go in the coach.

Their first lodgings were in Woodstock Street, near Hanover Square, where they did not remain very long. They then removed to No. 6, Castle Street, near Cavendish Square, and had rooms in the house of a Mrs. Crow. Johnson's first task was now to dispose of his play, completed after so much toil. In company with Peter Garrick, who had lent him Knolles's *History of the Turks* at the outset, and who now had left the Navy in order to set up as a wine merchant with brother David in a little street off the Strand, he repaired to the Fountain Tavern to read it over. Charles Fleetwood, a man of birth who had succeeded in dissipating a large fortune pretty quickly, had in 1734 purchased the major share of the patent for Drury Lane Theatre. As a Staffordshire man, nephew and heir to Lord Gerard, he may have been known to the Garricks. At any rate, to Fleetwood they both went, with the play, hoping that he would accept it for his theatre. But he was insufficiently impressed, and would scarcely read it : the play was not attraction enough in itself to encourage him to put it on the boards when there was no powerful patron to back it.

So *Irene* was once more sadly relegated to the cupboard, though he did get it out a few months later to show to Cave. The next shaft in his quiver was the scheme for translating Sarpi's *History of the Council of Trent*, and here he was successful, for he approached Cave again, who now agreed to sponsor it. When Cave at last came into actual contact with Johnson over this matter, he soon realised his capacity, and the acquaintance rapidly ripened into a close intimacy. This was, in a modest way, the making of Johnson, for Cave, with his

Gentleman's Magazine, which in half-a-dozen years he had raised to such a high point of success and to such an unprecedented circulation, now stood in need of him as a general literary adviser, as well as a contributor on special subjects.

It was a big advantage to the printer-editor, a shrewd business man but not possessed of much culture, to have some one at his elbow who, for only a small reward, could supervise and improve—in short, "sub-edit"—the contributions of others to the magazine, could answer correspondents, and if called upon translate from the French and Italian. In common with many other educated men of his day Johnson had taught himself some of those modern European languages that were still unrepresented in the curricula of the schools and universities, which continued to look upon Latin and Greek as alone essential to scholarship. French and Italian were rather the accomplishments of fashionable folk who travelled on the continent, where society was much more cosmopolitan than it is today ; or the necessary equipment of the tutors accompanying rich young men whose education had to be completed by the "grand tour." The linguistic knowledge which Johnson had acquired in early life, partly from mere intellectual curiosity, and partly to earn bread, stood him in good stead when he came to mix freely with the world of fashion, however little he shone in the actual speaking of languages whose refinements of pronunciation were not easily mastered by a man of strongly accentuated English speech and without any musical ear.

In every way Cave's demands upon him increased : he had to act as poetical referee in the place of Moses Browne and his kinsman John Duick, those pen-cutters turned *littérateurs* ; to sit in judgment on the verses that were sent in competition for the prizes which Cave offered, to increase his circulation ; and to choose extracts suitable for printing from the leading books of the day as they were issued. If there was not great profit there was hope in this work, and the association with Cave gave Johnson a lasting respect for him as an honourable and kindly man.

With his spirits revived, Johnson was now in a mood again for literary composition on his own account, apart from the hack work on the magazine, or the occasional trifles he personally contributed. He was wise enough not to attempt a second play : indeed, though *Irene* was eventually produced on the stage in 1749, he accepted the lesson of his failure and never wrote for the theatre again. His effort was now in satiric poetry, and he chose for his theme the unrelieved wickedness of the great city in which he hoped to be able to remain, as contrasted with the simplicity and beauty of life in the country he had left without regret, combining with it all an attack on the Walpole administration. Keeping to the metre of the heroic couplet, then still much in favour, and rather conventional in its general viewpoint, *London : A Poem, In Imitation of the Third Satire of Juvenal*, had yet vigour and originality enough to raise it high above most of its current models. Unlike *Irene*, it was written with Johnson's usual ease and fluency, if not with the full passion of perfect sincerity, and was quickly finished, without long toil and interminable revision. But that he should have so belied what were, later on at least, his real feelings regarding the relative attractions of town and country life, suggests that he had not yet escaped from the tyranny of mere poetical fashion. Its best known line, printed by him in capital letters,

SLOW RISES WORTH, BY POVERTY DEPRESS'D,

is quoted for its supposedly autobiographical application rather than for any special merit or beauty of its own.

It is rather to be regretted that in his endeavour to get his poem published he again resorted to a subterfuge—a fairly innocent one, perhaps, but quite out of character with the traditional Johnson. He wrote to Cave this time in his own name, from Castle Street, but put forward the poem as the work of an author with whom he was in touch, who lay "under very disadvantageous circumstances of fortune." This was to constitute an extra claim on Cave's generosity, beyond that excited by any merit the poem might possess. He asked Cave to "look over this poem with another eye, and reward it in a different manner, from a mercenary bookseller, who counts the lines he is to purchase, and considers nothing but the bulk." He explained that he had made alterations, and so been obliged to copy it out, and offered to correct it for the press, as well as to tone down the satire if required. Some neatly turned compliments were offered to Cave, and request made for an immediate answer, so that he could consult the author.

Whether Cave "smelt a rat" we do not know, but he considered the poem favourably, though without actually accepting it, and sent a present for "the author." He stipulated that Robert Dodsley, the poet-publisher, should read it, and see whether he would agree to his name appearing on the title-page. The suggestion was to print 500 copies, and Johnson professed himself "so much the author's friend" that he would undertake in the case of a loss to reimburse Cave, who if there were a profit was very generously willing for it to go to the author, less the sum advanced as a present. He asked for an exact statement to be prepared showing what his liabilities would be. Cave duly sent him an estimate, and Johnson confirmed the undertaking. After some slight delay Johnson got his manuscript back and took it to Dodsley, who expressed himself very favourably about the poem, and desired to be associated with the publication of such "a creditable thing." Johnson consulted Cave, thinking that Dodsley, if financially interested, would be more anxious to push the sale. Eventually, Dodsley took the whole responsibility, and paid ten guineas for the poem, as Johnson refused to take less than Paul Whitehead had recently received for a similar piece.

London is said to have been refused by a large number of booksellers, but one would have expected Cave to be the first to whom he would go and not the last. If it is true, perhaps he had got to feel that his own name was no recommendation, and that he had better try a new and less direct method of approach. His name did not even appear on the title-page, which simply has, "Printed for R. Doddesley, at Tully's Head in Pall-Mall." Presumably, however, the authorship was now known to Cave and Dodsley. Little time was wasted over the printing. The manuscript had reached Cave's hands by 6 April 1738, and Johnson was anxious for no time to be lost, in view of Parliament rising in the middle of May, and the town consequently emptying. So on 13 May it was published, at the price of one shilling, on the same morning as a satire by Pope, *One Thousand Seven Hundred and Thirty Eight*, also priced at one shilling.

The success of Johnson's poem was immediate and a second edition was called for within a week. A third edition appeared later in 1738, and a fourth in 1739. Literary circles were all agog, and generously prepared to welcome "an unknown poet, greater even than Pope."

And Pope himself, to his lasting credit, was no less generous, and on discovering by enquiry that the author was an obscure man named Johnson exclaimed, "He will soon be *déterré*." Pope could hardly be expected to recollect that nine years earlier he had praised a college translation of his own *Messiah* by the same hand, or even if he remembered the name to connect the two Johnsons together. To Lord Lyttelton, who was enraptured by the poem, he also expressed high commendation—here again one wonders whether any memory remained with Lord Lyttelton of the boy with whom long ago he had engaged in "colloquial disputes" at Hagley. General Oglethorpe, too, though not yet personally known to Johnson, touched him by warm approval. Elizabeth Carter, then a precocious young woman of twenty, who had already been contributing to Cave's magazine since 1734, mentioned the poem to her father at Deal, but the parson's taste did not allow him to approve of anyone who was fond of *Martial*, and as for the name Johnson he had never even heard it in connexion with any point of scholarship or letters. It was through Cave's introducing him to her at this time that Johnson began his long and valuable friendship with the most genuinely learned of the bluestockings.

Some doubt exists as to when Johnson first met that strange literary adventurer, Richard Savage. There are a number of references in *London*, which, if they do not refer to Savage, evidence a very striking chain of coincidences. The "Thales" of the poem, who "bids the town farewell,"

> Resolved at length, from vice and LONDON far,
> To breathe in distant fields a purer air,
> And, fix'd on Cambria's solitary shore,
> Give to St. David one true Briton more,

exactly matches the Savage who retired to Wales over a year later, but there obviously can be nothing in the reference unless Savage's retirement had been projected before *London* was written, which, indeed, the circumstances render possible. Again, the lines,

> Some frolic drunkard, reeling from a feast,
> Provokes a broil, and stabs you for a jest,

are strangely reminiscent of the affair in 1727 when Savage, in a drunken fray, stabbed a Mr. Sinclair, and was convicted of murder. And, more, Savage had been in receipt of a pension from Queen Anne, on condition that he, in the guise of "The Volunteer Laureate," wrote an ode each year on her birthday; and after her death, on the first anniversary of that birthday, on 1 March 1738, he produced an elegy instead, hoping that the pension would be continued by the authorities, but ineffectually. Thus speaks "Thales" in *London*,

> But what, my friend, what hope remains for me,
> Who start at theft, and blush at perjury?
> Who scarce forbear, tho' BRITAIN'S court he sing,
> To pluck a titled Poet's borrowed wing.

Who was it, except Savage, who plucked the wing of the laureate, or "titled poet," that sang the court of Britain? Apart from these special points he seems throughout to have selected all in Juvenal's satire most applicable to Savage, and omitted those which were irrelevant.

However, the case is not so clear as this evidence might at first suggest. There are definite statements that Johnson made the acquaintance of Savage on his first visit to London in 1737, but he himself is quoted as having positively denied that he knew Savage when *London* was written, or had any actual person in mind when he created "Thales." Yet he was credited by Boswell, and is still credited, with the authorship of the epigram, "*Ad Ricardum Savage*" (however poor its quality), which appeared in *The Gentleman's Magazine* for April 1738, almost at the very time *London* was published. The whole question remains a mystery, though we can compromise by assuming that Savage's circumstances were so well known to all Grub Street, that Johnson might have written about them without any personal acquaintance with the poet.

The question of when he made friends with Savage is a minor problem. It is a major problem to know why he made friends with him at all. Savage, though he had some genuine gift for literature, and was not without a share of the poet's honest pride, was a shiftless and unscrupulous adventurer. His claim to be an illegitimate son of the Countess of Macclesfield, by Lord Rivers, on account of whom she was divorced in 1698, will not bear a moment's investigation. The elaborate story he concocted to back up his claim, which Johnson whole-heartedly accepted, became an obsession with him. He made it his principal stock-in-trade, and pressed it forward in season and out of season. But to those at all familiar with the stories of such "claimants," it is so typical in its wealth of vague assertion, and its corresponding lack of definite information, as to be unworthy of serious consideration. His story, if true, could so very easily have been made at least more credible by a few simple names and dates, that his cunning in not attempting to supply the means of testing it is his own condemnation. He was true to type in the way in which he quarrelled with all his benefactors, and then pursued them with malignant ingratitude.

It is at least beyond dispute that Johnson was intimate with Savage some time after his return to London in 1737. They were certain to make acquaintance when Johnson had become a regular visitor at St. John's Gate, where *The Gentleman's Magazine* was printed. He first beheld the place " with reverence," as a long-heard-of literary shrine, to which at last he was making pilgrimage, but probably its aspect became less sacred with use, and after gaining a more intimate knowledge of some of the acolytes. His earliest contribution to the magazine (two very doubtful items of 1736 excepted) was a set of verses in Latin addressed to Cave, in his capacity as editor, and entitled *Ad Urbanum*. This appeared in the number for March 1738, just when *London* was being finished, and over his initials, " S.J." In the April number he had two other small contributions, one an epigram in Greek and Latin on Elizabeth Carter and the other an epigram "To a Lady who spoke in Defence of Liberty," the "Lady" being his beloved Molly Aston.

The reasons we must find for Johnson accepting the friendship of Savage lie in some attractive qualities the latter possessed, which he would display to those who believed his story. A handsome man, with elegant and polished manners, he was, in his way, a brilliant talker, with a fund of reminiscence acquired less from books than from constant contact with men of all classes and types. Much older than Johnson, he had had for many years acquaintance with the literary world, and claimed at least to have moved with ease in another world to which literary men were not ordinarily admitted. It is quite possible, indeed probable, that he had met Johnson's brilliant cousin, " Parson " Ford, dead now only some seven years or so, who had also moved in those two worlds. Savage's showy profusion is indicated by his having " subscribed " in 1731 for no less than twenty copies of Husbands's *Miscellany*, in which Johnson's translation of Pope's *Messiah* had appeared. To Johnson, accepting him as a mis-begotten and still more ill-used scion of the aristocracy, he was, with all his faults, a romantic figure. Johnson generally prided himself upon a habit of scepticism, but it was not a scepticism proof against the kindly impulses of his heart. Certainly the spirit of incredulity which often shocked his friends was strangely suspended in this instance.

Very little is really known of their association, beyond general stories of common hardships endured, and Johnson's biography of his strange friend does not do much to lift the veil at that point. They are said to have been so poor at times that they had to walk the streets at night for want of money to pay for a lodging. Particularly they used to perambulate the squares of Westminster, passing the long hours of darkness in spirited conversation, which on one occasion, in St. James's Square, concluded with a condemnation of the ministry and a resolution to "*stand by their country*." These stories were probably exaggerated in retrospect, but so far as they are true must refer to an occasion soon after Johnson and his wife came to London, when they were quite temporarily separated, she being put up by a friend near the Tower, while he was in lodgings in Fleet Street. There is no evidence that Savage did anything to corrupt Johnson's mind or principles, and it must be credited to him that he should have so valued the friendship of a young man without money or influence, who had nothing to offer except his own society, and who at this period suffered from the social disqualification of being a total abstainer. It was after being introduced to the night life of the city by Savage that he used at times to run the risk of having his motives misinterpreted by taking street-walkers into taverns to hear their histories, a form of sociological investigation not wisely undertaken by those who value their moral reputation.

It was probably a symptom of Johnson's disorder that he should all his life have shown a tendency not only to "overcharge his defects," but also to paint his years of struggle in too dark colours. He was ever inclined to exaggerate his mean origin, his ill-health, his mental condition, his sinfulness, his poverty, his hardships, his laziness, and any other quality or condition in which he felt conscious of deficiency. We must always discount a good deal of his self-depreciation, as well as of his gloomy reminiscence.

Though Cave had approved of Johnson's scheme for translating Sarpi's *History of the Council of Trent*, it was some time before anything was done in the matter. Cave was not to blame, but Johnson was delayed through various causes, and it was not till 2 August 1738 that the translation was actually begun. He then had expectation of being able to go steadily ahead, but hoped that Cave, who had also complained of his not devoting enough attention to the magazine, would jog his elbow if necessary. It certainly was necessary to jog it at times. His decision was even then being awaited in a poetical competition that should have been settled long before. As far back as December 1735 Cave had announced in the magazine that a prize of £40 would be awarded in next year's poetry competition, and in the following February the subject was given as the "Divine Attributes," the one prize to be divided into three sums, £20, £12, and £8. The thing dragged on : a number of poems were received, and two of them printed between April and June 1737. Nothing more was done for nearly a year, when in April 1738 a hope was expressed by the editor "that the Gentlemen who are to judge and allot the Forty Pounds, proposed in Prizes for the Poems sent in on the Divine Attributes, will now have leisure to consider 'em." Two more of the poems were printed in May and June 1738, but still the prizes remained unawarded.

We now know the reason of all this delay : for "the Gentlemen" sitting in judgment we must read Johnson, who found the task of discriminating between the poems irksome and distasteful. Cave was pressing him for a decision in August 1738, but he was still very unwilling, and said that he could not settle the matter even to his own satisfaction, and certainly not so as to please the competitors. Not until April 1739 was the result announced, and then only after a vote among the competitors themselves, "by reason of the difficulty of procuring a decision from proper judges." Cave was similarly badly served in other competitions, but exercised much forbearance towards those responsible. We do not know whether Johnson was the villain of the piece throughout. It was during this period, as will presently appear, that his first recorded prayer confessed to "sloth" as one of his faults.

In *The Gentleman's Magazine* for August 1738 he had "English Verses to Eliza" (Elizabeth Carter), and in September some fatuous lines "To Lady Firebrace, at Bury Assizes," which show how low he could sink in the literary scale when executing an absurd and distasteful commission which he himself admitted "neither deserves much thought nor requires it." Why Cave desired these lines we do not know, unless to stimulate "Count" W. Bryan, a Suffolk contributor of harmless society verses, to fresh effort. Lady Firebrace, who in the preceding year, as a middle-aged widow, had married Sir Cordell Firebrace, a Suffolk baronet, would have the right, as wife of a Member for the County, to sit with the Judge at the Assizes by her husband.

Johnson has been credited on good authority with the authorship of other items that appeared in 1738 in the magazine, but have not yet been accepted by the bibliographers—a Latin Epigram on "Venus in Armour," in April; the Latin lines, "*Ex Cantico Solomonis*," also in April; and the verses, "The Logical Warehouse," in May—and with having sponsored two items in April and May, the first some Latin lines on Dr. John Radcliffe, by Noel Broxholme, and the second some verses on the death of George, Prince of Denmark, by Henry Aldrich, both old pieces. The same authority states that his first prose contribution to the magazine was an article in July 1738, signed "Eubulus," and entitled "Remarkable Example in a Prince and Subject", which opens with a reference to Du Halde's *China*.

There was another definite task now allotted to Johnson in the conduct of the magazine. The House of Commons, ever jealous of its privileges, had recently passed a resolution forbidding reports of its proceedings being published. This was a blow to Cave, but like an honest tradesman he did his best to evade it. From June 1738 his magazine made a feature of "Debates in the Senate of Magna Lilliputia," in which the proceedings in the House were abstracted from reports by William Guthrie, a Scotchman, one of Cave's hacks, with the names of the speakers given under a thin disguise. It was Johnson's duty each month to "edit" Guthrie's reports, and he usually found it necessary to make a good many alterations. It was not till November 1740 that Johnson began to write the reports himself, when his imagination, untrammelled by any direct knowledge of the debates, credited the speakers with a powerful and sonorous eloquence of which most of them could honestly plead "not guilty."

Cave at this time was also engaged in another venture. In September 1735 he had projected a translation of the Jesuit Jean Baptiste Du Halde's *Description of China*, issued at Paris in the same year, but subscribers did not come in quickly enough, perhaps because someone issued another translation in 1736. Cave's work made no definite advance till a year or so later, when it began to be issued in monthly parts. In 1736 and 1737 some passages of the translation were printed in *The Gentleman's Magazine*, to encourage interest in the work. Johnson had something to do with the enterprise, but the actual translation was done by William Guthrie, helped by an Irishman named Green, and in its complete form of four volumes was not issued till May 1742.

There was yet another work in which Johnson was more directly interested. Jean Pierre de Crousaz, Professor of Philosophy and Mathematics at Lausanne, had published *A Commentary on Mr. Pope's Principles of Morality, or Essay on Man*, and in September 1738 the question of its translation was being considered by Cave. However, he decided at the time, and Johnson agreed with him, that it would not be likely to pay, and it was not till 1741 that Cave took the risk of printing it, and then in a translation by another hand. But another work by de Crousaz, on the same subject, *An Examination of Mr. Pope's Essay on Man*, they had already decided to translate, and Johnson urged that its issue should be "pushed forward with the utmost expedition." It came out a month or two later, in November 1738, and in the December number of *The Gentleman's Magazine* appeared an advertisement which followed very closely one which Johnson had drafted for Cave, when pressing for speed. The translator's name was not given, but she was the redoubtable Elizabeth Carter.

Much has been made of the fact that Johnson, in writing to Cave about the translation of Crousaz, signed himself, "Yours, *impransus*, Sam. Johnson." It has been assumed that this was the tragic cry of a man too poor to buy himself a dinner. But it is very unlikely, and Johnson's pride would hardly have allowed him almost to beg the price of a meal from Cave. There is no reason why he should have been in want at this time, when he was receiving on an average over twenty-five shillings a week from Cave for his translation of Sarpi alone, apart from pay for his regular work on *The Gentleman's*

Magazine. It was possible, as he knew very well himself, for a family to live on fifty pounds a year and get something more than the mere necessities of life, and he condemned Savage for contriving to be in poverty when in enjoyment of such an income. Perhaps he had been too busy to dine, or was merely excusing himself from writing more by an intimation that he must go out and get a meal. It was on 7 September (O.S.) 1738, his twenty-ninth birthday, that he composed the first real prayer of which he kept a copy. He thanked God for having protected him " in the days of childhood and youth, in the midst of weakness, blindness and danger "; and alluded (characteristically) to " the time which I have spent in sloth, vanity, and wickedness."

Whatever the implications of *impransus*, Johnson was able very soon after this to give thought to another struggling writer than himself. Alexander MacBean, one of those unfortunate Scotchmen who laboured so hard in the kitchen-gardens of literature, with so little reward, had accumulated much material for a " Military Dictionary," and Johnson in his kindness tried to enlist Cave's patronage for him, though unsuccessfully as far as we know. In November Johnson was anxious for Elizabeth Carter to translate *Boethius*, but here again nothing resulted. *The Gentleman's Magazine* for that month contained a " Life of Father Paul Sarpi," which he had written to encourage interest in the translation he was at work upon, and in December he wrote a Greek epigram on Dr. Birch, and the " Address to the Reader." In the number for January 1739 he began " The Life of Dr. Herman Boerhaave " (whose science of chemistry was one of the few he favoured), which concluded in April ; he also contributed a " Letter to Mr. Urban " in January, and perhaps a Latin paraphrase of his Greek epigram on Dr. Birch ; " An Appeal to the Publick " in March ; and another " Address to the Reader " in May.

His hereditary Jacobite prejudice against the house of Hanover found vent in a satire entitled *Marmor Norfolciense*, published anonymously in April 1739. The title followed the content, which professed to be an ancient rhymed inscription discovered near Lynn in Norfolk—that being the county of the obnoxious Walpole. It made little impression, and though Pope professed to find it very humorous few others have been moved to hilarity by it. One story goes that his name was discovered, and warrants issued for his arrest, in consequence of which he and his wife sought "an obscure lodging in a house in Lambeth-marsh," till the scent had grown cold, but there is no corroboration of this. At any rate, his pen was not put out of commission, for his was the "Impartial Hand" responsible for an ironical work published next month, in May 1739, *A Compleat Vindication of the Licensers of the Stage, from the Malicious and Scandalous Aspersions of Mr. Brooke, Author of Gustavus Vasa.* The recently appointed Licensers of Plays, who were the objects of this attack, had made a characteristic start by suppressing Henry Brooke's tragedy, and Johnson had been engaged by Charles Corbett, of Addison's Head, in Fleet Street, quite a reputable bookseller, to work up the case against them. There were nearly a thousand subscribers to the work, which was constructed on a background of Swedish history, with Walpole introduced under the name of Trollio.

The translation of Sarpi's *History of the Council of Trent* had been in continuous progress since 2 August 1738, and it was Cave's undoubted intention to publish it. In the *Weekly Miscellany* for 21 October 1738 a full advertisement appeared, giving Johnson's name as translator, with his address, "at No. 6 in Castle Street, by Cavendish Square," the whole to form two quarto volumes, priced at eighteen shillings each ; or three volumes, on large paper, at a guinea each. The work was stated to be already in the press, but as the translation was little more than begun not much type can have been set up. The last payment to Johnson was not until 21 April 1739, when the total he had received for his big task amounted to £49 odd, which meant, as already pointed out, an average of over twenty-five shillings a week. No doubt this represented the completion of the translation.

But misfortune overtook the enterprise just when everything was ready for publication. By an extraordinary coincidence, there was another translator in the field at the same time, and a translator who also bore the name of Samuel Johnson. This other Samuel Johnson was curate of St. Martin's-in-the-Fields, and custodian of the parish Library founded in 1695 by Archbishop Tenison. One was as jealous of his own work as the other, and as tenaciously determined not to give way. They had some skirmishes in the newspapers, and an impossible situation was created. Neither would yield, and the result was that neither could hope to proceed with any chance of success. The curate of St. Martin's-in-the-Fields had the patronage of his vicar, Zachary Pearce, afterwards Bishop of Rochester (and a contributor of etymologies to the famous *Dictionary*), with other of the clergy, while his rival translator was supported by the ever faithful Gilbert Walmesley, by William Caslon, the letter founder, and by Thomas Birch, D.D., F.R.S., already a man of some mark. It was such a complete case of stalemate as rarely occurs in a matter of literature. Cave had promised his subscribers two hundred quarto sheets, and the highest estimate of what was actually printed off is only a dozen sheets, most of which were destroyed, and the balance lost. But as he had paid the translator, in addition to all his other incidental charges, it involved him in a considerable loss.

In the June number of *The Gentleman's Magazine* for 1739 there appeared a first "Extract" from four sermons preached by Joseph Trapp, D.D., the poet-pamphleteer, which he had just published, the abridgement being by Cave himself. The second and concluding extract was promised for next month. But Cave's right to abridge them was challenged. So he, as ever when in a difficulty, sought Johnson's help to find legal justification for his act, and it was duly supplied under thirty-one heads. But the promised conclusion never appeared. Johnson took after his father in his readiness, and capacity, to usurp the functions of a lawyer.

CHAPTER XII.

THE APPLEBY SCHOOL ATTEMPT
LONDON FINALLY CLAIMS HIM
1739-1740

THE long and arduous task of translating Sarpi's *History of the Council of Trent*, continued for all but nine months, had grown very distasteful to Johnson. When, through the extraordinary coincidence of the rival translator, the scheme to publish fell through altogether, he must have felt, with an added disgust, that his work had been entirely thrown away.

So he became once more restless and dissatisfied, and anxious to escape from circumstances which seemed so painfully confining. London had not yet quite assimilated him, or he London, and if the suitable chance came he was prepared to sacrifice any ambition of winning a place in the great literary world to the solid if less glorious satisfaction of security as a country schoolmaster. Mrs. Johnson, too, may have found life in London uncongenial, especially as she considered country air as necessary for her health, which was always rather poor. His friends at home were aware of his feelings, and ready to inform him of any vacancy.

A chance came within about three months of his finishing Sarpi. On 11 June 1738 the Rev. Samuel Martin, who had been headmaster of Appleby Grammar School, in Leicestershire, since 1725, notified to the governors his intention to resign his post that day twelve months. And resign he did, on 11 June 1739. This was the founder's baptismal day, when the audit was held, and the time appointed by the statutes for the election of a new " Latin Master," as the head was called. A candidate offered in the person of the Rev. Thomas Mould, M.A., a young man of about twenty-five, who was of founder's kin—that is, related to Sir John Moore, Lord Mayor of London, who had founded the school at the end of the preceding century—and therefore, under the statutes, to have preference over any candidate not so related. But, out of the thirteen governors, five only were present at the meeting. They were, Sir John Harpur, bart., of Calke Abbey, Derbyshire ; George Moore, esq., of Appleby ; William Browne, esq., of Stretton-en-le-Field, Leicestershire ; the Rev. George Gell, Rector of

Appleby ; and John Moore, of the Middle Temple, younger brother of George. They did not constitute the necessary quorum of seven required for the election. It was therefore decided by them to hold another meeting on 16 July, and immediate notice to that effect was given to all the governors. But the muster then was worse even than before, only four governors turning up to vote, Sir John Harpur, George Moore, William Browne and the Rev. George Gell. John Moore would have been present except for illness. The four governors, declaring that the work of the school was largely held up, and that its reputation was consequently suffering, decided to bother no more with abortive meetings, but to petition the Bishop of Lincoln, then Richard Reynolds, their diocesan, to make the appointment himself, under the statutes of the school, which gave him the power so to act in the case of the governors failing to make a fresh appointment within six months of a headmaster's death or dismissal. And they humbly recommended Thomas Mould for the post, he being nearly related to the founder, and, as they believed, qualified academically.

This was the condition of affairs when Johnson's friends offered to run him for the appointment. It is clear that there must have been dissension among the governors, for under ordinary circumstances a quorum could always have been obtained on an occasion of such importance. Thomas Mould cannot have been at all a unanimous choice, and it looks as if the five governors in question were the only ones who favoured him, for family and local reasons. Two of them were his kinsmen, and the Rev. George Gell became connected with the family next year through his daughter's marriage. The remaining eight governors probably preferred absenting themselves to voting directly against a nominee of the Moores. The eight were, Sir Thomas Gresley, bart., of Drakelow, Derbyshire ; Sir Robert Burdett, bart., of Foremark, Derbyshire ; Christopher Horton, esq., of Catton Hall, Derbyshire ; Theodore William Inge, esq., of Thorpe Constantine, Staffordshire ; John Wylde, esq., of Long Whatton, Leicestershire ; Godfrey Clarke, esq., of Chilcote, Derbyshire (father of Gibbon's friend, Godfrey Bagnall Clarke) ; Thomas Gresley, esq., of Netherseal, Leicestershire, uncle of Sir Thomas ; and Charles Jennens, esq., of Gopsal, Leicestershire, uncle by marriage to Sir Robert Burdett.

Johnson's friends evidently saw their chance in the fact of Thomas Mould having only a minority of this formidable board of governors to support him. And there was plenty of time in which to canvass and wire-pull, for the Bishop could not actually make the appointment, even if he were prepared to do so, until six months after 11 June. Johnson's principal supporter in the matter was Sir Thomas Gresley, who spent the day of the first meeting in getting married for a second time, at Haddon, near Bakewell, when, by a tragic coincidence, his fellow governor, John Wylde, a connexion of the Moores, died at Long Whatton. But Johnson's friends, however well disposed, could not easily get over the fact, which had told against him so much ever since his prematurely leaving Oxford, that he had no degree. Under the statutes of Appleby School no headmaster could be appointed who was not a graduate of an English university. Something had to be done to repair this deficiency, which they seem to have considered the only bar to his appointment. The first step was to approach his old friend at Pembroke, Dr. William Adams, to see if Oxford could be prevailed upon to grant him a degree ; but it was thought too big a favour to confer, even on a poet of some achievement. Pope, who associated Johnson with the authorship of *London*, and *Marmor Norfolciense*, had also been approached, and he, from a regard for his merit, and without any direct solicitation from Johnson himself, wrote to Lord Gower, who was one of the great territorial magnates of Staffordshire, as well as a figure in public life, asking him to exert his influence on Johnson's behalf, a fact of which Johnson was very proud when he learned of it in after years.

The governors had discovered that Lord Gower was well acquainted with a friend of Swift's, and they formed the idea that this friend might be persuaded to write to the Dean and ask him to use his influence with the authorities at Trinity College, Dublin, with a view to their sending the " poor man " Johnson a diploma constituting him a Master of Arts. Whether it was realised that a degree from Trinity College was of no direct use in the matter we do not know, or whether Johnson's sponsors were looking further ahead and hoping that, armed with his Irish degree, Oxford would incorporate him a Master of Arts, after a nominal period of residence, following a practice common at the time, and a practice of which Swift himself had taken advantage in 1692.

At any rate, no one could have behaved more kindly, or with more delicacy, in this quest for academic favours, than the great Lord Gower, who was then at his Staffordshire seat of Trentham, and who, it is curious to note, was a kind of nephew-by-marriage to Sir Wolstan Dixie, who had made Johnson's life so miserable at Market Bosworth. He wrote to his friend, as requested, on 1 August 1739, a fortnight after the meeting at which it had been decided to seek the Bishop's aid. He explained the situation, how Johnson was "a native of this country, and much respected by some worthy gentlemen in his neighbourhood, who are trustees of a charity school now vacant," and how they wished to make him master. It will be noticed that Lord Gower, himself a North Staffordshire man, speaks objectively of South Staffordshire and its adjoining counties as "his neighbourhood." He went on to state that the salary was £60 a year certain, "which would make him happy for life," but the statutes insisted on a Master of Arts—where graduated he did not specify. The trustees, he added, highly extolled the "learning and probity" of Johnson, who was "not afraid of the strictest examination," and who, though not relishing the idea of such a long journey, would even adventure as far as Dublin, if deemed necessary, "choosing rather to die upon the road, than be starved to death in translating for booksellers; which has been his only subsistence for some time past." This outburst of Johnson's, as quoted, is scarcely fair to Cave, who had treated him well enough and paid him a reasonable wage for his work.

Though anxious to do his utmost to help such a deserving scholar—in whom he did not apparently recognize the son of old Michael Johnson, the bookseller, who used to visit Trentham—Lord Gower undertook his task as intermediary with considerable misgiving. In the first place he modestly doubted his interest with his correspondent; and in the second place he evidently questioned in his own mind whether the College authorities would be inclined to grant a degree to a stranger, even at the Dean's request, in the easy way "those good-natured gentlemen"—the school governors—expected. It was even taken for granted that the diploma would be sent direct to Lord Gower, as if it were a pound of cheese. He had communicated his doubts to the governors, but without effect: no doubt they thought, in the manner of the period, that all the gifts of heaven were obtainable by what some people like to call influence, and others personal recommendation. In conclusion, he hoped his correspondent, if he felt, as he himself felt, that the application was impracticable, would forgive him and simply burn his letter ; but if, on the other hand, he thought that there was a probability of obtaining the degree, he trusted that his "humanity, and propensity to relieve merit in distress," would incline him "to serve the poor man." And he pointed out that the "election could not be delayed longer than the 11th. of next month," which increased the difficulty. When Johnson was inclined to put Lord Gower into his *Dictionary*, under "renegade," because of his forsaking the Jacobite cause, he cannot have known of this early kindness.

Lord Gower was correct in his date : the school statutes laid it down that there must not be a delay of more than three months in the appointment of a master by the governors, and the 11th. of September was just three months after the 11th. of June, when Mr. Martin had handed in his resignation to them at the meeting. Whether Lord Gower knew that the question had been referred to the Bishop, who could not appoint until six months had elapsed, does not appear.

It was, however, all in vain : this wonderful chain of influence broke somewhere, though we do not know at which link. It is curious that Lord Gower made no mention of Pope being behind the application. There is reason to believe that Lord Gower's letter actually reached Swift himself, for whose eyes it was obviously not intended, and if that were so we can hardly be surprised if its diffident tone discouraged him from taking any action.

Sir Thomas Gresley and his other friends advised Johnson to apply for the post in person, so he duly made the journey, to a country quite familiar to him, Appleby being only seven or eight miles from Market Bosworth, and nearer still to Ashby-de-la-Zouch, where Michael Johnson had a bookstall. It was in July 1739 that, with tears in his eyes, he said farewell to his friend Savage, who had at last been persuaded to leave London for South Wales. This, no doubt, preceded his visit to Appleby. The statutes required an applicant to notify his name and address to every governor who lived within ten miles of the school, and at least three weeks before the election, the information to be given in writing and delivered at, or sent to, the governor's house. No more than three of them lived over ten miles away, Sir Robert Burdett, at Foremark, John Wylde, at Long Whatton, and John Moore, in London. Appleby, it should be remembered, was only about a dozen miles from Lichfield, and eight of the governors lived no further away from Johnson's birthplace, so that most of them were more or less his neighbours, and all in the district where Michael Johnson had been so well known. Sir Robert Burdett was second cousin to Gilbert Walmesley's wife, while Theodore William Inge had not only been a contemporary of Johnson's at Oxford, but also was a son of that eminent county gentleman, William Inge, who some years before had told him the anecdote about Ambrose Philips.

With such a backing as Johnson would seem to have enjoyed his success might have been assured had he been normally qualified, academically and personally, for such a position. But the attempt to procure him a degree failed, and that in itself was fatal to his prospects. Even with a degree, his fitness for a headmastership might have been successfully challenged. The old physical trouble remained. Pope, writing afterwards, apropos of the application, said that "he had an infirmity of the convulsive kind, that attacked him sometimes, so as to make him a sad spectacle." So that all the efforts of his friends on his behalf were brought to nought, and the Bishop, after the expiry of the six months, on 12 December 1739, had no choice but to appoint Thomas Mould, who, through the default of the governing body, was the only qualified candidate in the field. Mould remained till his death in 1779.

Had Johnson been successful, and held his appointment, it would have made a great difference in his career, though with what result to his reputation it were idle to speculate. Fate can achieve her ends by such vastly different methods, and it is difficult to believe that the essential bigness of the man would not eventually have expressed itself even in the country schoolmaster.

It is interesting to observe that Samuel Martin, whose retirement led to all these happenings, two years later married a daughter of the dreaded Hunter of Lichfield, and so became a kind of connexion of Johnson's through their wives. Perhaps there was already some association with the Lichfield circle, which proved a factor in determining Johnson's application. It is to be remarked that a number of Lichfield boys came on to Appleby. We have seen how George Garrick arrived early in 1737, after his brief spell under Johnson at Edial, and he may still have been at the school in 1739. Two brothers of Johnson's school friend, Gilbert Repington, had entered at an earlier date, Edward in 1725 and Charles in 1727. Two Simpsons from Lichfield entered in 1736, Joseph, the unfortunate barrister afterwards befriended by Johnson and Garrick, and his younger brother Stephen, to become a doctor. Like other local schools of this character—"charity schools" as Lord Gower called them—its pupils included boys from neighbouring county families, and three sons of peers had entered during the period of which we are speaking.

The visit to Appleby synchronised with the death in London of his second cousin, Cornelius Jesson, one of the largest makers of sail cloth in England, son of the Cornelius Jesson who had been Steward of Christ's Hospital. And it inaugurated another very unsatisfactory period for Johnson, when he wandered about the Midland counties for months, with his wife left behind in London and their relations clouded by some conduct for which he felt himself to blame, with his literary work for Cave suspended, and with no settled occupation or plan of life. We know few details of these wanderings, or what compelled them, but, though they were brightened by some pleasant social interludes, they cannot have been very happily undertaken. He was now thirty years of age, and his rejection at Appleby seemed the culminating failure in his long, if spasmodic, series of attempts to become a schoolmaster. Stourbridge would not have him; Market Bosworth tortured him into sudden leaving after a few months; Ashburne disdained his application; Solihull could not risk his nervous peculiarities; Edial proved an unsuccessful venture under his management; Brewood liked the idea of a master with "convulsive motions" no better than did Solihull; and then, to crown all, the powerful influences that would secure him the Mastership at Appleby proved of no avail. Much though he valued the work of schoolmasters in theory, much though he honoured them for their devotion, and much though he reprobated the failure of a biographer to record the masters under whom his subject sat, there can be little wonder after such a dismal record that he himself should always have shrunk from the title of dominie, and been only anxious to forget, and to have others forget, that he had ever sought, under economic pressure, to enter a profession for which he was so ill-fitted.

Early in the year 1740 his wanderings had brought him back to Lichfield, to stay with his mother and Lucy Porter. He had scarcely written to his wife since leaving her in London five or six months ago. At this time the dead bones of *Irene* were stirring once again, and on Thursday, 31 January 1740, he received a letter from Garrick saying that Mr. Fleetwood had at last promised to guarantee that if it could not be produced immediately it should at least be the first for next season ; while William Rufus Chetwood, the prompter at Drury Lane, was anxious to bargain for the right of printing it after its appearance on the stage, and offered fifty guineas. Johnson was delighted to hear that his tragedy had at last found favour with the players, and hoped its success was going to prove the solution of his difficulties. But it was a false hope, and save for an occasional loan to a friend the MS. of *Irene* slumbered on the shelves again for nine years.

On this very same day, however, he had put through a piece of business which relieved him of immediate financial anxieties. He had mortgaged the house at Lichfield, his birthplace, to that good old family friend, Theophilus Levett, for the sum of £80, and received £20 of it for himself. There was an immediate use for this cash. He had only recently learned that his "dearest Tetty"—his "charming love," as he was now moved quaintly to address her—had suffered an injury to a leg-tendon, which had caused her much pain, as well as anxiety, and he had sent her some money. He could not bear to think of her confined to the room at Mrs. Crow's, in Castle Street, where she still remained, having to endure this physical ill, on top of her other troubles. He sat down at night to write to her, imploring her not to disregard his happiness so much as to run any risk in the matter, and to spare nothing that might alleviate her condition. If the surgeon who was attending her could not quickly effect a cure, she was to have another in consultation, and he suggested two or three visits from such leading men as John Ranby, Surgeon-in-Ordinary to the King's Household, or John Shipton, who had been called in at Queen Caroline's last illness in 1737. She was not to worry, on so pressing an occasion, over a guinea fee, for he would forward the £20 on Monday, and also write and tell her how he had spent his time since he left her, how her daughter Lucy was, and of his affairs generally. But he hoped before then to hear that her leg was better. "I still promise myself many happy years from your tenderness and affection, which I sometimes hope our misfortunes have not yet deprived me of."

The suggestion that her "expectation of life" was so much smaller than his own does not sound very tactful, but we will let that pass. It was, at any rate, a contrite, as well as an affectionate Johnson who wrote the letter. "I hope you do not think so unkindly of me as to imagine that I can be at rest while I believe my dear Tetty in pain." In conclusion he assured his "dear girl" that during these compulsory peregrinations he had not met anyone but had confirmed him in his devotion to her. If his "most amiable woman in the world" had not been anxious as to her young husband's conduct while he wandered free she would have proved herself to be more, or less, than human.

True to his principle of never treating the weather as a topic for discussion, Johnson made no mention of the terrible conditions of cold which had prevailed for over a month. Years afterwards he could recall "the dreadful winter of Forty," but unlike other literary men of the day he did not complain of it at the time. The frost had begun just after Christmas Day, and the country was soon under arctic conditions. An ice-fair was held on the Thames, and everywhere was ice-bound. In Staffordshire there were wonders to be seen where nature had been surprised by such unwonted inclemency of weather, and "the great frost" lived long in Lichfield memories.

The lavish generosity which Johnson always showed with any money he had in hand is well illustrated by his promise to send on the whole of the £20 he had received to his wife. She ordinarily "disliked the profusion with which he constantly gave away all the money about him," but on this occasion she may have forgiven his open-handedness. If he was profuse in his gifts, she was as little inclined to parsimony in her own expenditure, and he was equally surprised and concerned that the money with which he supplied her vanished so quickly. They were as unthrifty a couple as they well could be with such small means, and that was the real reason for their chronic impecuniosity, and, secondarily, no doubt for the friction that sometimes marred their relations. But his attitude towards her in ordinary converse was one of respectful homage, which she rather archly accepted as a tribute to her charms. His letter to her is quite in the same tradition.

Johnson in this letter expressed a hope with which he had often flattered himself, that their troubles would never separate them again. But their bit of good fortune probably did not immediately re-unite them, for he does not seem to have returned to London till later. It was on this tour that he made that stay at Ashburne on which he commenced a number of valuable friendships. His headquarters, of course, was the large and comfortable home of his old school friend, John Taylor, who about this time gave up his hereditary law practice to enter the Church, in July 1740 becoming Rector of Market Bosworth. Taylor knew everybody in that part of Derbyshire, and Johnson visited freely at the homes of the neighbouring squires. But the family with which he became most intimate was that of Littleton Poyntz Meynell, whose seat of Bradley was about three miles from Ashburne. Mr. Meynell was middle-aged with a growing family. He was a county man of position, but it was his son Hugo Meynell who made the name so famous in the annals of foxhunting, and who, curiously enough, succeeded Johnson's connexion, Thomas Boothby, as Master of the Quorn in 1753, marrying his granddaughter a few years later. " Old Meynell " showed his quality, his truly British quality, by his one known saying, " *For any thing I see, foreigners are fools*," which continues to delight by its unconscious humour.

Johnson on this occasion paid frequent visits to Bradley, " where his company was much desired by the ladies of the family, who were, perhaps, in point of elegance and accomplishments, inferior to few of those with whom he was afterwards acquainted." Mrs. Meynell, daughter to a Barbadoes planter, was then alive, with her daughter Mary, who four years later was to marry William Fitzherbert, afterwards M.P. for Derby and the holder of various public offices. Mrs. Meynell died in June 1740, only a few months after Johnson's visit, and in the introductory note to some lines to her memory in *The Gentleman's Magazine* we can almost certainly read Johnson's own regard for it. The Fitzherberts, at Tissington, half-a-dozen miles from Bradley, were county neighbours of the Meynells, and they too became the friends of Johnson. Mary Meynell won his highest admiration and respect by her character and accomplishments, and in a moment of friendly exuberance he said that " she had the best understanding he ever met with in any human being." She gave her husband the greatest devotion, and rather disturbed the good man's equanimity by her anxiety for his spiritual welfare. Johnson she welcomed as an excellent influence in the household, who would exercise some restraint on the clever but cheery company Mr. Fitzherbert loved to gather round him.

On this same occasion, through the Meynells, he made the acquaintance of Miss Hill Boothby. The Boothby baronets lived at Ashburne Hall, almost in the town, and her uncle then held the title, which later passed to her brother and her nephew. Hill Boothby, who was a year older than Johnson, could claim distant connexion with the Fitzherberts, and Mrs. Meynell was her dearest friend, so much so that after Mary's premature death in 1753 she ran the Fitzherbert household and mothered the children. It was soon after she had taken over these responsibilities that her correspondence with Johnson began, a correspondence which breathes as serene and beautiful a friendship as could well be imagined. It is a curious circumstance that Hill Boothby was not very distantly akin to Thomas Boothby, the great sportsman who had married Hester Skrymsher, apparently Johnson's cousin, but there is no suggestion of any such link being known to them. Johnson, of course, had mixed before in polite circles at Lichfield, but at Ashburne, among comparative strangers, he would feel better able to stand on his own feet. He confessed that he had never tried to please socially until he was over thirty, thinking the attempt would be hopeless : perhaps it was on this Ashburne visit that he began to make the effort, and to find that even his awkward and uncouth presence did not debar him from a social success founded on talents and qualities which made people overlook his surface defects.

The circle at Ashburne in which Johnson moved was to have another contact with literature a little later. Richard Graves, who came to Tissington in 1741 as curate of the parish, and lived as chaplain and companion with the Fitzherberts at the Hall, drew on his memories of the group when he came to write his *Spiritual Quixote*. Mr. and Mrs. Fitzherbert, Mr. Meynell, and Hill Boothby, are all identified with characters in the book, which was a satirical attack on the Methodists. Hill Boothby, who could read her Hebrew Bible, had methodist leanings, as had also her friend Mrs. Fitzherbert, whose youngest son, the diplomatist, Lord St. Helens, was the authority for the identifications.

It was at Bradley, too, that Johnson began his life-long friendship with the Rev. John Kennedy, who had been Rector there since 1732. Kennedy was a man of much learning, but with little capacity for applying it. His wife was also a talented woman, but they were an eccentric couple, and spent their long married life in very straitened circumstances. Another Ashburne family with which he became associated was the highly reputed medical one of Chauncy. Dr. Charles Chauncy settled there after his marriage in 1682, living in the very house where Taylor afterwards entertained Johnson. His son, Dr. William Chauncy, succeeded him, dying in 1736, and it was William's daughter Frances who in 1744 married Thomas Lawrence, the distinguished London doctor with whom Johnson became so intimate.

A little more than a quarter of a century later this same countryside, which even in the literary associations it had acquired might be considered as typically English as well could be, was to see the strangest sight it had ever yet encountered, the mysterious figure of a Frenchman—a "wicked Frenchman" would have been considered tautological—queer in his dress, queer in his manner, queerer in his ideas, the very antithesis of Johnson mentally and physically, who seemed completely out of place wandering amid such surroundings. Had not "old Meynell" wisely spoken for his kind when he said that, for all he could see, foreigners were fools ; and did not Johnson himself describe Jean-Jacques Rousseau as "one of the worst of men : a rascal who ought to be hunted out of society"? As ever, the younger generation did not take its ideas from the elder, and Hill Boothby's nephew, Sir Brooke Boothby, was a fervent admirer of the "rascal."

Johnson's prolonged absence from London is evidenced in his literary work. From May 1739, when he wrote the address "To the Reader," until June 1740, when he contributed his "Life of Admiral Blake," there is no communication to *The Gentleman's Magazine* that can be attributed to his pen, a gap for which there is not any parallel between 1738 and 1743. It is possible that Cave's patience may have been too severely tried by Johnson's long delay in making the award for the poems on the "Divine Attributes," or by the abortive translation of Sarpi, and that a temporary estrangement between them may have been one cause for Johnson remaining so long in the country. From the literary evidence it is reasonable to infer that he was out of

London from the time of his Appleby application in the summer of 1739 until the spring of 1740, though on the evidence of his letter alone he might have returned in February. Whatever the exact date of his return to London it was at least final. His personal connexion with the country, except as an occasion for holidays in his later life, ceased entirely, and he became a Londoner with such provincial thoroughness as to make the natives seem by comparison but lukewarm lovers of the great capital which to him stood for all that gives zest to life.

Thus ended the first great cycle of his career, when the direction in which fate was going to lead him appeared still uncertain. His blood and bone were by long inheritance of Middle England, and warred to some extent with the intellectual urges that directed him towards London. It will have been seen what a hold the country laid upon him, in spite of his later development into the great apologist of city life, with all its stimulating social contacts, and the lively bustle of its streets and marts. His first thirty years were almost entirely conditioned by his early environment, by the complicated interactions of kinship, and by the sympathetic interest of friends in his own neighbourhood. The pattern of his life for this period was thus closely woven on to a web of local and hereditary association, from which it was not easily to be detached by forces born of purely intellectual activities.

It is extraordinary how many of the families whose names are familiar through the whole period of Johnson's life helped to form great interconnected groups with all of which he could claim some kinship or common tie. The Hectors, the Carlesses, the Lloyds, with the Crowleys, the Actons and the Moseleys, were all akin in some way to his mother through the Fords and the Hickmans. The Porters, to whom his marriage allied him, were connected with the Rev. John Hunter through both of his wives; with Hunter's undermaster, the Rev. Edward Holbrooke; with the Rev. Samuel Martin, whom Johnson sought to succeed at Appleby; with the Sewards; and with the Whites of Lichfield. Less to be expected were family ties between Johnson's own kindred and the kindred of the Porters, and between Mrs. Johnson's cousins on the Jervis side and cousins of the Porters. The whole story shows such an amazing criss-cross of relationships as strikingly to illustrate the homogeneity of social groups and the influence of the family in shaping people's lives. The climax of genealogical incongruity is reached when we are able to see those great protagonists, Samuel Johnson and Lord Chesterfield, who have always stood typically for the poor scholar and the aristocratic patron, sundered by an unbridgeable social gulf, as linked together by common connexion with the Crowleys, through the peer's brother, Sir William Stanhope, having married Mary Crowley and so become great-nephew by marriage to "Parson" Ford.

The part played by kinsfolk in shaping his early career is apparent all through the story. And apart from relatives, whatever he did and wherever he went we find the same local influences at work time and time again, though these influences, it must be confessed, were often of small practical avail. Almost at every critical turn, for instance, Gilbert Walmesley was there to advise and assist. He took a fancy to Johnson as a boy, and gave him his first easy experience of cultivated society. He sponsored the Edial experiment, and helped to supply a nucleus of pupils. He encouraged him to write his play. He recommended him for the mastership of Solihull School. He arranged for his going to London with Garrick. He gave him a letter of introduction to the Rev. John Colson, though with no apparent result. He also gave him a letter of introduction to Henry Lintot, his London bookseller. He encouraged him in the abortive enterprise of translating Sarpi's *History of the Council of Trent.* And no doubt his influence had something to do with the kind reception accorded to Johnson in London by his brother-in-law, the Hon. Henry Hervey. Much later one of Johnson's greatest friends was Topham Beauclerk, whose mother was Mrs. Walmesley's first cousin, but this seems to have been mere coincidence.

Even the grammar schools where Johnson sought masterships were largely linked together by common associations. When he went to Market Bosworth the fame of its last head but one, Anthony Blackwall, was still fresh in memory, and William Budworth, under whom Johnson sought to serve at Brewood, had been Blackwall's pupil. And the Rev. William Lockett, who married Johnson, had been assistant master under Blackwall at Derby School, while William Fitzherbert, Johnson's friend, had also been Blackwall's pupil there. John Crompton, who was head of Market Bosworth from 1734, came from Solihull, where Johnson tried to become his successor in 1736.

Hunter, the head of Lichfield School, had started as an usher at Solihull. At Appleby, where we find Lichfield boys as pupils, including George Garrick after the closing down of Edial, Johnson endeavoured to succeed Samuel Martin, who soon afterwards married Hunter's daughter. When we come to that dark and sinister figure in Johnson's early life, Sir Wolstan Dixie, we find that his mother had been living in the Bishop's Palace at Lichfield ; that his brother, the Rector of Market Bosworth, had been married at Lichfield Cathedral to the sister of Johnson's school friend, Andrew Corbet ; that he was connected with the Pyotts of Streethay, one of whom was a trustee of Michael Johnson's marriage settlement ; that just after the period I deal with here he married a first cousin of Molly Aston ; and that there was even a distant tie between him and Lord Gower, who did what he could to get a degree for Johnson when he made his application at Appleby.

Gilbert Walmesley, of course, belonged to the great world, and his influence was equally at Johnson's service in town or country. But most of the other factors in the shaping of his early career, whether personal or not, were of a purely local character. They constituted a powerful drag upon him, and helped to keep him in his native district, deluded first by one hope and then by another. Though London was in some ways such an irresistible magnet, with all that it offered in the prospect of literary fame to an ambitious young man, in spite of its not very warm initial welcome, the country would not surrender him without a long struggle. Even after his rejection at Appleby there were evidently forces still at work which might have drawn him back into the provincial circle from which his abilities had promised to rescue him. But when these at last were broken the issue of the struggle did not remain long in doubt. London absorbed him, while the country saw him no more as a participator in its various activities and ceased to exert any direct influence on his life. It is an extraordinary fact, and one for which even greater poverty than he ever endured would have been no sufficient excuse, that after his return to London in the first half of 1740 he did not once visit the aged mother at Lichfield whom he yet held in such affection and reverence, nor did he even attend her funeral in 1759. It was not till the winter of 1761–2, when he had become famous and relieved from money anxieties, that he showed himself again to his townsmen.

Much though Johnson owed to his sturdy provincial heritage, which had contributed so powerfully to his intellectual and moral integrity, and much though he had gained from the cultured society to which he had been admitted in his youth and early manhood, it was not until he had broken free from the vast net of hereditary associations which enveloped him, and had ceased in any way to rely upon their influence, that he came to his full stature as a man or as a writer. He may to some extent merely have been undergoing a natural process of development that proceeded independently of his immediate surroundings. But we cannot help feeling that in his case, almost more than in that of any other great man of letters, the transplanting into the congenial soil of the metropolis had a stimulating influence upon his mind and work such as might not have operated to anything like the same extent had circumstances caused him to remain in the provinces. It is strange to think that the countryman who had found it so hard to break the ties which bound him to his native shires should have become for us the most familiar and characteristic figure that ever trod the streets of London.

APPENDIX A.

THE JOHNSON PEDIGREE

In The Reades of Blackwood Hill and Dr. Johnson's Ancestry *I did not present any actual pedigree of the Johnsons, as the material was too scanty. But in Part IV. of these* Gleanings *I tabulated the descendants of the Doctor's uncle, Andrew Johnson. The pedigree that follows, beginning with the Doctor's grandfather, William Johnson, is as complete as it can now be made, in the light of everything I have printed about the family to date.*

The relationship to the Skrymshers is shown in the form to which the evidence so strongly points, yet which it is so hard to credit in the absence of direct proof and in the light of Johnson's apparent ignorance of such a notable connexion as a first cousin's marriage to Thomas Boothby, the great foxhunting squire, would have constituted, especially to one himself so obscurely born.

When Johnson visited London with his mother in 1712 *he played with a toy given him by his " cousin Isaac Johnson." Perhaps this cousin was another son of Andrew Johnson and Sarah Fisher, who had a near kinsman Isaac Fisher.*

It seems probable that the Thomas Johnson married to Ann Burton at St. Mary's, Lichfield, on 4 *Feb.* 1728, *was the Doctor's cousin, and it can hardly be doubted that that cousin's known children, Ann, Mary and Benjamin, were those of the same names baptised there in* 1736, 1739 *and* 1742. *But three other children born to " Thomas Johnson " were baptised there during the same period : Charles on* 24 *Nov.* 1728, *Thomas on* 31 *Jan.* 1731, *and Amy on* 24 *Jan.* 1746. *If they were also children of " Cousin Tom " they must have died young or without issue.*

It is very probable that there are Johnsons still in existence, descendants of the Doctor's first cousin, Fisher Johnson, but none of the family have been definitely traced to a later date than 1810.

In all cases where any association can be established between Dr. Johnson and the kinsfolk shown in this pedigree, its nature is briefly indicated, and emphasised by italics.

WILLIAM JOHNSON, of Cubley, co. Derby, which he left about 1664 to settle in Lichfield, where he lived first in Tamworth Street, 1666–7, then in the Bird Street–Sandford Street ward, *circa* 1668–9, and in Bore Street, 1670–71 ; described by his sons as a ' yeoman,' or ' gentleman,' but probably not more than a small farmer when at Cubley, while at Lichfield he had about the lowest assessment in the parish and was evidently in very poor circumstances. Burd. 28 Feb. 1671/2, at St. Michael's, Lichfield. *When Dr. Johnson told Boswell, "I can hardly tell who was my grandfather," he was referring to William Johnson, though he knew that his grandfather had come from Cubley, and himself had the registers there searched for relative extracts.* Mard. Catherine, dau. of ......; after her husband's death she lived in the Bird Street–Sandford Street ward of Lichfield, off and on, *circa* 1673–83, when she was so poor that on three occasions, in 1672, 1673 and 1679, she received the gift of a "woman's waistcoat" from the churchwardens of St. Mary's, under the charity of Henry Smith. After 1682 she probably lived with her son Michael in Sadler Street: she was burd. on 10 Jan. 1691/2, according to the register of St. Mary's, Lichfield, where there was no graveyard, and eleven days later Michael paid for her grave, which was probably by her husband's at St. Michael's. William and Catherine Johnson had issue,

I. Michael Johnson, of Sadler Street and the Market Square, Lichfield, bookseller, stationer and parchment manufacturer. *According to Dr. Johnson his father was born at Cubley in* 1656 (i.e., 1656/7), where he was bapt. on 2 Apl. 1657. Entered under date of 8 Dec. 1671 as one of eight boys to receive a grant from the Feoffees of the Conduit Lands Trust of Lichfield towards their "placing and preferment"; on 8 Dec. 1672 entered as the first of seven to receive a grant from the same Charity "towards their preferment and binding apprentice" (in his case £4, the highest amount); on 11 Apl. 1673 apprenticed to Richard Simpson, of The Harp, St. Paul's Churchyard, London, stationer, for 8 years, his mother receiving her £4 from the same Charity on 12 Apl. 1673, £3–10–0 of which was for the apprenticeship, the remaining 10s. being for the expenses of his journey to London; apprenticeship expired on 11 Apl. 1681, when he returned to Lichfield and began business on his own account as bookbinder and bookseller, in Sadler Street; in 1684–5 appointed a Warden of the Conduit Lands Trust of Lichfield; on 5 Oct. 1685 made free of the Stationers' Company; on 30 Dec. 1686 licenced to marry Mary [b. 1663], dau. of Luke Neild, of Derby, but marriage did not take place; had branches at Uttoxeter, co. Staffs., and Ashby-de-la-Zouch, co. Leic., as early as 1687; churchwarden of St. Mary's, Lichfield, 1688/9; Sheriff of Lichfield in 1709; elected a magistrate of the city, 19 July 1712; Junior Bailiff in 1718; Senior Bailiff in 1725. Published a number of works, from 1687 onwards, and by 1697 had established a parchment factory in a building by Stowe Pool, which he carried on for thirty years or more. Burd. 7 Dec. 1731, at St. Michael's, Lichfield. *From his father Dr. Johnson inherited his physical bulk and strength of body, as well as something of the strength and activity of his mind, with the melancholic tendencies that afflicted him through life.* Mard. 19 June 1706 (ante-nuptial settlement dated 11 June 1706), at Packwood, co. Warwick, to Sarah, third dau. of Cornelius Ford, then of Packwood, yeoman, who was born Mch. 1669 at Kings Norton, co. Worc., and bapt.

there 6 Apl. 1669. As a widow she lived on in ' the Birthplace,' and continued her late husband's business ; she was burd. 23 Jan. 1759, at St. Michael's, Lichfield, aged 89. *For his mother, a woman of gentle and unassuming character, with no intellectual outlook, Dr. Johnson had the greatest affection and respect.* She had issue by Michael Johnson,

1. **SAMUEL JOHNSON** [1709–1784], LL.D.
2. Nathaniel Johnson, of Lichfield, bookseller ; bapt. 14 Oct. 1712, at St. Mary's, Lichfield ; apparently running a branch of the business at Burton-on-Trent in 1735–6 ; possibly a bookbinder and stationer at Frome, in Somerset, for a year or so about 1736 ; died unmard.; burd. 5 Mch. 1736/7, at St. Michael's, Lichfield. *Dr. Johnson praised his manly spirit, but the brothers had little in common, and their relations were strained.*

II. Benjamin Johnson, bapt. 24 Feb. 1658/9, at Cubley, co. Derby ; one of nine boys recorded as " put forth " on 8 Dec. 1675 by the Feoffees of the Conduit Lands Trust of Lichfield, he having been apprenticed on 6 Dec. 1675, for 7 years only, to the same Richard Simpson, of London, stationer, with whom his elder brother Michael was serving his articles, his mother receiving £3 from the Feoffees therefor on 14 Apl. 1676 ; apprenticeship expired on 6 Dec. 1682 ; made free of Stationers' Company on 4 June 1683 ; nothing known of him after 3 Dec. 1683, when his younger brother Andrew was apprenticed to him.

III. ANDREW JOHNSON, *of whom presently.*

Margaret Johnson, bapt. 2 Aug. 1663, at Cubley, co. Derby ; perhaps mard. 23 Feb. 1692/3, at St. Chad's, Lichfield, to John Lyndon, of Lichfield, joiner, son of Francis Lyndon, of Lichfield, and uncle to Mary Wilson who mard. the celebrated Henry Sacheverell, D.D. John Lyndon, who was bapt. 13 Apl. 1658, at St. Mary's, Lichfield, and living on 3 Oct. 1716, had issue by Margaret Johnson his wife,

a. Catherine Lyndon, bapt. 21 Feb. 1694/5, at St. Mary's, Lichfield ; living 3 Oct. 1716, unmard.

b. Mary Lyndon, living 3 Oct. 1716, unmard.

William and Catherine Johnson, there is strong evidence to suggest, may have had another dau., older than any of the children recorded above,

Catherine [? Johnson], who mard. Gerard Skrymsher, of Woodseaves, in par. of High Offley, co. Staffs., who matriculated pensioner from Trinity Coll., Cambridge, in 1635, scholar 1638, and B.A. 1638/9 ; degree of M.D. conferred upon him by Royal Mandate, 1660 ; some 33 years his wife's senior ; youngest son of James Skrymsher, of Norbury Manor, Staffs., esq., by Eleanor his wife, dau. of John Hockenhull, of Prenton, co. Cheshire. He was bapt. 30 July 1618, at Norbury, and died 2 Oct. 1700, aged 82, being burd. at High Offley. *His nuncupative will, declared on* 28 *Sept.* 1700, *was drafted on* 3 *Oct.* 1700 *by Michael Johnson, of the City of Lichfield, stationer, one of the witnesses by the dying man's bedside, and who, when administration of the estate was granted to Catherine, the widow, on 6 Jan. 1701/2, stood surety for the education of the children, who were minors.* She died 27 July 1725, aged 74, at Woodseaves, admon. of her estate being granted on 27 May 1726 to her son Charles. She was burd. at High Offley, where there is a white marble mural tablet to the memory of her and her husband, by whom she had issue,

1. Charles Skrymsher, of Woodseaves, in par. of High Offley, co. Staffs., gent.; bapt. 17 Apl. 1688, at High Offley; ed. Uttoxeter School, Staffs.; admitted pensioner at Trinity Coll., Cambridge, 22 June 1709, aged 18; matric. 1709; B.A. 1713/14; burd. 20 June 1762, at High Offley. Mentioned on the tablet to his parents' memory. *A fortnight before his own death in 1784 Dr. Johnson made enquiries as to whether this "Charles Scrimshaw of Woodsease" was still living, and claimed him as "very nearly related."* Admon. of his estate was not granted until 31 May 1800, in P.C.C. Mard. 1st., 12 May 1708 (by licence from Chester of same date), at Eccleston, co. Chester, to Dorothy, widow of ...... Mossond (or Mossam), she being then of the par. of St. Michael's, Chester, and he of Eccleshall, co. Staffs. Mard. 2nd., 28 Sept. 1719, at High Offley, to Mary, only dau. and heir of Samuel Mytton, of Ryton, co. Salop, yeoman, she being dead on 31 May 1800. Charles Skrymsher had issue (of whom Thomas and Mary may possibly have been born of his first marriage),

   (a) Thomas Skrymsher, of Woodseaves, par. of High Offley, co. Staffs.; burd. 16 June 1762, at High Offley. Mard. Deborah, dau. of ......, and had issue,
      Charles Skrymsher, bapt. 10 Oct. 1754, at High Offley.

   (b) Mary Skrymsher, mard. ...... Beckett; both were living on 19 Dec. 1775, with children, and she on 30 Aug. 1784, at Hulme-Walfield, par. of Astbury, co. Chester, with a son,
      Charles Skrymsher Beckett, living 30 Aug. 1784.

   (c) Ann Skrymsher, bapt. 26 Dec. 1723, at High Offley, and burd. there 21 July 1726.

   (d) Agnes Catherine Skrymsher, bapt. 27 Dec. 1726, at High Offley; mard. 12 Apl. 1746, at Sheinton, co. Salop, to Henry Babb, by whom she had a son,
      Henry Babb, living 19 Dec. 1775.

   (e) Mytton Skrymsher, bapt. 3 Dec. 1727, at High Offley; living 31 May 1800, as his father's only child.

1. Hester Skrymsher, bapt. 20 June 1686, at High Offley; mard. 1705, as his second wife, Thomas Boothby, of Tooley Park, par. of Peckleton, co. Leic., esq. (son of Thomas Boothby, of Tooley Park). He was bapt. 3 Mch. 1680, at Peckleton, died 4 Aug. 1752, aged 72,

and was burd. in Peckleton church, his will, dated 21 Oct. 1738, with a codicil of 12 June 1747, being proved 13 Nov. 1752, in P.C.C. A great sportsman, celebrated in the history of foxhunting, Thomas Boothby had mard. for his 1st. wife, in 1697, Elizabeth, dau. of Sir Charles Skrymsher (a kinsman of Hester's), of Norbury, co. Staffs., knt., and had issue by her. Hester (who, with her husband, is mentioned on the tablet to her parents' memory at High Offley) died 1 May 1712, aged 25 (her widower marrying a 3rd. wife, Sarah . . . . . . , about 1716), and was burd. in the chancel of Peckleton church, leaving issue by Thomas Boothby,

(1) Charles Skrymsher Boothby, of Groby, in par. of Ratby, and of Foston, both in co. Leic., esq.; bapt. 13 Dec. 1705, at High Offley, co. Staffs.; died 6 Dec. 1774, aged 69 ; burd. in Foston church ; will dated 2 May 1768, proved 17 Dec. 1774, at Leicester. Mard. 18 Apl. 1753, at Peckleton, to Anne, only child of the Rev. Wingfield Buswell, M.A., Rector of Tickencote and Normanton, both in co. Rutland, and niece of Sir Eusebius Buswell, 1st. and last bart. She died without issue on 16 Nov. 1785, aged 65, and was burd. at Foston ; her will, dated 30 Aug. 1784, with a codicil of 23 Oct. 1784, was proved 17 Mch. 1786, in P.C.C.

(2) Gerard Boothby, bapt. 13 Aug. 1707, at High Offley, co. Staffs.; living 12 June 1737 ; died without issue.

(3) William Boothby, bapt. 26 May 1709, at High Offley, co. Staffs., and burd. there 15 Aug. 1709.

(4) John Boothby, bapt. 23 Mch. 1711/12, at High Offley, co. Staffs., and burd. there 3 May 1712.

(1) Hester Boothby, bapt. 25 July 1710, at High Offley, co. Staffs.; mard. 21 Oct. 1754, at Belgrave, co. Leic., to John Beaumont Byerley, of Belgrave, co. Leic., who died 8 Nov. 1760, aged 45, and was burd. at Belgrave. She died 14 Jan. 1760, aged 50, without issue, and was burd. at Belgrave.

2. Elizabeth Skrymsher, bapt. 19 Apl. 1691, at High Offley, co. Staffs., and burd. there 22 Feb. 1692/3. Commemorated on the tablet to her parents' memory.

3. Mary Skrymsher, bapt. 10 May 1694, at High Offley, co. Staffs.; mard. in or before 1728 to John Bromfield, of Midgebrook, par. of Swettenham, co. Chester, gent., who died 1 Oct. 1752, aged 52, at Brereton Hall, Brereton, co. Chester, and was burd. at Astbury, his will, dated 6 May 1752, being proved 1 May 1753, at Chester. She (who, with her husband, is mentioned on the tablet to her parents' memory at High Offley) died 16 Jan. 1776, aged "83," without issue, at Dane Bank, Congleton, co. Chester, her will, dated 19 Dec. 1775, being proved 17 Apl. 1777, at Chester.

ANDREW JOHNSON, *third and youngest son of William Johnson preceding and Catherine his wife;* bapt. 7 Dec. 1660, at Cubley, co. Derby ; apprenticed 24 June 1676, for seven years, to John Marriott, of Ashburne, co. Derby, baker, his mother receiving from the Feoffees of the Conduit Lands Trust of Lichfield £3 for his ' putting forth '; apprenticed again for another seven years, 3 Dec. 1683 (when he was 23), to his elder brother Benjamin Johnson, bookseller; *said by Dr. Johnson to have been in his early life a celebrated pugilist and wrestler, " who kept the ring in Smithfield for a whole year, and never was thrown or conquered."* After expiry of his apprenticeship in Dec. 1690 settled in Lichfield, where he lived with his eldest brother, Michael Johnson, in Market Street, and assisted in the business ; in 1696 began business on his own account as a bookseller in Birmingham, where he issued in 1702 what used (wrongly) to be looked upon as Birmingham's first book publication ; had a good shop in the High Street, but never prospered, and in 1720–22 was in imminent danger of arrest for debt ; burd. 22 June 1729, at St. Philip's, Birmingham. Will dated 17 Apl. 1729, proved 17 Sept. 1731, at Lichfield. Mard. 1st., Mary, dau. of . . . . . . , and by her, who was burd. 22 June 1693 (as recorded in the register of St. Mary's, Lichfield, where there was no graveyard, the actual burial being probably at St. Michael's), had issue,

A. Michael Johnson, bapt. 8 Aug. 1691, at St. Mary's, Lichfield ; died young, without issue.

B. Catherine Johnson, bapt. 1 Apl. 1693, at St. Mary's, Lichfield, and burd. 28 June 1693 (St. Mary's register—probably for St. Michael's).

Andrew Johnson mard. 2ndly., on 13 Nov. 1696, at Harborne, co. Staffs., Sarah, dau. of Thomas Fisher, of Elmdon, co. Warwick, yeoman. He mard. 3rdly., about 1717, Sarah White, who was living his widow in Birmingham in 1732. By Sarah Fisher, his second wife, he had further issue,

C. Mary Johnson, bapt. 23 Dec. 1697, at St. Martin's, Birmingham.

D. FISHER JOHNSON, *of whom presently.*

E. Anne Johnson, bapt. 14 June 1701, at St. Martin's, Birmingham.

F. Thomas Johnson, bapt. 19 Feb. 1702/3, at St. Martin's, Birmingham ; *as a boy came to live with his uncle Michael at Lichfield, probably to learn the trade of a currier, and described by Dr. Johnson as " Cousin Tom " and his " playfellow in childhood;" returned from Birmingham to Lichfield, St. Mary's parish, in 1728, probably to help his uncle Michael in the business after Samuel had gone up to Oxford;* on 1 Aug. 1755 described as a currier in the West Orchard in Coventry ; during last years of his life, at least, in very poor circumstances, *and constantly helped by Dr. Johnson, who visited him at Coventry as opportunity offered, the last time on his death-bed ;* burd. 28 May 1779, at Holy Trinity, Coventry, as " Mr. Thomas Johnson." Perhaps the Thomas Johnson who mard. Ann Burton at St. Mary's, Lichfield, on 4 Feb. 1727/8. He had issue,

1. Benjamin Johnson, bapt. 14 Sept. 1742, at St. Mary's, Lichfield; apprenticed 25 Dec. 1756, for 7 years, to John Jee, of Leicester, tin plate worker; appears in Leicester Poll Book of 1768 as Benjamin Johnson of Coventry; died without issue before Dr. Johnson made the codicil to his will on 9 Dec. 1784.

1. Ann Johnson, bapt. 18 Nov. 1736, at St. Mary's, Lichfield; mard. to William Whiting, of Hinckley, co. Leic., currier, *and mentioned* 9 *Dec.* 1784 *in the codicil to Dr. Johnson's will.* They were both living on 17 July 1786, and had a dau.,

Sarah Whiting, born 6 (or 20) Apl. 1780, *and mentioned as "the grand-daughter of the said Thomas Johnson" in the codicil to Dr. Johnson's will of* 9 *Dec.* 1784; living 17 July 1786.

2. Mary Johnson, bapt. 21 June 1739, at St. Mary's, Lichfield; mard. 27 Feb. 1758, at St. Martin's, Leicester, to John Bill (or Bills), of Leicester, flax dresser, and died before 29 Sept. 1785. John Bill, son of John Bill, flax dresser and soldier in H.M. service, was apprenticed on 22 Feb. 1747, for 7 years, to Thomas Stretton, of Leicester, flax dresser, and burd. 25 Aug. 1778, aged 45, at St. Martin's, Leicester, having had issue by Mary Johnson,

(1) Joseph Bill, of Hinckley, co. Leic., stocking weaver; mard. 14 Aug. 1785, at Hinckley, to Ann, dau. of .... Warpole, of Hinckley, and was burd. 7 Sept. 1828, at Hinckley, aged 70, having had issue,

John Bill, of Hinckley, framework knitter; born 21 Mch. 1797; bapt. 2 Apl. 1809, at Hinckley; mard. 1 Feb. 1820, at Hinckley, to Mary Davy, of Hinckley, and had issue,

a. Joseph Bill, bapt. 24 June 1821, at Hinckley, and burd. there 11 July 1821, aged 14 (?) days.

b. Charlotte Bill, bapt. 30 Nov. 1823, at Hinckley, and burd. there 30 May 1825, aged 1½ years.

c. Mary Ann Bill, bapt. 24 Apl. 1826, at Hinckley.

(1) Mary Bill, living a spinster at Coventry, 29 Sept. 1785.

FISHER JOHNSON, *eldest son of Andrew Johnson preceding by Sarah Fisher his second wife*; bapt. 7 Nov. 1699, at St. Martin's, Birmingham; left Birmingham in 1736 for Leicester, where he remained; described on 10 Oct. 1754 as a labourer; burd. 14 Nov. 1758, at St. Margaret's, Leicester. *Dr. Johnson, in the codicil to his will, dated* 9 *Dec.* 1784, *referred to him as "Fisher Johnson, late of Leicester;"* mard. 3 May 1737, at St. Martin's, Leicester, to Anne Farres, of that par., and had issue,

I. Thomas Johnson, born 14 Mch. 1738; bapt. 22 May 1738, at St. Martin's, Leicester; lived in Leicester until at least 1775; *mentioned in the codicil to Dr. Johnson's will on* 9 *Dec.* 1784; *described in the deeds relating to Dr. Johnson's Birthplace, on* 29 *Sept.* 1785, *as "Thomas Johnson, of*

Nottingham, in the County of Nottingham, stationer and printer, cousin and heir at law of the said Samuel Johnson deceased." Nothing known of him after 17 July 1786, unless he were the Thomas Johnson burd. 30 Jan, 1820, aged 81, from the Workhouse, at St. Martin's, Leicester. Mard. 21 Oct. 1760, at St. Martin's, Leicester, to Frances Allen, of that par., and had issue by her,

a. Benjamin Fisher Johnson, of St. Mary's, Nottingham; bapt. 8 Sept. 1762, at St. Margaret's, Leicester; mard. 25 Oct. 1785, at St. Mary's, Nottingham, to Ann Bowers, of that par., and had issue by her,
   (a) Benjamin Johnson, bapt. 10 Sept. 1787, at St. Mary's, Nottingham; probably died in infancy.
   (b) Thomas Johnson, bapt. 10 Nov. 1788, at St. Mary's, Nottingham.
   (c) Benjamin Johnson (twin with Elizabeth), bapt. 13 Mch. 1792, at St. Mary's, Nottingham.
   (d) Elizabeth Johnson (twin with Benjamin), bapt. 13 Mch. 1792, at St. Mary's, Nottingham.
b. Elizabeth Johnson, burd. 16 Aug. 1768, at St. Margaret's, Leicester.
c. Fisher Johnson, bapt. 14 Dec. 1769, at St. Margaret's, Leicester, and burd. there 27 Apl. 1771.
d. Thomas Johnson, burd. 18 Nov. 1770, at St. Margaret's, Leicester.
e. John Johnson, bapt. 17 Nov. 1771, at St. Margaret's, Leicester.
f. Frances Johnson, burd. 31 Jan. 1775, at St. Margaret's, Leicester.

II. Benjamin Fisher Johnson, born 29 Feb. 1740; bapt. 6 Apl. 1740, at St. Martin's, Leicester; apprenticed 10 Oct. 1754 to Benjamin Spencer, of Leicester, woolcomber, for 7 years; made free of Leicester, 18 Aug. 1767; of Leicester, woolcomber, 1785 and 1789; *mentioned in the codicil to Dr. Johnson's will on* 9 *Dec.* 1784; of Belgrave Gate, Leicester, worsted maker, in 1794, and in 1800 a victualler at same address; an innholder there at time of his death on 1 Sept. 1809; burd. 4 Sept. 1809, at St. Margaret's, Leicester. Admon. of his estate granted 2 Mch. 1810, at Leicester. Mard. 1 June 1770, at St. Martin's, Leicester, to Elizabeth Craven, of that par., who was living his widow at Leicester on 2 Mch. 1810, and was probably burd. on 26 Apl. 1810, at St. Margaret's, Leicester, having had issue,

a. Lucy Johnson, bapt. 31 Oct. 1771, at St. Margaret's, Leicester.
b. Elizabeth Johnson, born 16 Nov. 1773, and bapt. 21 Nov. 1773, at St. Margaret's, Leicester.
c. Sophia Johnson, born 8 Dec. 1775; bapt. 17 Dec. 1775, at St. Margaret's, Leicester, and burd. there 1 Aug. 1776.
d. Samuel Fisher Johnson, born 11 June 1777; bapt. 13 June 1777, at St. Margaret's, Leicester; made free of Leicester, as his father's eldest son, on 29 Nov. 1800; in the employ of Thomas Gardiner

[b. 1743], of Leicester, hosiery manufacturer, as a comber; of Belgrave Gate, Leicester, framework knitter, in 1800; later became a publican, like his father, and described as an innholder, 2 Mch. 1810; said to have drunk himself "into a coffin."

e. Benjamin Craven Johnson, born 23 June 1780, and bapt. 28 June 1780, at St. Margaret's, Leicester; made free of Leicester, as his father's second son, on 3 Dec. 1800. Mard. 25 Dec. 1801, at St. Margaret's, Leicester, to Ann, dau. of ...... Ward, of that par., and had issue by her.

Benjamin Craven Johnson, born 9 Feb. 1802, and bapt. 15 Feb. 1802, at St. Margaret's, Leicester.

APPENDIX B

THE FORD PEDIGREE

In The Reades of Blackwood Hill and Dr. Johnson's Ancestry *the last of the tabular pedigrees, No. XXIX., embodied all the genealogical information then available in regard to the Fords.*

During the intervening forty years, in the various volumes of these Gleanings, *I have printed much new material about the family.*

The pedigree that follows is as complete as it can now be made, and its narrative form allows the inclusion of much more detail.

The connexion of Dr. Johnson's great-grandfather, Henry Ford, who commences the pedigree, with the Fords of Corley and Fillongley, in Warwickshire, is strongly suggested by the evidence at ante, *IV.*, 39–41.

The last known male member of the family was the Rev. Samuel Ford, who died in 1793, *but Phoebe Ford, long housekeeper to Edward Gibbon, lived till* 1796*: they were both first cousins of Dr. Johnson's. Descendants of the Fords in the female line, through the marriage of George Jesson to Dr. Johnson's great-aunt, Mary Ford, in* 1643, *are as the sands of the sea, as can be gathered from reference to* The Reades of Blackwood Hill and Dr. Johnson's Ancestry, *pp.* 138–9.

Descendants, too, still exist of Dr. Johnson's aunt, Phoebe Ford, wife of John Harrison, as indicated at pp. 182–3 *of* The Reades of Blackwood Hill and Dr. Johnson's Ancestry, *and at* ante, *IX.*, 46.

In all cases where any association can be established between Dr. Johnson and the kinsfolk shown in this pedigree, its nature is briefly indicated, and emphasised by italics.

HENRY FORD, of Ward End, in par. of Aston-juxta-Birmingham, co. Warwick, later of West Bromwich, co. Staffs., and latterly of Birmingham, co. Warwick, yeoman and miller; took Oath of Protestation against Popery, at West Bromwich, in 1641. *The first known member of "the ancient family of Ford," as Dr. Johnson distinguished it.* Admon. of his estate granted 1 May 1648, in P.C.C. Mard. 1st . . . . . . , and by her had issue,

I. Henry Ford, of Birmingham; bapt. 5 Aug. 1607, at Aston-juxta-Birmingham; admon. of his estate granted 12 Sept. 1661, in P.C.C.

Henry Ford mard. 2ndly. Mary, dau. of . . . . . . , who lived during her widowhood at Haunch Hall, in par. of Kings Norton, co. Worc. (which was purchased in 1649 for her younger son, Cornelius); she was burd. 24 July 1658, at Kings Norton. By her, whose will, dated 17 July 1658, was proved 20 Nov. 1661, in P.C.C., he had further issue,

II. Henry Ford, of Winson Green, Birmingham, of Sandwell, in par. of West Bromwich, of The Manwoods, Handsworth, co. Staffs., and of Clifford's Inn, London, solicitor and attorney-at-law; bapt. 3 Feb. 1627/8, at Aston-juxta-Birmingham; admitted Fellow of Clifford's Inn, 18 Apl. 1665, surrendering his room there in Feb. 1690; agent for Brome Whorwood, M.P., of Sandwell Park, West Bromwich, and of Holton Park, co. Oxon, from about 1672; burd. 28 Sept. 1691, at Handsworth. Mard. 13 Sept. 1661 (settlement dated 11 Dec. 1661), at Lapworth, co. Warwick, to Rebecca, dau. of William Ingram, of Nuthurst, in par. of Hampton-in-Arden, co. Warwick, yeoman, and by her, who was bapt. 27 Sept. 1637, at Lapworth, co. Warwick, and burd. 9 Apl. 1672, at St. Martin's, Birmingham, had issue,

a. Elizabeth Ford, mard. 13 July 1681 (by licence dated 12 July 1681), at West Bromwich, to William Abnet, of Audley, and later of Handsworth, both in co. Staffs., eldest son of William Abnet, of Eardley End, par. of Audley, and of Catherine Shakerley his wife. By him, admon. of whose estate was granted at Lichfield on 24 Nov. 1721, she (who was then alive) had issue,

(a) Humphrey Abnet, living 23 Oct 1726.

(b) Charles Abnet, of The Manwoods, Handsworth, who died unmard., admon. of his estate being granted 2 Oct. 1730, at Lichfield.

(c) Robert Abnet, of Stafford, co. Staffs., apothecary, admon. of whose estate was granted 17 Nov. 1733, at Lichfield. Mard. Elizabeth, dau. of the Rev. William Wight, of Arley, co. Warwick, by Ursula his wife, dau. of Sir Francis Wolryche,

2nd. bart., by Elizabeth his wife, dau. of Sir Walter Wrottesley, 1st. bart. She was living his widow, 9 Apl. 1743.

(d) Elizabeth Abnet, who died unmard. in par. of St. Mary's, Stafford, admon. of her estate being granted 29 Sept. 1724, at Lichfield.

(e) Catherine Abnet, mard. 12 Nov. 1709, at Trysull, co. Staffs., to William Robins, Mayor of Stafford in 1719, 1731 and 1740. She, who was living 23 Oct. 1726, had issue by him, who died in 1744, a son,

John Robins, born in 1714, at Stafford; admitted to Middle Temple, 29 Nov. 1731; called to Bar, 10 June 1737; M.P. for Stafford, 1747–54; died 17 Dec. 1754, unmard. See *ante*, VI., 70, for his "marriage," in 1752, to Anna, widow of *John Whitby, of Great Haywood, co. Staffs., whom Johnson had prepared for the University in* 1735.

b. Samuel Ford, bapt. 1 May 1666, and burd. 4 May 1666, at St. Martin's, Birmingham.

c. . . . . Ford, burd. 28 June 1668, at St. Martin's, Birmingham.

d. . . . . Ford, burd. 3 Apl. 1672, at St. Martin's, Birmingham.

III. CORNELIUS FORD, *of whom presently.*

I. Mary Ford, bapt. 6 Feb. 1619/20, at Aston-juxta-Birmingham; mard. 13 June 1643, at West Bromwich, to George Jesson, of West Bromwich, yeoman, son of John Jesson, of West Bromwich, by Amy, his wife, dau. of Thomas Darby, of Rowley, co. Staffs., and was burd. 23 Oct. 1663, at West Bromwich. George Jesson, who was bapt. 11 Jan. 1619/20, at West Bromwich, was burd. there on 28 Nov. 1678, his will, dated 25 Nov. 1678, being proved 12 Feb. 1678/9, in P.C.C. He mard. 2ndly., at West Bromwich (settlement dated 21 Sept. 1671), Mary, sister of William Feldon, of Warley, co. Worc., and by her, who was living 10 Oct. 1685, had no issue. By Mary Ford, his first wife, George Jesson had issue,

1. Thomas Jesson, of Oakwood, West Bromwich, and latterly of Sutton Coldfield, co. Warwick; bapt. 25 May 1645, at Sutton Coldfield, and burd. there 30 Mch. 1703, admon. of his estate being granted 18 Nov. 1703, in P.C.C. By Rebecca his wife, dau. of Francis Wasse, of Sutton Coldfield, whom he mard. on 23 Mch. 1671, and who predeceased him, he had issue one son,

   Thomas Jesson, bapt. 16 Feb. 1674, at Sutton Coldfield, and burd. there 28 June 1703, having had no issue. *Attended in his last illness by Dr. Johnson's uncle, Dr. Joseph Ford.*

2. Henry Jesson, bapt. 10 Apl. 1648, at West Bromwich; matric. 15 Mch. 1666/7, from Pembroke College, Oxford (*where he preceded his cousin, Dr. Johnson, by* 61 *years*); B.A. 1671; living 14 Sept. 1671; dead 25 Nov. 1678.

3. John Jesson, of Bilston, and later of Graiseley, par. of Wolverhampton, both in co. Staffs.; bapt. 6 July 1651, at West Bromwich, and burd. 21 Apl. 1712, at Wolverhampton. Will dated 24 Mch. 1711/12, proved 14 May 1712, at Lichfield. Mard. Elizabeth, dau. of Thomas Brett, of Wolverhampton, on 20 Nov. 1675, and by her, whose will, dated 26 May 1727, was proved 28 July 1729, at Lichfield, had issue,
   (1) Rev. Cornelius Jesson, born 25 Nov. 1689; matric. 15 Apl. 1708, aged 18, from Balliol Coll., Oxford; B.A. 16 Feb. 1711/12, M.A. 1714; Vicar of Wombourne-cum-Trysull, co. Staffs., 1725–56; died 23 Nov. 1756; burd. at Trysull. *Dr. Johnson would probably meet him when visiting their cousin, Mrs. Harriotts, at Trysull, before her death in* 1728. Mard. 1717 Mary, dau. of John Egginton, of Cannock, and later of Rodbaston, par. of Penkridge, all in co. Staffs., esq., and by her, who was burd. 14 July 1753, at Trysull, left issue.
   (2) John Jesson, of Wolverhampton; died unmard.; admon. of his estate granted 29 Aug. 1712, in P.C.C.
   (3) Thomas Jesson, of Oakwood, West Bromwich; born 1697; died 31 Aug. 1766; burd. at West Bromwich. Mard. (settlement dated 22 Dec. 1726) to Mary, dau. of Timothy Chambers (*whose sister Jane mard. Dr. Johnson's uncle, Samuel Ford, in* 1707), of Moseley, par. of Kings Norton, co. Worc., gent., by Mary his wife, dau. of William Eborall (*whose son, Samuel Eborall, mard. Susanna, sister of Harry Porter, whose widow mard. Dr. Johnson*), of Hampton-in-Arden, co. Warwick, esq. By her, who was born 29 Oct. 1698, bapt. 16 Nov. 1698, at Kings Norton, and died 27 Nov. 1764, being burd. at West Bromwich, he left issue.
   (1) Mary Jesson, mard. 1704 to John Chattock, of Haye House, Castle Bromwich, co. Worc., by whom, who was burd. 29 Apl. 1723, at Aston-juxta-Birmingham, she, who was living his widow 29 Sept. 1729, at Solihull, left issue.
   (2) Martha Jesson, mard. 21 Oct. 1708, to Thomas Brett, of West Bromwich, who was living 26 May 1727.
   (3) Elizabeth Jesson, mard. 5 May 1711, to John Pearson, of Wolverhampton.
   (4) Sarah Jesson, mard. 16 Apl. 1720 to Josias Bull, only son and heir of William Bull, of Kingshurst, par. of Coleshill, co. Warwick; they were both living on 26 May 1727.

4. Cornelius Jesson, of Christ Church, Newgate, London, ironmonger, and later, from 16 June 1703, Steward of Christ's Hospital; bapt. 30 Apl. 1655, at West Bromwich; admitted to freedom of Ironmongers' Company, 5 Oct. 1693, and to livery 14 Oct. 1693; died

22 Nov. 1723; burd. at Christ Church, Newgate; admon. of his estate granted 4 Apl. 1724, in P.C.C. *When the infant Johnson was taken to London by his mother in 1712, to receive the benefit of the Royal touch, they stayed in Little Britain, quite close to Christ's Hospital, and probably met this cousin.* Cornelius Jesson mard. in 1678 (licence dated 18 June, for St. Giles, Cripplegate) Anne, dau. of . . . . . . Whiting, of St. Martin's, Ludgate, London, and by her, who was burd. 18 Nov. 1715, at Christ Church, Newgate, had issue,

(1) Cornelius Jesson, of par. of St. Botolph's, Aldersgate Street, London, sailcloth maker; died Sept. 1739; will dated 27 Mch. 1727, proved 15 Sept. 1739, in P.C.C. Mard. Christabella, dau. of . . . . . ., and by her, whose will, dated 29 Oct. 1739, was proved 31 Oct. 1739, in P.C.C., left no issue.

(2) George Jesson, of London; living in 1709.

(3) Abraham Jesson, matric. 13 Mch. 1705/6, from Trinity Coll., Oxford, aged 16; living 1711.

(4) Thomas Jesson, of London; burd. 10 Sept. 1718, at Christ Church, Newgate.

(1) Sarah Jesson, died 9 Feb. 1756, aged 81, unmard.; burd. at Helmdon, Northants.

(2) Ann Jesson, mard. Edward Harriott, of Helmdon, co. Northants., who died 27 Apl. 1729, aged 47, and was burd. at Helmdon. She died 8 Aug. 1774, aged 85, having had issue, and was burd. at Helmdon.

1. Sarah Jesson, born 28 Mch. 1659; bapt. at West Bromwich.

II. Elizabeth Ford, bapt. 13 Mch. 1621/2, at Aston-juxta-Birmingham; mard. 1st. to . . . . . . Tomkis, by whom she left no issue. He died before 30 Dec. 1657, on which date she mard, 2ndly., at Trysull, William Barnesley, of Trysull, co. Staffs., gent., son of Thomas Barnesley, of Trysull, by Margaret his wife, dau. of Walter Southwick, of Tettenhall, co. Staffs. He was bapt. 10 Oct. 1618, at Trysull, died 20 Aug. 1685, and was burd. 22 Aug. 1685, at Trysull, his will, dated 24 June 1684, being proved 1 Feb. 1685/6, in P.C.C. Robert Plot, the antiquary, visited him at Trysull, about 1675, and got help for his *Natural History of Staffordshire*. His widow was burd. 28 Sept. 1697, at Trysull, her will, dated 23 Jan. 1696/7, being proved 12 Oct. 1698, at Lichfield, having had issue by William Barnesley her second husband,

1. Thomas Barnesley, born 8 Sept. 1658, at Trysull; burd. 2 July 1667, at Trysull, after death by drowning.

2. William Barnesley, of Trysull; bapt. 11 Oct. 1665, at Trysull; burd. there 6 Dec. 1690. Admon. of his estate was granted 23 June 1691, at Lichfield.

1. Elizabeth Barnesley, born 2 Feb. 1660/1, at Trysull; mard. 28 May 1687 (by licence dated 21 May 1687), at Trysull, to Robert Harriotts, of Chorley, in par. of Stottesden, co. Salop, and later of Trysull, in right of his wife. He was burd. 24 Dec. 1699, at Trysull, and admon. of his estate was granted 4 Mch. 1699/1700, in P.C.C. She died without issue, and was burd. 16 Feb. 1727/8, at Trysull, her will, dated 23 Oct. 1726, being proved 8 Mch. 1727/8, in P.C.C. *Mrs. Harriotts was the "great lady" of the family, and Dr. Johnson paid tribute to the regularity of her household, which he first entered as an infant in 1710–11, to have his eyes examined by a doctor. Her prosperity excited the jealous hostility of Michael Johnson, though it was very likely her legacy of £40 in 1728 which enabled Samuel to be sent to Oxford.*

III. Sarah Ford, bapt. 28 Dec. 1624, at Aston-juxta-Birmingham; died unmard. at Winson Green, Birmingham; burd. 21 Nov. 1654, at St. Martin's, Birmingham. Admon. of her estate was granted 15 Feb. 1654/5, in P.C.C.

CORNELIUS FORD, *third son of Henry Ford preceding by Mary his second wife;* of Haunch Hall, par. of Kings Norton, co. Worc., of Dunton House, par. of Curdworth, co. Warwick, and latterly of Packwood, co. Warwick, gentleman; bapt. 29 Apl. 1632, at Aston-juxta-Birmingham; died at Packwood; burd. 11 May 1709, at Curdworth. His will, dated 28 Apl. 1709, was proved 1 May 1709, in P.C.C. *In a letter of 1775 Dr. Johnson stated that his grandfather, Cornelius Ford, lived at "the Haunch," in the par. of Kings Norton, and he described him to friends as an independent gentleman of small means.* The books he bequeathed in his will evidence evangelical sympathies. By Anne his wife, dau. of . . . . . ., who died at Dunton, and was burd. 28 Oct. 1701, at Curdworth, he had issue,

I. JOSEPH FORD, *of whom presently.*

II. Benjamin Ford, bapt. 10 Aug. 1663, at Kings Norton; died young.

III. Samuel Ford, of Light Farm, Packwood, co. Warwick, of Erdington, in par. of Aston-juxta-Birmingham, and sometime of Stroxton, co. Lincs., where he was churchwarden in 1714 and 1717/18, gent.; bapt. 25 Dec. 1672, at Kings Norton. Witnessed the settlement on the marriage of his sister, Sarah Ford, to Michael Johnson, on 11 June 1706. Mard. 30 Oct. 1707, at Kings Norton, to Jane, elder dau. of Richard Chambers, of Farmons Green, Moseley, in par. of Kings Norton, gent., by Jane his wife, second dau. of the Rev. Timothy White, M.A., Vicar of Northfield, co. Worc., and Master of Leicester Hospital at Warwick, who was born about 1675 and was aunt to the Rev. Richard Chambers, Prebendary of Hereford. Samuel Ford was living 27 Sept. 1731, in or near Birmingham, and had issue by Jane Chambers,

1. Nathaniel Ford, bapt. 4 Sept. 1709, at Packwood, of whom nothing more is known.

2. Rev. Samuel Ford, bapt. 25 Aug. 1717, at Stroxton, co. Lincs.; educated at Sutton Coldfield Grammar School ; matric. 11 Mch. 1735/6, aged 18, from Trinity Coll., Oxford, *previously seeking his cousin Dr. Johnson's advice as to a preparatory course of study.* After two years at Oxford he was admitted sizar at Emmanuel Coll., Cambridge, 11 May 1738, aged 20 ; matric. 1739, proceeding B.A. in 1740/1, and M.A. in 1744. Rector of Brampton Abbotts, co. Hereford, from 1742 till his death, and Vicar of Monkland, same co., from 1754 to 1780 ; died 6 May 1793, aged 76, without issue, at his house in Great Castle Street, Hereford ; burd. 9 May at Holme Lacy, co. Hereford. *His features are said to have " exhibited a mild resemblance " to his cousin Dr. Johnson.* Will dated 6 Dec. 1792, proved 28 June 1793, in P.C.C. Mard. Mary, dau. of . . . . . . [? Thomas], who died at her house in Castle Street, Hereford, without issue, on 9 July 1796, being burd. 11 July at Holme Lacy. Admon. of her will, dated 17 Jan. 1794, was granted 23 Sept. 1796, at Hereford.

1. Jane Ford, bapt. 15 Aug. 1708, at Packwood, co. Warwick ; perhaps alive 12 Sept. 1741.

2. Elizabeth Ford, bapt. 2 May 1712, at Stroxton, co. Lincs.; mard. (as his 1st. wife) Humphrey Heely, of . . . . . . co. Warwick, wholesale ironmonger, born in 1714. She died about May 1768, on road home from Scotland and Newcastle. *She is said by Dr. Johnson to have had " daughters " in Oct. 1767, but Boswell states she " died without having children."* Humphrey Heely, who mard. again after Elizabeth's death, held some office in an Edinburgh theatre before Oct. 1767. He was keeper of the tap at Ranelagh House in or after 1775, and later, in 1784, entered Whicher's Almshouses, Chapel Street, Westminster, where he died about 1797, being burd. at St. Margaret's Chapel adjoining. *He was helped by Dr. Johnson for many years.*

IV. Cornelius Ford, sometime of Stroxton, co. Lincs., where he was churchwarden in 1700, 1707 and 1710 ; ? whether perhaps burd. at Oldswinford, co. Worc., on 10 Dec. 1734. *Said by Dr. Johnson to have accomplished a prodigious leap on one of his journeys, and " in his boots."* Mard. Sarah, dau. of . . . . . . , and had issue (of whom only Phoebe was surviving on 17 May 1780),

1. Cornelius Ford, bapt. 30 July 1703, at Stroxton, and presumably dead on 23 Oct. 1726.

2. Joseph Ford, bapt. 14 Dec. 1704, at Stroxton, and burd. there 6 Feb. 1705/6.

3. Andrew Ford, bapt. 14 May 1706, at Stroxton, and burd. there 14 June 1706.
4. Joseph Ford, bapt. 19 Aug. 1707, at Stroxton; living 23 Oct. 1726.
5. Andrew Ford, bapt. 19 May 1710, at Stroxton; living 23 Oct. 1726.

1. Sarah ("Sally") Ford, bapt. 14 Feb. 1701/2, at Stroxton; in 1719 kept house for her widower uncle, John Harrison, in Birmingham, *and left such an impression of sweetness of temper on Dr. Johnson as to make him feel that this cousin had no fault*; living 23 Oct. 1726.
2. Anne Ford, bapt. 27 Aug. 1708, at Stroxton; living 23 Oct. 1726.
3. Phoebe Ford, born 1710–20; in 1721 under the guardianship of her uncle, Dr. Joseph Ford, who bequeathed his trust to his younger brother, Nathaniel Ford; from *circa* 1742 housekeeper in the household of Edward Gibbon, sen., and afterwards in that of his son, Edward Gibbon the historian, from whose service she retired on a pension in 1781. *On 17 May 1780 she wrote to her cousin, Dr. Johnson, complaining of her treatment by Gibbon's butler, Richard Caplen.* On 10 Aug. 1795 of No. 1, Little Sutton Street, Clerkenwell, co. M'sex, and on 15 Mch. 1796 of Hercules Building, par. of St. Mary, Lambeth, co. Surrey. Died unmard.; will dated 10 Aug. 1795, proved 11 Nov. 1797, in P.C.C. She left a small sum of money to be divided between her nieces, Pheeby Thomas, wife of Mr. James Thomas, of Powick, nr. Worcester, and Sarah King and Jane Howell, sisters of said Pheeby. The parentage of these three sisters remains to be discovered, and whether they were daughters of a brother or sister of Phoebe Ford. James Thomas, of Pear Tree Farm, Powick, died 26 Aug. 1815, aged 67, and was burd. at Powick, his will, dated 8 May 1815, and proved 19 Sept. 1815, in P.C.C., mentioning his wife Phoebe but giving no clue to her maiden name. She died 16 Oct. 1826, aged 90, and was burd. with him. They had no children, but her will, dated 10 Apl. 1816, with a codicil of 5 May 1826, and proved 2 Apl. 1827, at Worcester, leaves the residue of her estate to be divided equally among the following, some at least of whom were obviously descendants of her nieces:—James Kings, of Great Malvern, co. Worc., labourer; William Kings, of All Saints, city of Worcester, labourer; Henry Howell, of St. Martin's, city of Worcester, painter; Thomas Dynley Howell, a private soldier in the Twelfth Regt. of Foot; Thomas Kings, of St. Martin's, city of Worcester, labourer; Phoebe Simmonds, of city of Hereford, widow; Robert Dunn, of Powick, glover; Henry Dunn, of St. Martin's, city of Worcester, glover; and Sarah Caudle, of par. of St. John, Worcester, widow. Thomas Dynley Howell joined the 12th. Regt. of Foot on 25 Nov. 1811, at Port Lewis, Mauritius; he was discharged at Athlone on 1 Feb. 1818.

V. Nathaniel Ford, of Stourbridge, co. Worc., and later of Sutton Coldfield, co. Warwick, and later again (1727) of Stourbridge once more, mercer and clothier ; Warden of the Corporation of Sutton Coldfield in 1709–10 ; bapt. 2 Dec. 1676, at Kings Norton ; probably burd. at Oldswinford, co. Worc., on 4 July 1729. Mard. 3 Sept. 1701, at Doverdale, co. Worc., Jane, second dau. of Gregory Hickman, of Stourbridge, clothier, by Jane his wife, eldest dau. and coheir of Thomas Launder, of Kidderminster, co. Worc., cooper, and capital burgess of the Borough (thus becoming son-in-law to his eldest brother, Dr. Joseph Ford). *She was remembered by Dr. Johnson as a brusque but good natured woman, with little delicacy of feeling.* By her, who was bapt. 23 May 1682, at Oldswinford, and burd. there on 29 Sept. 1729, Nathaniel Ford had issue (with perhaps another Nathaniel, burd. 25 Dec. 1731, at Oldswinford),

1. Joseph Ford, born 13 Sept. 1702 ; bapt. 23 Sept. 1702, at Oldswinford ; burd. 30 Dec. 1707, at Sutton Coldfield.
2. Nathaniel Ford, born 23 July 1704 ; bapt. 1 Aug. 1704, at Sutton Coldfield, and burd. there 28 Apl. 1705.
3. Gregory Ford, of Stourbridge, clothier ; born 12 June 1706 ; bapt. 20 June 1706, at Sutton Coldfield ; burd. 3 Oct. 1748, at Oldswinford.
4. Henry Ford, bapt. 9 Dec. 1707, at Sutton Coldfield ; ? whether perhaps burd. 29 May 1727, at Oldswinford.
5. Hickman Ford, bapt. 25 Oct. 1710, at Sutton Coldfield, after which nothing is known of him.

I. Phoebe Ford, bapt. 28 Apl. 1665, at Kings Norton ; mard. 16 May 1698, at Curdworth, co. Warwick, to John Harrison, of Lichfield, and later of Birmingham, saddler, only son of Samuel Harrison, of Lichfield, chandler, Sheriff of Lichfield in 1693, by Elizabeth Goodman his wife. *Dr. Johnson remembered his uncle Harrison with disgust, for his meanness, his vulgarity, his vanity, and his chronic tippling.* Witnessed the settlement on the marriage of his sister-in-law, Sarah Ford, to Michael Johnson, on 11 June 1706. Will dated 8 Nov. 1727, proved 14 July 1733, in P.C.C. Left issue by Phoebe Ford his wife (who was dead in the Spring of 1719),

1. Rev. Cornelius Harrison, born 20 Oct. 1700, and registered among Dissenters' children at St. Mary's, Lichfield. Admitted to Pembroke Hall, Cambridge, 4 July 1718, aged 17 ; B.A. 1722/3 ; M.A. 1726 ; elected to Foundation Fellowship at Pembroke Hall, 29 May 1731. Perpetual Curate of Darlington, co. Durham, from 1727. Died 4 Oct. 1748, aged 47 ; burd. at Darlington. *Described by Dr. Johnson, rather unjustly, as " the only one of my relations who ever rose in fortune above penury, or in character above neglect."* Will dated 6 June 1747, proved 4 Feb. 1748/9, at York. Mard. 13 Sept. 1743 to Mary, dau. of John Marley, of Eppleby, in par. of

Forcett, co. York, by Margaret his wife, dau. of Richard Holmes, of Stubb House, par. of Winston, co. Durham (and niece and heir of Richard Holmes, of Stubb House). She mard. 2ndly (after 10 Oct. 1757) the Rev. Robert Rawling, but had no issue by him, and died 6 Aug. 1798, aged 77, at Stubb House; burd. at Darlington. Her will, dated 21 Apl. 1796, was proved 5 Feb. 1799, at Durham. Robert Rawling, her second husband, son of Luke Rawling, of Boldon, co. Durham, matric. 1 Dec. 1738, aged 18, from Lincoln Coll., Oxford; B.A. 1742; will, in which he is described as of Eppleby Low Field, in chapelry of Forcett, co. York, clerk, dated 22 June 1794, and proved 9 Aug. 1794, at York. The Rev. Cornelius Harrison had issue by Mary Marley his wife,

(1) Cornelius Harrison, of Stubb House, par. of Winston, co. Durham; of Grange Hall, in Bowes, co. York; and of Eppleby Low Field, in chapelry of Forcett, co. York. Born 27 Dec. 1744; matric. 8 Apl. 1761, from Trinity Coll., Oxford; B.A. 1765. Patron of St. Giles Church, Bowes. He died 5 June 1806, at Stubb House, Winston, and was burd. at Bowes, his will, dated 2 Jan. 1806, being proved 25 June, 29 July and 27 Aug. 1806, in P.C.C. Mard. 28 Aug. 1766 to Anne, eldest dau. and heir of Philip Brunskill, of Bowes, co. York, by Mary his wife, dau. of Christopher Whytell, of Gilmonby Hall, Bowes. She died 9 Jan. 1784, aged 36, and was burd. at Bowes, leaving issue by Cornelius Harrison. Their grandson was the eccentric antiquary, "General" George Henry Plantagenet-Harrison [1817-90], as he styled himself.

(1) Mary Harrison, bapt. 14 May 1746; mard. 16 Oct. 1772, to James Robson, of Ellerton, and of Leeds, both in co. York, merchant; she was living 21 Apl. 1796, and he of Leeds, woolstapler, on 2 Jan. 1806. It is not known whether they had issue.

2. John Harrison, bapt. 24 July 1704, at St. Mary's, Lichfield; living 8 Nov. 1727; died young.

3. Samuel Harrison, bapt. 23 Nov. 1708, at St. Mary's, Lichfield; dead 28 Apl. 1709.

1. Elizabeth Harrison, bapt. 25 Jan. 1705/6, at St. Mary's, Lichfield; burd. Mch. 1705/6, at St. Michael's, Lichfield.

2. Sarah Harrison, bapt. 25 Jan. 1705/6 (presumably twin with Elizabeth), at St. Mary's, Lichfield; dead 28 Apl. 1709.

3. Phoebe Harrison, bapt. 8 Nov. 1709, at St. Mary's, Lichfield; mard. Apl. 1731, at South Wingfield, co. Derby, to Benjamin Herne, of Birmingham, and afterwards of Banwell, nr. Axbridge, co. Somerset, schoolmaster, who was burd. 27 Oct. 1765, aged 55, at Axbridge. She lived on at Axbridge, her will being made there on

3 Apl. 1781, and proved 3 Dec. 1781, at Wells. *Corresponded with her cousin, Dr. Johnson, whom she called her " best friend," and left him the residue of her small estate.* She had issue by Benjamin Herne,

(1) Elizabeth Herne, a lunatic ; *admitted on* 19 *Apl.* 1766 *to Bethlem Hospital, as of Compton Bishop, co. Somerset, on Dr. Johnson's recommendation ; discharged* 28 *Feb.* 1767, *as incurable, and placed by him in a madhouse at Bethnal Green, where he contributed to her support, finally making provision for her in the codicil to his will on* 9 *Dec.* 1784 ; died unmard.; burd. 22 Feb. 1792, at St. Matthew's, Bethnal Green.

(2) Phoebe Herne, mard. . . . . . . Watts, of Bristol, and burd. 8 June 1769, at Axbridge, co. Somerset. By him, who survived her, she had a son,

John Watts, living a minor, 3 Apl. 1781 ; to inherit his grandmother's shoe buckles, with £10, at 21, *which otherwise were to go to Dr. Johnson.*

II. Mary Ford, bapt. 11 Sept. 1667, at Kings Norton ; mard. 17 Feb. 1702/3, at Curdworth, co. Warwick, to John Hardwicke, of Great Moor, in par. of Pattingham, co. Staffs., gent., third son of William Hardwicke, of Great Moor, by Eleanor Wood his wife. She was living 23 Oct. 1726, and perhaps burd. at Pattingham on 16 June 1753, having had issue by him, who was bapt. 2 Apl. 1678, at Pattingham, and perhaps burd. there on 12 May 1752,

1. William Hardwicke, of Great Moor, Pattingham, gent.; bapt. 27 Apl. 1704, at Pattingham, and burd. there 28 May 1740, admon. of his estate being granted 17 June 1740, at Lichfield. He was mard. 11 Dec. 1730, at Penn, co. Staffs., to Jane, widow of . . . . . . Norris, and had issue by her,

(1) John Hardwicke, of Great Moor, Pattingham ; bapt. 6 Jan. 1731/2, at Pattingham ; heir to his uncle, Thomas Hardwicke ; said to have sold his estate and left the district.

(2) William Hardwicke, bapt. 23 May 1734, at Pattingham ; burd. there 5 Oct. 1735.

(1) Jane Hardwicke, bapt. 10 Apl. 1733, at Pattingham.

2. Thomas Hardwicke, of Great Moor, Pattingham ; bapt. 17 Dec. 1708, at Pattingham ; died without issue, after, it is said, having " amassed a great fortune " (? whether perhaps burd. 5 Feb. 1779, at Pattingham).

1. Sarah Hardwicke, bapt. 26 Aug. 1706, at Pattingham ; mard. 1st., 13 Apl. 1727, at Pattingham, to John Parsons [1683–1757], of Ackleton, in par. of Worfield, co. Salop (son of Thomas Parsons, of

Ackleton), whose will, dated 20 Dec. 1756, was proved 2 Aug. 1757, at Lichfield. She mard. 2ndly., 8 Aug. 1758, at Chelmarsh, co. Salop, John Gibbons [1712–86], of Stableford, in par. of Worfield, co. Salop, gent. (son of Benjamin Gibbons, of Stableford, gent.), whose will, dated 26 Jan. 1780, was proved 1 May 1787, at Lichfield. She herself was burd. Apl. 1780, and her will, dated 24 Nov. 1778, was proved 25 Oct. 1780, at Lichfield. She had issue only by her first husband,

(1) Thomas Parsons, born 1728, died in 1778, leaving an illegitimate son, Thomas Dean.
(2) John Parsons, born and died in 1732.
(3) John Parsons, born 1734 ; lived at Manchester.
(1) Mary Parsons, born 1730 ; mard. 1st. Richard Smytheman, and 2nd. Richard Slater ; living 24 Nov. 1778.
(2) Sarah Parsons, born 1737, died 1800 ; mard. Isaac Clarke, and had issue,
(*a*) Anne Clarke, living unmard. 24 Nov. 1778.
(*b*) Catherine Clarke, living unmard. 24 Nov. 1778.
(3) Elizabeth Parsons, born and died in 1740.

III. Sarah Ford, born Mch. 1669, at Kings Norton, co. Worc.; bapt. 6 Apl. 1669, at Kings Norton ; mard. 19 June 1706 (ante-nuptial settlement dated 11 June 1706), at Packwood, co. Warwick, to Michael Johnson ; burd. 23 Jan. 1759, aged 89, at St. Michael's, Lichfield. Michael Johnson, eldest son of William Johnson, of Cubley, co. Derby, and afterwards of Lichfield, by Catherine his wife, was bapt. 2 Apl. 1657, at Cubley ; apprenticed 11 Apl. 1673 to Richard Simpson, of London, stationer ; made free of Stationers' Company, 5 Oct. 1685 ; of Lichfield, bookseller, stationer, and parchment manufacturer ; churchwarden of St. Mary's, Lichfield, 1688/9 ; Sheriff of Lichfield in 1709, Junior Bailiff in 1718, and Senior Bailiff in 1725 ; burd. 7 Dec. 1731, at St. Michael's, Lichfield. *For fuller particulars of Michael Johnson and his wife, see " JOHNSON PEDIGREE," ante, pp.*162-3. They had issue,

1. **SAMUEL JOHNSON** [1709–1784], LL.D.
2. Nathaniel Johnson, of Lichfield, bookseller ; bapt. 14 Oct. 1712, at St. Mary's, Lichfield ; died unmard ; burd. 5 Mch. 1736/7, at St. Michael's, Lichfield.

JOSEPH FORD, *eldest son of Cornelius Ford preceding and of Anne his wife ;* bapt. 29 Apl. 1662, at Kings Norton ; admitted pensioner at Queen's College, Cambridge, 6 June 1679 ; matric. as pensioner from Queen's, Oct.–Nov. 1679. Of Stourbridge, co. Worc., physician, and described as M.D.; latterly of Oldswinford, co. Worc., where he was burd. 9 Mch. 1720/1. Will dated 10 Feb. 1720/1, proved 4 July 1721, in P.C.C. *The uncle cited by Dr. Johnson as having left his affairs in perfect order and omitted nothing in his will, which required " great leisure, and great firmness of mind."* Mard. about the end of 1690 to Jane, widow of Gregory Hickman, of Stourbridge, clothier, and eldest dau. and coheir of Thomas Launder, of Kidderminster, co. Worc., cooper, and capital burgess of the Borough, by Joan his wife, dau. of Richard Coles, of Hopton, co. Salop, yeoman. She was by her first marriage the mother of Jane Hickman, who mard. her husband's younger brother, Nathaniel Ford, in 1701, *and also of the Gregory Hickman to whom Dr. Johnson's first known letter was addressed in Oct.* 1731. Bapt. 25 Aug. 1657, at Kidderminster, and burd. 20 Sept. 1722, at Oldswinford ; her will, dated 11 Sept. 1722, was proved 2 Oct. 1722, at Worcester. By Dr. Joseph Ford, her second husband, she had issue,

I. Joseph Ford, bapt. 2 Sept. 1691, at Oldswinford, and burd. there 11 Sept. 1691.

II. Rev. Cornelius Ford, bapt. 22 Jan. 1693/4, at Oldswinford ; educated at Mansfield School, co. Notts.; admitted pensioner at St. John's Coll., Cambridge, 6 Mch. 1709/10, whence he was admitted B.A. in 1713. Afterwards migrated to Peterhouse, whence he proceeded M.A. in 1720 ; Fellow, 1720–24. Living at Pedmore, nr. Stourbridge, 1723 and after. Ordained deacon, at Peterborough, on 1 Jan. 1724/5, and priest on 1 Jan. 1726/7 ; Rector of South Luffenham, co. Rutland, from 10 Jan. 1726/7, on presentation of the celebrated Philip Dormer Stanhope, 4th. Earl of Chesterfield (to whom he is said to have acted as chaplain), but mostly resided in London, at an hotel in the Piazza, Covent Garden. Died 22 Aug. 1731, at the Hummums, in Covent Garden, without issue. To have been burd. on 26 Aug. at St. Paul's, Covent Garden, but no record of it there. Well known to his contemporaries as a scholarly and widely read man, a brilliant and witty talker, but whose self-indulgent habits precluded the chance of any solid intellectual achievement. *Dr. Johnson discussed with Boswell the story that his ghost had appeared afterwards to a waiter at the Hummums. To the end of his days Dr. Johnson retained his admiration for the intellectual gifts and sound judgment of this cousin (popularly known as "Parson" Ford), with whom he had stayed as a schoolboy at Pedmore in* 1725. *Ford's insistence on the importance of cultivating the art of conversation, and his ability to illustrate it, left a lasting impression on Johnson, and probably influenced him to aim at a similar proficiency.* Mard. 3 June 1724, at Rushock, co. Worc. (by licence of same date from Worcester), Judith, dau. of Ambrose Crowley, of Stourbridge, co. Worc., ironmonger (whose will in 1713 nominated Dr. Joseph Ford as an exor.), by Sarah his second wife, and half-sister of Sir Ambrose Crowley, the great ironmaster. She was born 28 Feb. 1680/1, at Stourbridge, bapt. into the Church at Rushock on the day of her marriage (having been brought up as a Quaker), had no issue by Cornelius Ford, and was living his widow on 25 July 1732, after which nothing is known of her.

III. James Ford, born 24 Mch. 1698/9 ; bapt. 9 Apl. 1699, at Oldswinford ; died between 10 Feb. 1720/1, and 11 Sept. 1722, unmard.

I. Ann Ford, bapt. 28 Oct. 1692, at Oldswinford ; of Wolverhampton ; died unmard.; burd. 21 Apl. 1744, at Oldswinford, aged 51. Will dated 16 Mch. 1743/4, proved 23 Aug. 1744, in P.C.C.

II. Phoebe Ford, born 26 Mch. 1696 ; bapt. 4 Apl. 1696, at Oldswinford ; of Stourbridge ; died unmard.; burd. 5 Sept. 1766, at Oldswinford. Will dated 23 June 1762, proved 11 Apl. 1767, in P.C.C.

APPENDIX C

MICHAEL JOHNSON'S PURCHASE OF LORD DERBY'S LIBRARY IN 1706

To *The Times Literary Supplement* for 27 July 1940 (pp. 363, 365) I contributed a letter giving particulars of a most important discovery bearing upon Michael Johnson and his status in the book trade. In November 1939 Mr. Edward B. Goodacre, of Beech House, Orrell Mount, near Wigan, kindly wrote to tell me of certain entries in a diary he was editing for the Chetham Society. This diary, in the possession of Colonel C. P. Prescot, of Shipton Bellinger Manor, Tidworth, Hants., was kept by his direct ancestor, Henry Prescott, Deputy Registrar of the Diocese of Chester from about 1686. Henry Prescott was born at Rough Park, Upholland, near Wigan, in 1649, and died at Wrexham, while on a journey from Chester, in 1719, being buried at Upholland. The relevant entries are as follows:—

1705. 9 Dec. I receive a letter unexpected from the Earl of Derby.

1705. 10 Dec. Write to my Lord Derby & promise my service to procure the Library at Knowsley.

1706. 31 Aug. Randle Minshal returns with an account of the Library of my Lord Derby, represents it great & noble, of most of the Fathers entire, History, especially French, constituted of Folios above the proportion of the other volumes : he reckons the whole 2900.

1706. 10 Sept. I am informed my Lord Derby's Library is sold to a bookseller (Johnson) of Lichfield.

1706. 13 Sept. I receive my Lord Derby's answer which quits me of the Library & pleases me.

1707. 1 June. I look over the printed pretended Catalogue of my late Lord Derby's books.

Enquiry at Knowsley revealed that there is nothing known there of the sale. But a MS. Catalogue of the Library of William George Richard Stanley [1656-1702], 9th. Earl of Derby, entitled "*Bibliotheca Gulielms. Comitis Darbia apud Knowsley anno* 1679," records the titles of some 1554 volumes, while a similar Catalogue of the books of his brother, James Stanley [1664-1736], who succeeded him as 10th. Earl, taken at Knowsley, 25 July 1727, numbers only some 838 volumes. This shows that the Library had suffered diminution between the two dates, though we must conclude that the 9th. Earl had increased it considerably before his death; that his brother, soon after succeeding, decided to sell the lot; and that later on he began to collect again on his own account. After 1727 he went ahead rapidly, and a MS. Catalogue of his Library, made in 1730, extends to 631 pages and contains a far greater number of titles. The Library now contains no bookplate of any Earl before the 10th.

This transaction of Michael Johnson's is much the most important of his career, so far as we have any record, and indicates a higher position in the trade than has been accorded him. Undertaken only three months after his marriage, it may have represented a recrudescence of his earlier ambitions and a desire to improve his status with a view to being better able to meet his fresh responsibilities; and his wife's portion may have encouraged a spirit of enterprise. It is a pity that, beyond these chance entries in an obscure diary, there is no record of the deal, and that no copy of the Catalogue is known to exist. At least we can assume that Michael Johnson would have to pay personal visits to Knowsley, first to inspect the books and afterwards to arrange their removal. That Henry Prescott speaks of "the pretended Catalogue" evidences some criticism of the quality of Michael Johnson's cataloguing, which it would be interesting to be able to judge for ourselves.

APPENDIX D

THE CAMBDEN-ROEBUCK-MAXWELL-BOSWELL CONNEXION SOLVED

(see *ante*, V., 105, 265-70; IX., 20-23, 230-31)

At the last reference cited I called attention to the fact that Elizabeth, daughter of Henry Cambden, of The Castle Inn, Birmingham, the first wife of Benjamin Roebuck (brother to John Roebuck, the celebrated inventor), was an early friend of Johnson's, while Helen Maxwell, who became his second wife, was "cousin" to James Boswell, and so of a very different social status. I confessed inability to discover "the nature of the 'cousinship' between Boswell and the Maxwells," and opined it was "probably distant."

In September 1939 Professor Pottle kindly called my attention to another reference in *Boswell Papers*, I., 87, where Boswell himself provides the key to the relationship, which turns out to have been much nearer than was expected. In his "Journal," under date of 6 October 1762, he wrote:—

> Sir John's [i.e., Sir John Douglas of Kelhead's] Mother and my Mother were half-Sisters, both daughters of Colonel Erskine, from whom, by the way, it is probable that I derive my military genius.

Professor Pottle also drafted out a short pedigree to illustrate the relationship, relying principally upon Sir James Balfour Paul's *Scots Peerage*, and I again communicated with Mr. Cameron Smith, who had helped me with the Maxwell-Douglas connexion. There was great difficulty in perfecting the pedigree, because of the fact that Colonel John Erskine ("the White Colonel"), Deputy Governor of Stirling Castle, the common ancestor of James Boswell and Mrs. Roebuck, was found to have married three times, and to have had a cousin and contemporary, another Colonel John Erskine ("the Black Colonel"), who was at the same time Lieut. Governor of Stirling Castle, who married four times, and with whom there was naturally much confusion. The two Colonels are said to have lived side by side at Culross, which made it necessary to distinguish them as "Black" and "White." But eventually, with the added help of the Rev. J. M. Webster, Minister of Carnock, Dunfermline, and more especially of the Rev. William Stephen, late Minister of Inverkeithing, but now of Edinburgh, who made close investigations, and whose MS. note on the subject, with the citation of his authorities, is deposited in the Register House at Edinburgh, the whole pedigree was straightened out, as follows :—

JOHN ERSKINE [1562–1634], 7th. Earl of Mar, Lord High Treasurer of Scotland, mard. in 1592, for his second wife, Lady Marie Stewart, dau. of Esmé, 1st. Duke of Lennox [1542 ?–83], and had issue a sixth son,

Hon. Sir CHARLES ERSKINE, of Alva and Cambus Kenneth, who died July 1663. He mard. 1st. Mary, dau. of Sir Thomas Hope, 1st. bart. of Craighall, Lord Advocate of Scotland, and had issue by her,

Mary Erskine, born 1639.
Thomas Erskine, of Cambus Kenneth, born 1641, died in early life.
John Erskine, born 5 July 1642, died young.
Sir Charles Erskine [1643–90], of Alva, eldest surviving son, cr. bart. 1666. Mard. and had issue.
James Erskine, born 26 Mch. 1645.
David Erskine, born 8 Sept. 1646.
Elizabeth Erskine, born 8 Aug. 1648.
William Erskine.

Hon. Sir Charles Erskine mard. 2nd. (contract 15 May 1655) Helen, dau. of Sir James Skene, of Currichill, and widow of Sir Robert Bruce, of Broomhall, and had issue by her,

JOHN ERSKINE, *of whom presently.*
Marie Erskine.

JOHN ERSKINE, *son of Hon. Sir Charles Erskine preceding, by Helen his second wife, dau. of Sir James Skene ;* born 19 Sept. 1660 ; Ensign in Mar Regt. in 1680 ; Captain in 1690 ; Colonel before 1695 ; usually designated " the White Colonel " to distinguish him from his cousin Colonel John Erskine of Carnock, " the Black Colonel," Lieut. Governor of Stirling Castle, who appointed him Deputy Governor thereof in 1689 ; died between 8 Oct. 1737 and 7 July 1741. Col. John Erskine mard. 1st. (contract 21 Apl. 1681) Jean, 11th. dau. and youngest child of John Murray, of Touchadam, by Janet Nisbet of Dean, his wife, and had issue by her,

I. John Erskine, born 1690, died young ; ? burd. 27 Jan. 1694, at Greyfriars, Edinburgh.
I. Helen Erskine, mard. (contract 8 Sept. 1705) Sir William Douglas [1675 ?–1733], 2nd. bart. of Kelhead, and died 26 July 1754, having by him had issue,

Sir John Douglas [1708–78], 3rd. bart. of Kelhead, who mard. and had issue.
William Douglas.
Charles Douglas, " in the East Indies."
James Douglas, mard. and had issue,

Stewart Douglas.
Erskine Douglas.
Francis Douglas.
David Douglas, mard. and had issue.
Helen Douglas, mard. Capt. John Erskine.
Catherine Douglas, mard. Sir William Maxwell, of Springkell.
Jane Douglas, mard. 30 Apl. 1727 to Hugh Maxwell of Dalswinton; died 16 Jan. 1795. Hugh Maxwell, son of George Maxwell [d. 1721], of Dalswinton, by Jean his wife (mard. 1700), dau. of Lord Neil Campbell and granddau. of the Marquess of Argyll, died 12 Mch. 1765, aged 65, leaving issue by Jane Douglas his wife,
Capt. William Maxwell [1728–96], of Dalswinton.
Hugh Maxwell, living 1769–87.
Helen Maxwell, mard. as his second wife, Benjamin Roebuck, of Sheffield, merchant, and died 24 Sept. 1801. Benjamin Roebuck, who died 10 Sept. 1796, at Bath, and was burd. at Weston, had mard. for his first wife, Elizabeth Cambden, *an old friend of Johnson's*, dau. of Henry Cambden, of The Castle Inn, Birmingham; she was born 12 Feb. 1714/15, bapt. at St. Martin's, Birmingham, and died shortly before Aug. 1777.

II. Margaret Erskine, born 18 Dec. 1685; mard. (contract 2 and 9 Apl. 1707) Capt. William Erskine, Captain of Blackness, third son of Henry, Lord Cardross, and known also as Mr. William Erskine, merchant of Edinburgh, who died Nov. 1724. By Margaret Erskine his wife, who died 14 Apl. 1730, at Hope Park, Edinburgh, he had issue,
Harry Erskine, born 23 July 1708.
John Erskine, Captain.
David Erskine, of Edinburgh, writer.
Jean Erskine.
Frances Erskine, mard. 14 Jan. 1748 to James Loch of Drylaw, and died 19 Sept. 1750.

III. Janet Erskine, born 13 Oct. 1688.

Col. John Erskine mard. 2ndly., 29 Apl. 1697, Lady Mary, dau. of George Maule, Earl of Panmure, and widow of Charles Erskine, 10th. Earl of Mar, and by her, who was living 16 Mch. 1708, apparently had no issue. He mard. 3rdly. (proclamation of banns, 2 July 1714) Euphemia, dau. of William Cochrane of Ochiltree (and sister of Thomas Cochrane, 8th. Earl of Dundonald), by Lady Mary his wife, dau. of Alexander Bruce, 2nd. Earl. of Kincardine, and by her had further issue,

IV. Mary Erskine, born 8 June 1715, and bapt. 1715, at Edinburgh; mard. 13 June 1737 the Rev. Alexander Webster [1707–84], Minister of the Tolbooth Church, Edinburgh (see *Dict. Nat. Biog.*); and died 28 Nov. 1766.

V. Elizabeth Erskine, born 1 Dec. 1716, and bapt. 1717 at Edinburgh; died shortly before 8 Oct. 1737.

VI. Euphemia Erskine, born 21 Apl. 1718; mard. 1738, or 1739, as his first wife, Alexander Boswell [1706–82], of Auchinleck, advocate, and afterwards a Lord of Session, and died 11 Jan. 1766, having had issue an eldest son, **JAMES BOSWELL** [1740–95], *the biographer of Johnson.*

I have myself referred to G.E.C.'s *Complete Peerage*, and his *Complete Baronetage*, as well as to Balfour Paul's *Scots Peerage*, for some elucidatory details, and where any discrepancies are noticed the pedigree I have presented is likely to be the more correct.

APPENDIX E

THE REV. JOHN CLEMENTS, VICAR OF COLWICH

(see *ante*, V., 112-113)

I AM now able to furnish a much fuller account of this cleric, whose career after his successor came to Colwich in 1760 was unknown to me until I came across the following entry in Venn's invaluable *Alumni Cantabrigienses* :—

> CLEMENTS, JOHN. M.A. from St. John's, 1748 ; " B.A. of Corpus Christi, Oxford." Incorp. and adm. pens. at St. John's, Jan. 26, 1747–8. Probably matric. from St. Mary Hall, Oxford, Nov. 3, 1726 ; s. of John, of St. Swithin's, Worcester, age 17. Ord. priest (Worcester) May 20, 1733. V. of Colwich, Staffs., 1734. R. of Long Watton, Leics., 1748–86. R. of Appleby, Leics., 1777–93. F.S.A. 1782. Died May, 1793 (*Scott-Mayor*, III., 574).

Scott's volumes on the St. John's register were very familiar, for he presented them to me as they appeared, but I had not spotted the reference to Clements, whom I had no reason to suspect had transferred to Cambridge. The actual entry in the register is as follows (III., 124) :—

> 1747/8. CLEMENTS, JOHN, A.B. of Corpus Christi College, Oxford ; admitted pensioner, tutor and surety Mr. Ludlam, 26 January.

Further details of him given by Scott, at Venn's reference, in addition to the date of 4 June 1732 for his ordination as deacon by the Bishop of Worcester, are as follows :—

> He was instituted Vicar of Colwich, Staffordshire, in January 1733/4, and Rector of Long Whatton, co. Leicester, 16 February 1747/8. On 11 February 1747/8, when he is described as chaplain to John, Earl of Breadalbane,

> he received a dispensation from the Archbishop of Canterbury to hold Colwich with Long Whatton, their values being stated to be £40 and £120 and their distance apart 26 miles. He was instituted Rector of Appleby, co. Leicester, 24 April 1777. He resigned Long Whatton in 1786, but held Appleby (and perhaps Colwich) until his death. He became an F.S.A. in 1782. He died at Worcester in 1793 (Nichols, *History of Leicestershire*, iii, 1107; *Gentleman's Magazine*, 1793, p.481).

Scott, of course, was wrong in suggesting that Clements held Colwich till his death, which was thus recorded in *The Gentleman's Magazine* for May 1793, p. 481 :—

> At Worcester, Rev. John Clements, F.S.A. rector of Appleby, co. Leicester and Derby, and of St. John's College, Cambridge, where he took the degree of M.A. 1748.

Scott's reference to Nichols's *Leicestershire* provided authority for Clements's dates at Long Whatton, and for his becoming F.S.A. in 1782.

A very valuable reference I happened upon myself was contained in a tabular pedigree of the old family of Pipe of Bilston, facing p. 172 of vol II. of Shaw's *Staffordshire*. From this I learned that Samuel Pipe [1670–1730], of Stafford, married in 1711 Jane [d. 1774], eldest daughter of the Rev. John Spateman, Rector of Yoxall, she being married secondly on 23 April 1734, at Colwich, to John Swinnerton, gent., sometime of Stafford. By her first husband Jane had, with other issue, " Mary Pipe, eldest child, coheir to her brother James [the Rev. James Pipe [1721–1759], died unmard.], married at Stafford Dec. 14, 1731." And this Mary Pipe's husband is shown as " John Clements, clerk, vicar of Colwich, co. Stafford ; afterwards rector of Long Whatton and Appleby, both in the county of Leicester ; died in 1793." That they had children is indicated by the customary descending arrow, and we learn something of them in a bracket-enclosed note below, which runs as follows :—

> These were man and wife some years above 60. Of their eight children, most died young : but a son, Michael Spateman Clements, late on the superannuated admirals' list, has left, by an heir of Hopton, of Canon Frome, co. Hereford, a son and daughter, both living 1800. A younger son, James Clements, was also living, a widower and issueless, 1800.

From the pedigree of Hopton of Canon-ffrome, Ledbury, co. Hereford, in Burke's *Landed Gentry*, we learn that Capt. Michael Clements, R.N., of Weybridge, Surrey, married Ann, daughter of Edward Cope Hopton

[1707–1754], M.P. for Hereford city : she died 11 July 1786, leaving two children who died unmarried.

When we turn to the *Dict. Nat. Biog.* we find there, "Clements, Michael (d. 1796 ?), captain in the royal navy," whose professional career is dealt with in some detail by Sir John Knox Laughton. But his origins and parentage, and even his full name, are not stated, and the first date given of his career is May 1757, when he was first Lieut. of the *Unicorn* frigate. He damaged his naval career by appearing as a witness in the trial of Admiral Keppel, in 1779, and speaking strongly in his defence. He continued on the list of captains till 1787, a year or two later being made a rear-admiral on the superannuation list. He is believed to have died about 1796.

It will be seen that now, by collating all the evidences I have quoted, we can give the facts of the lives of the Rev. John Clements and his son much more fully and accurately. At least we know enough to suggest that the Vicar of Colwich to whose sermons Johnson listened with such attention in 1735 was a cut above the ordinary country parson in his interests as well as in his family setting.

APPENDIX F

DR. GERARD SKRYMSHER AND HIS SON CHARLES

(see *ante*, III., 20-25; IX., 112-17)

It is a curious illustration of how the keenest spirit of research may yet allow very obvious sources of information to be overlooked in particular cases, that only since Part IX. of these *Gleanings* was issued have I happened to discover that Dr. Gerard Skrymsher and his son Charles, of whom and their family connexion with Johnson I have written so much, both figure in Venn's invaluable *Alumni Cantabrigienses*, the entries being as follows :—

> SCRYMSHERE, GARRARD. Matric. pens. from Trinity, Easter, 1635. S. of James, of Norbury, Staffs. Scholar, 1638 ; B.A. 1638–9 ; M.D. (*Lit. Reg.*). Living at Norbury, 1680. (*Staffs. Pedigrees*, 1664–1700).

SCRYMSHER, CHARLES. Adm. pens. (age 18) at Trinity, June 22, 1709. S. of George (Gerard), M.D., of Woodseaves, Shropsh. School, Uttoxeter, Staffs. (Mr. Burton). Matric. 1709 ; B.A. 1713–4. (*Staffs. Pedigrees*).

My doubts as to whether Gerard Skrymsher really was an M.D., or where the degree was acquired, are now resolved, and his medical qualifications no longer in question. A note explains that " *Lit. Reg.*" stands for " *Litterae Regiae.* Royal Mandates directing the conferring of a degree." The Registrary of the University of Cambridge, in response to my request, has most kindly supplied me with a copy of the Mandate in question, as follows :—

Charles R.

Whereas the violence of the late Commocions hath had soe sad an influence upon Our two Universities That divers Scholars of integrity & good learning have been hindred in the due way and time of proceeding to their respective Degrees. And whereas Wee are well satisfied of the full standing sufficiency & merit of Dudley Hoper (Bach^{r} in Divinity), Wm. Gery, John Bargrave, Timothy Welfit, Samuel Rogers, Wm. Johnson & Jo. Redman M^{rs} of Art to bee D^{rs} of Divinity, of Roger Burgoyne, Wm. Barlow, Otho Nicholson & Gerard Skrymsher for the Degree of D^{rs} in Physick ; Thomas Fiddes, Rich : Crosse & Thomas Plume to bee Bachel^{rs} in Divinity ; and Christ : Hildiard to be Master of Arts. And also well assured of their particular & eminent Sufferings for Us and the Church during the late publique Distraccions whilest Wee were kept from Our Dominions. Our will and pleasure is That dispencing with the irregularities that may relate to this Affaire you admit the said Hoper, Gery, Bargrave, Welfit, Rogers, Johnson and Redman to the Degree of Doctors in Divinity ; the said Burgoyne, Barlow, Nicholson and Skrymsher, Doctors of Physick, the said Fiddes, Crosse & Plume to ye Degrees of Bachelaurs in Divinity, and the said Hildyard to ye Degree of Master of Arts, without those previous Usages and performances wch are ordinarily required in that Our University reserving to each his Seniority. And further Wee require That all persons requisite to this Action doe give their assistance to the compleat investing them in their respective Degrees wch Wee require may be without any subsequent Condicions upon wch they shall not have conveniency to attend. And for soe doing this shalbee yor Warrant. Given at Our Court at Whitehall ye 13th. day of November in ye 12th. yeare of Our Reigne 1660.

By his Maties Command
Edw. NICHOLAS

To Our trusty & welbeloved the Vice Chancellor & Pro-Vice-Chancellor of Our University of Cambridge for the time being to bee communicated to ye next Convocacion.

It seems obvious from this that Gerard Skrymsher must have been loyal to the Royalist cause, but beyond that it does not show any special favour from the Crown. It was simply an act of justice that those who had been prevented from proceeding to degrees for which they had qualified, by the outbreak of civil war, should have their qualifications formally recognised, though no doubt an act of justice not extended to those who had shown themselves "disaffected." The Registrary quotes further authority for the fact that the recipients of these delayed degrees were accorded the seniority they would have enjoyed if they had proceeded in the normal way; and that between 25 June 1660 and 2 March 1660/1 the total number of degrees for which Royal mandates were issued was as follows:—Doctors of Divinity, 121; Doctors of Civil Law, 12; Doctors of Physic, 12; Bachelors of Divinity, 12; Masters of Arts, 2; and Bachelor of Civil Law, 1.

Two of those who were granted degrees under the same Royal Mandate as Gerard Skrymsher figure in the *Dict. Nat. Biog.*, John Bargrave [1610–80], Canon of Canterbury, who after ejection from St. Peter's College in 1643 lived mostly abroad until 1660; and Thomas Plume [1630–1704], Archdeacon of Rochester and founder of the Plumian professorship of astronomy at Cambridge.

It is interesting to find that Charles Skrymsher, Johnson's "very near relative", followed his father to Cambridge, for there was nothing in his career as known to me to suggest that he was likely to have had a university education.

APPENDIX G

MICHAEL JOHNSON'S APPRENTICESHIP

(see *ante*, III., 5-8; VIII., 26-30)

Mr. S. A. H. Burne has kindly communicated to me the interesting fact that the original indenture by which "Michaell Johnson son of William Johnson late of Lichfield in the county of Stafford Yeoman deceased" was apprenticed to "Richard Sympson Citizen and Stationer of London" has been discovered among the documents in the Salt Library at Stafford, dated 11 April 1673. It is signed by "Richard Simpson" alone, so no doubt there was a counterpart signed by Michael Johnson and retained by his master. The form is the printed one of the Stationers' Company, and Richard Simpson's signature is witnessed on behalf of the Master and Wardens by "Geo. Tokefield."

APPENDIX H

THE PARSONS-HARDWICKE MARRIAGE

(see *ante*, IX., 16-18)

I AM now able to give fuller particulars of the marriage of Johnson's first cousin, Sarah Hardwicke, to John Parsons, and of their children. Mr. Gerald P. Mander has added to my debt to him for help by sending me an extract from a pedigree of the Parsons family compiled by the Rev. J. B. Blakeway, and printed in or soon after 1899 in his "History of Albrighton" by the *Shropshire Archaeological Society*.

John Parsons, of Hughley, who removed to Rindleford in 1672, died in Aug. 1687, and was burd. at Worfield. He had a fourth son, Thomas Parsons, bapt. 28 Feb. 1656, at Hughley, who died 12 June 1710, at Ackleton, and was burd. at Worfield. He married, in 1681, Sarah (born 1658, died 1720), dau. of Richard Clemson, of Ackleton. His eldest son is thus described:—

JOHN PARSONS, of Ackleton; nat. 1683; sep. 1757; mar. Sarah, dau. of . . . . . . Hardwicke, of the Little Moor, parish of Pattingham (she remd. John, son of Benjamin Gibbons, of Stableford, gent. [nat. 1712, sep. 1786], and ob. 1780, aet. circa 75), and by her had issue:—

(1) Thomas, nat. 1728, sep. 1778.

(2) Mary, nat. 1730, mar. Richard Smytheman and Richard Slater.

(3) John, nat. et sep. 1732.

(4) John, nat. 1734, lived at Manchester.

(5) Sarah, nat. 1737, ob. 1800, mar. Isaac Clarke.

(6) Elizabeth, nat. et sep. 1740.

APPENDIX J

GEORGE JERVIS OF GREAT PEATLING

(see *ante*, VII., 40)

THERE was a George Jervies, of co. Leic., gent., who matriculated at Oxford, from Merton College, about 1579, aged 14, and again on 24 Nov. 1581, aged 17, this time as *pleb.* (Foster's *Alumni Oxonienses*). There was also one "Jervis *minor*" who entered Eton in the third quarter of 1575 and left in the first quarter of 1579: he was commensal at the third table (*Eton College Register* 1441–1698, ed. Sir Wasey Sterry, 1943, p. 190). As the dates and their sequence in the two records accord with the idea of their referring to the same individual it is reasonable to infer that they do denote only one person, as Sir Wasey suggests. And as the pupil came from Leicestershire it is natural to identify him (as Sir Wasey tentatively does) with George Jervis of Great Peatling, the great-great-grandfather of Mrs. Johnson, who was aged 53 on 26 July 1619 and so as nearly coeval with that pupil as it is possible to make him with only age figures from which to calculate the year of birth. There is another feature of the evidence which strongly supports the identification. It will have been noticed that (George) Jervis was "*minor*" at Eton; and George Jervis of Great Peatling had a brother William Jervis, some two years his senior, who was no doubt the Eton pupil listed by Sir Wasey as "Jarvis or Gervis *ma*": he was a King's Scholar 1576–1577. All the evidence pieces together perfectly, and I accept it as proof of the identifications suggested.

APPENDIX K

FRESH LIGHT ON JOHNSON'S MEDICAL HISTORY

(see *ante*, III., 56-61)

FROM *Sophie in London* 1786, *being the Diary of Sophie v. la Roche*, translated from the German by Clare Williams, London, 1933, p. 186, we learn that on 17 September 1786 the diarist called on Fanny Burney at Windsor, who talked affectionately of Johnson:—

Indeed she speaks of him with grateful reverence, and I too have become devoted to him, since I realised how he struggled to the fore in the face of two tremendous obstacles—poverty and sickness—for in his youth he was so badly operated upon for ulcers on the neck that he never saw again with his left eye nor heard with his left ear.

APPENDIX L

MARRIAGE OF CATHERINE ABNET

(see *ante*, VI., 70, and IX., 220)

In the *Bilston Register* 1684–1746, printed by the Staffordshire Parish Register Society, I find the following marriage (p. 39) :—

1709. Nov. 24. Mr. Wm. Robins & Mrs. Catherine Abnet, ye Daughter of Mr. Wm. Abnet, of Stafford, were Married by me at Trysull Chappell abt. Ten of ye Clock in ye Morning upon a Lichfield Licence.

The date quoted by me for the marriage at the first of the above references was 12 Nov. 1709. I cannot say if it was an error. The " me " who officiated was the Rev. Richard Ames [1662–1730], Curate-in-Charge of Bilston.

APPENDIX M

RICHARD CONGREVE

(see *ante*, III., 127, and V., 117)

ANY doubt as to Richard Congreve having been a pupil at Charterhouse is removed by the following extract from that noble volume, *Alumni Carthusiani*, ed. Bower Marsh and Frederick Arthur Crisp, privately printed 1913, p. 92 :—

RICHARD CONGREVE the Son of John Congreve Esq. & Abigail his Wife was baptised at Stretton in the County of Stafford on May the 28th. 1714 and admitted July 3d. 1728 on the nomination of Rt. Honble. the Earl of Dartmouth in the Room of Edward James Ward.

The record is of Foundation Scholars, and the entries are printed verbatim. William Legge [1672–1750], first Earl of Dartmouth, was a nobleman of some political distinction, with large landed interests in Staffordshire.

If Richard Congreve, as I have thought probable, was before this at Lichfield Grammar School, it can hardly have been as fellow-pupils that he and Johnson lived on such terms of youthful intimacy, for Johnson left in the autumn of 1725, at the age of sixteen, when Congreve would be only eleven.

An undoubted schoolfellow of Johnson's (see *ante*, III., 128, V., 114, and VI., 104) who is shown in the same work (p. 89) to have gone on to Charterhouse was Gilbert Repington. He was admitted on 30 June 1726, over eight years before he went up to Oxford to join Richard Congreve at Christ Church.

APPENDIX N

MICHAEL JOHNSON'S FINAL POVERTY

(see *ante*, V., 73-4)

Mr. Laithwaite has made yet another discovery in the records of the Conduit Lands Trust at Lichfield. In a hitherto unexamined minute-book a statement of disbursements from September 1730 to September 1731 contained this entry :—

> Pd. Mr. Johnson a decaid Traidsman 10. 10. 0

This minute-book is filled with badly written accounts, completely out of order and largely undecipherable. Mr. Laithwaite rather thinks he saw another version of the list in which the recipient's Christian name was actually given as "Michael," but whether or no there can be no doubt that it was the old bookseller who had thus come in his last year of life to be relieved from want by the very Charity which had long ago helped to raise him and his family to a position of some prosperity (*ante*, VIII., 29–31). The record shows the state of penury to which he was reduced before his death in the first week of December 1731. There were about sixty beneficiaries in this list, and among them also was Humphrey Hawkins, one of Johnson's masters at the Grammar School (*ante*, III., 87–8, VIII. 101–104), who lived another ten years—he received six pounds. Among the feoffees and sidesmen this year were such well known Lichfieldians as Richard Dyott, Theophilus Levett, James Robinson, John Floyer, Richard Hammond, Richard Burnes, Luke Robinson, Jonathan Mallett and Samuel Mousley.

APPENDIX O

NEW LIGHT ON ANDREW JOHNSON'S EARLY LIFE

(see *ante*, III., 6, 12, VIII., 26-8, 30)

THE curious problem presented by Michael Johnson's brother Andrew not having been apprenticed to the bookselling trade until 3 December 1683, when he was twenty-three, and then to his brother Benjamin, has now acquired a new facet. The only explanation I could offer was that his wrestling and boxing activities, in which, according to his nephew, he so distinguished himself at Smithfield, had engrossed his attention to the exclusion of proper preparation for a business career. But another discovery by Mr. Laithwaite, which he has kindly communicated to me, rather discounts my pretty theory. In a further search he had the opportunity of making through the records of the Conduit Lands Trust at Lichfield he happened upon the following entry in a muddled, crowded and badly written minute-book not previously examined :—

16 May 1677 Paid Mr. Jesson for placeing Andrew Johnson sonne of widow Johnson to John Marryott of Ashbourne for 7 yeares from 24 June 1676 03.00.00

This, of course, puts quite a new complexion on the story of his early life. It will be noticed that the dates allow him time to have served his full period with John Marriott, and enjoyed six months liberty before being re-apprenticed to his brother Benjamin. What interested me especially was to discover if possible John Marriott's trade—whether he too was a bookseller. His will gave a strong negative to my question.

Dated 20 June 1709, it described him as John Marriott, of Ashborne in the County of Derby, *baker*. He gave to his son John his ancient messuage house adjoining the Market Street, wherein he formerly and till of late lived. The house he then occupied, adjoining the other and like it with access to Sandy Lane (now Hall Lane), he left to his son James. To his loving wife Elizabeth he left a third of the profits from his said properties, for her life ; and she was to inherit the lot if his children died under twenty-one and without issue. He alludes to a settlement he had made of certain lands in Snelston, Norbury and Offcote-Underwood, after the death of his former wife, upon John Marriott his nephew and his heirs, which were however chargeable with divers sums of money to be paid " to my son or his heirs." I therefore conclude that by his first wife he had had a son who predeceased him leaving a son John Marriott, the " nephew " (or grandson) of the will. The residue he left equally between his wife, his two sons, and his daughter Elizabeth. His wife and her sister, Sara Turner, were to be executrixes. The witnesses were Alex. Taylor, John Longden and Jos. Haynes. The will was proved at Lichfield on 7 October 1709. The inventory made on 25 June 1709, by Jos. Haynes, Thomas Hood and Thurstan Lisett, amounts to £30.14.2.

The Vicar of Ashburne has kindly searched his register and found the following entry :—

June 1709. Burried 23rd. John Marrot, Baker, Senex, Ashborn.

This shows that his will was made on his deathbed. As has been seen, that will reveals nothing of special interest, or bearing upon his association with Andrew Johnson, except for disclosing his trade.

We already knew, from an account of 8 December 1676, that the Feoffees of the Conduit Lands Trust had provided old Mrs. Johnson with £3 for her son Andrew, who was one of ten boys then " putt forth " (*ante*, VIII., 30), and perhaps it should have been apparent that it could only refer to apprenticeship. We have no means of telling whether he completed his apprenticeship with John Marriott, or why if so, having qualified to practise one trade, he should within six months or so bind himself for another seven years to learn the trade of bookselling under his brother Benjamin. Fourteen solid years of apprenticeship seem a term almost beyond human endurance, and would require some very unusual explanation. If his apprenticeship to John Marriott had been terminated, either through his own or his master's defection, it would not have prevented him being apprenticed again to a different trade, but in that case we should have expected a much earlier date for the new articles.

APPENDIX P

"JOHN NUNNS, COMEDIAN"

(see *ante*, VI., 192)

MR. ERNEST AXON, F.S.A., kindly tells me that "John Nunns, comedian, who departed this life after a long and severe illness Sep. 20th 1803, in the 54th year of his age," was buried at Fairfield, by Buxton. It can scarcely be doubted that this would be the retired naval officer named Nunns who married Samuel Stanton's daughter Elizabeth and acted in his company.

APPENDIX Q

'PARSON' FORD'S INFLUENCE ON JOHNSON

(see *ante*, III., 150-151, IX., 11, 13)

MY strong belief that one of the paramount influences on Johnson's intellectual development was that exerted by his cousin Cornelius Ford during their sojourn together at Pedmore in 1725–6 is supported more particularly by Mrs. Thrale in her original diary for September–November 1777. The following extract is from Miss Katharine C. Balderston's edition of *Thraliana*, 1942, vol. I., p. 171 :—

> Mr. Johnson had a great Notion of general Knowledge being necessary to a complete Character, and hated at his Heart a solitary Scholar who knew nothing but his Books. The Knowledge of Books says he will never do without looking on Life likewise with an observant Eye ; much may indeed be

swallowed, but much must be worked off; there are fæculancies that should subside, and Froth that shoud be scummed before the Wine can become fit for Drinking: Nealy Ford his Relation the profligate Parson immortalised by Hogarth; was he told me the Man who advised him to study the Principles of every thing, that a general Acquaintance with Life might be the Consequence of his Enquiries—Learn said he the leading Precognita of all things—no need per[haps] to turn over leaf by leaf; but grasp the Trunk hard only, and you will shake all the Branches.

Now that we know so much more of Cornelius Ford, of his wide knowledge, of his love of literature, of his classical learning, of his general high level of taste and judgment, and of his remarkable gift for "pleasing conversation" (*ante*, IX., 1–15), we are better able to appreciate the nature of his influence on the young Johnson—an influence that never lost its potency even through over half a century of fresh intellectual contacts. Particularly did it help to save him from the pit of narrow specialisation, to encourage his attention to the humane side of learning as well as to cultivate the power of expression as an art in itself, and generally to make himself a master of conversational practice. The parallelism between the two cousins in their supreme belief in and love of good talk as the final flower of intellectual cultivation is most remarkable, and it looks as if it was due to a very large extent to the direct influence of the older man on the younger.

This extract has another interest for me, that of giving us the delightful "Neely" as the diminutive by which Cornelius was known to his cousin.

APPENDIX R

JOHNSON'S DISLIKE FOR HIS SCHOOLMASTERS

(see *ante*, III., 111-114, 156)

In this connexion it is well to quote, also from Miss Balderston's *Thraliana* (I., 192), the actual entry made by Mrs. Thrale in her diary, in December 1777:—

I know not whether I put it into this Book or no, but Johnson always hated his Schoolmaster—a Mr. Hunter of Stourbridge I think his name was and I

> have heard him say that the hatred was reciprocal—he left that Hunter at the Age of 18: and spent a Year at Oxford where he felt, I find; and I am sure he *expressed*, most sovereign Contempt for his Instructors.

Hunter, of course, was Headmaster of Lichfield School, and the Rev. John Wentworth was Headmaster at Stourbridge during Johnson's pupilage there in 1726, which introduces a note of confusion not lessened by giving his age at the time of his leaving Hunter as eighteen, when sixteen was the correct figure. At eighteen he had said goodbye to all his schoolmasters for a year or so. But I accept Mrs. Thrale's reference as being to Hunter, for Johnson was more definitely hostile to him than to any other of his masters.

Miss Balderston, in a footnote, calls attention to Mrs. Thrale's statement here that Johnson "spent a year at Oxford," and calls it "an interesting corroboration of the findings of Croker, G. B. Hill, and A. L. Reade." It is a pity that the diarist did not transfer the statement to the pages of her *Anecdotes*, for it would have done something towards rebutting the evidence of his other biographers on the point, which, though not too decisively set forth, indicated that Johnson put in his full three years at the University (*ante*, V., 31–32). At *ante*, V., 45 *et seq.*, I proved conclusively for the first time, from a close analysis of the buttery book entries, that he left for good after thirteen months continuous residence in College.

INDEX TO NARRATIVE

The names in the Appendices will appear in the "Consolidated Index", Part XI.

1719–25. Moved to upper school of Grammar School, 43. Studies under Rev. Edward Holbrooke, 44–5. Forms school friendship with Edmund Hector, 46–7. Wins Lord Berkshire's prize for Latin verse, 47. Takes dancing lessons, 48. Resumes church attendance, 48. Makes friends with John Taylor and other fellow-pupils, 49–51.

1725–26. Spends six truant months at Pedmore under tuition of cousin, "Parson" Ford, 56–7. Refused re-admission at Lichfield Grammar School, 58. Fails to get into Newport Grammar School, 58. Accepted as "pupil-teacher" at Stourbridge Grammar School, 58. Studies under Rev. John Wentworth, 59–60. Admitted to local society at Stourbridge, 59–60.

1726–28. Returns home for two years of "idleness", 61–7. Helps in father's shop, 61. Reads widely, but intermittently, 61–2. Admitted to homes of Gilbert Walmesley and other leading Lichfield men, 63–5. Intimate with David Garrick and his family, 65–6. Visits to local kindred, 66–7. Retained local accent, 67.

1728–29. Enters Pembroke College, Oxf., 68–70. Father accompanies and introduces him, 70. Rev. William Jorden appointed his tutor, 70. Misses lectures to go sliding, 70–71. Performs first exercise in verse on Guy Fawkes' Day, 71. Translates Pope's *Messiah* at Mr. Jorden's request, 71–2. Actual matriculation delayed seven weeks, 72. Soliloquises about visiting foreign universities, 72–3. Neglects regular studies at University, 73 *et seq.* Is rude to Mr. Jorden, 73. Resents night inspection of undergraduates' rooms, 74. Influenced by regular religious practice, 75. Reads on plan of his own, 75. Galled by poverty, 75–6. Recommends John Taylor to go to Christ Ch., 76. Flings present of shoes angrily away, 76. His *Messiah* translation praised by Pope himself, 77. Has contacts with several fellow-collegians, 77–81. Grows rather less rebellious against order and discipline, 78. Has good private library at College, 78–9. Resolves to be less slothful, 80. Claims his College as "nest of singing-birds", 80–81. Just missed tutorship of William Adams, 81–2. After thirteen months continuous residence leaves Oxford for good, 83.

1729–31. Returns home in poor mental health, 84–5. Submits his case in writing to Dr. Swynfen, 85. Spends two years at home without definite employment, 86.

1731–32. Applies unsuccessfully for ushership at Stourbridge Grammar School, 86–7. Writes verses to Miss Hickman, 87. Loses his cousin, "Parson" Ford, 87–9. His father dies, 89. Writes "gallant" verse for Morgan Graves, 90. Meeting with William Inge, great local personage, 91. Accepts ushership at Market Bosworth Grammar School, 91. Attached to Sir Wolstan Dixie's household and bullied by him, 92–3. Receives share of father's personal estate, 93. Resigns from Bosworth School at opening of second term, 93. Applies for ushership at Ashburne Grammar School, without success, 94.

1732–35. Spends more time at home, 95. Stays at Birmingham with Edmund Hector, 95–6. Meets Thomas Warren, the printer, 96. Helps Warren with *Birmingham Journal*, 96. Moves to lodgings with Mr. Jarvis, 96. Translates Lobo's *Voyage to Abyssinia*, 97–8. Meets Harry Porter, 98. Legacy from his godfather Wakefield, 98–9. Borrows *Politian* from Pembroke Coll., and proposes new ed., 99. After Harry Porter's death, courts the elderly widow, 101. Seeks literary work from Edward Cave, ed., of *Gent. Mag.*, 101. Neglects his appearance, 102. Sees *Lobo* published, with his dedication, 102–3. Successful courtship of Mrs. Porter estranges her family, 103. Recovers his private